Man-Made

Man-Made gives a graphic, very realistic and convincing account of the injustices that women still endure in our society. The information is well researched, revealing and, often, frankly breathtaking. Anyone concerned about equality and civil rights should study the radical proposals set out clearly in this very readable and truly illuminating call to action.

Baroness Kinnock, former Foreign Office Minister and MEP

These fascinating and troubling personal stories of successful women must be read. Women shouldn't have to compensate for not being men. If we listen to the honest and thoughtful voices of a hundred women, each with their own perspective, we will realise the system has to change. We will all be the better for it.

James Smith, Chair of Carton Trust and formerly Chair of Shell UK

Man-Made

Why So Few Women Are in Positions of Power

EVA TUTCHELL

and

JOHN EDMONDS

Routledge
Taylor & Francis Group

LONDON AND NEW YORK

First published in paperback 2024

First published 2015 by Gower Publishing

Published 2016 by Routledge
4 Park Square, Milton Park, Abingdon, Oxon OX14 4RN

and by Routledge
605 Third Avenue, New York, NY 10158

Routledge is an imprint of the Taylor & Francis Group, an informa business

British Library Cataloguing in Publication Data
A catalogue record for this book is available from the British Library

Library of Congress Cataloging-in-Publication Data
Tutchell, Eva.
  Man-made : why so few women are in positions of power / by Eva Tutchell and John Edmonds.
    pages cm
  Includes bibliographical references and index.
  ISBN 978-1-4724-3212-4 (hardback) -- ISBN 978-1-4724-3213-1 (ebook) -- ISBN 978-1-4724-3214-8 (epub) 1. Sex discrimination against women--Great Britain. 2. Male domination (Social structure)--Great Britain. 3. Power (Social sciences)--Great Britain. 4. Leadership in women--Great Britain. 5. Equality--Great Britain. 6. Feminism--Great Britain. I. Edmonds, John, (Trade unionist) II. Title.
  HQ1237.5.G7T88 2015
  305.420941--dc23

                                                                    2014037240

ISBN: 978-1-4724-3212-4 (hbk)
ISBN: 978-1-03-283716-1 (pbk)
ISBN: 978-1-315-59373-9 (ebk)

DOI: 10.4324/9781315593739

Contents

The Interviewees

Women Interviewed

Adebowale, Maria – Director, Living Space Project

Anderson, Sarah – Business woman; joint founder and Director, Simple Solutions; Commissioner for the Equality and Human Rights Commission; formerly Chair, CBI SME Council

Barnes, Sally – Campaigner for Women Bishops; previously primary school headteacher

Bartoletti, Ivana – Director, Fabian Women's Network

Baxter, Maggie – Founder and Chair of Trustees of Rosa, the UK fund for Women and Girls

Benn, Melissa – Writer and campaigner

Bergman, Michaela – Chief Counsellor for Social Issues, European Bank for Reconstruction and Development; Social anthropologist and lawyer

Berry, Lynne – Consultant; Senior Trustee, Canal and River Trust; previously Chief Executive of WRVS

Blake, Libby – formerly Head of children's services, Kensington and Chelsea and at Haringey

Blower, Christine – General Secretary, NUT

Bolsø, Agnes – Professor, Department of Interdisciplinary Studies of Culture, University of Science and Technology, Trondheim

Boot, Rosemary – Executive Director, Circle Housing; previously Finance Director, Carbon Trust

Buchanan, Elizabeth – Farmer; previously Secretary to Prince of Wales

Bull, Deborah – Director of Cultural Partnerships, King's College, London; previously Creative Director, Royal Opera House

Bushyager, Revd Ruth – Anglican Missioner, Aide to Bishop of London

Butters, Jane – Surgeon at Kingston Hospital

Calkin, Natalie – The Homelessness project

Carberry, Kay – Assistant General Secretary, TUC; Commissioner for Equality and Human Rights Commission

Carrie, Anne Marie – Director of Kensington and Chelsea Education Ltd; previously Director of Barnardo's

Castle, Pamela – Environmental Lawyer; former Chair of the Environmental Law Association

Chadwick, Mary – Managing Director, Paine Webber International (UK)

Charlton, Helena – Portfolio Manager, DECC and No 10 Equality Unit

Chibah, Katherine – Music teacher and former professional viola player

Cotton, Hilary – Head of campaign for WATCH (campaign for women Bishops); delivers assertiveness courses for senior women civil servants

Dawes, Melanie – Director General of the Economic and Domestic Affairs Secretariat, Cabinet Office

Dean, Baroness Brenda – Peer; previously General Secretary of Sogat trade union

Dommett, Ellie – Lecturer in Psychology, Open University

Drewett, Ulli – Head of Production, Penguin Publishing

Dugdale, Anna – Chief Executive of Norfolk and Norwich University Hospital Trust

Elliott, Carole – Director of Teaching, Durham University

Elliott, Julie – MP for Sunderland Central

Evans, Mary – Former Deputy Director of Children's Services, Wandsworth

Ford, Sue – Vice President (Environmental) Upstream, BP

Fuller, Jane – Financial consultant and journalist

Gill, Rebecca – Young Women's Trust

Graham, Teresa – Chair, Salix Finance; Chair, Women of the Year

Greenfield, Susan – Professor of Synaptic Pharmacology, Oxford University; previously Director of the Royal Institution

Grussing, Kate – Founder and CEO of Sapphire Partners

Hale, Baroness Brenda – Deputy President of Supreme Court

Hancock, Heather – Chair, Rural to the Core; previously Global Partner, Deloittes

Hargreaves, Deborah – Director of High Pay Commission; former journalist

Harman, Harriet QC – MP for Camberwell and Peckham; Deputy Leader of the Labour Party; Shadow Secretary of State for Culture, Media and Sport

Hierons, Clare – CEO, Carbon Leapfrog

Holland, Diana – Assistant General Secretary, Unite

Hollis, Patricia – Peer; former Local Government Leader

Howard Boyd, Emma – Director, Sustainable Investment and Governance, Jupiter Asset Management

Hudson Wilkin, Revd Rose – Chaplain to the Speaker of the House of Commons

Hurvenes, Elin – Founder and Owner of Professional Boards Forum

Hutton, Dame Deirdre – Chair, Civil Aviation Authority (CAA); previously Chair, National Consumer Council

Ibsen, Mai-Lill – Non-Executive Board member of Norwegian Companies

Jones, Susanna – District Judge

Kelan, Elisabeth – Lecturer in Work Organisation and Gender, King's College, London

Kennedy, Baroness Helena QC – Human rights lawyer; Principal of Mansfield College, Oxford

Kinnock, Baroness Glenys – Peer; previously MEP and Foreign Office Minister

Knott, Judith – Director of Corporate Taxes, International and Anti-Avoidance, HMRC

Lees, Beatrix – Nursery nurse and owner of childcare small business

Littlewood, Margaret – formerly Lecturer in Gender Studies, Open University

Mack, Eleanor – Head of I&C Transformation, npower

Mackinlay, Deirdre – Former Director of Nursing and Midwifery at West Middlesex Hospital

Mactaggart, Fiona – MP for Slough

Malhotra, Seema – MP for Feltham and Heston

Marsh, Dame Mary – Founding Director of the Clore Social Leadership Programme; formerly Chief Executive, NSPCC

Martin, Sally – Vice President, Shell Downstream

May, Jill – Non-Executive Director of the Competition and Markets Authority; previously Head of Strategy UBS Bank

McGowan, Maura QC – Chair of the Bar Council

McKnight, Judy – Former General Secretary of NAPO

McMeikan, Liz – Chair, Moat Housing Association; Non-Executive Director, Wetherspoons; previously Managing Director, Tesco Express

Morgan, Adrienne – Barrister

Morrissey, Helena – CEO of Newton Investments; Founder of the 30% Club

Morton, Jay – Architect

Nelson, Liz – Executive Chairman, Fly UK

Neville-Rolfe, Baroness Lucy – Member, Efficiency Board, Cabinet Office; previously Executive Director, Tesco

O'Grady, Frances – General Secretary, TUC

Onwurah, Chi – MP for Newcastle Central

Paes, Stella – Head of Science, AQA

Palmer, Susan – Trustee Bowes Museum; previously Trustee, Heritage Lottery Fund; formerly Marketing Communications Director, Grant Thornton

Phillips, Helen – Executive Director, Yorkshire Water; previously Chief Executive, Natural England

Pye, Annie – Professor, University of Exeter Business School's Centre for Leadership Studies; leader, ESRC Funded research studies into Corporate Directing

Robinson, Ann – Director of Consumer Policy, uSwitch; previously senior Civil Servant and Charity Director

Royall, Baroness Jan – Labour leader in the House of Lords

Ruddock, Dame Joan – MP for Lewisham, Deptford

Savage, Wendy – Gynaecologist; Campaigner for women's rights in childbirth and fertility

Savkin, Tanya – Vice President/Senior Analyst, Moody's Investors Service

Segal, Lynne – Anniversary Professor of Psychology and Gender Studies, Birkbeck College, London; socialist feminist writer

Sharp, Baroness Margaret – Peer, LibDem Spokesperson, Education

Shoesmith, Sharon – former Director of Children Services, Haringey

Stead, Valerie – Lecturer, Lancaster University Business School

Street, Dame Susan – Non Exec, Ministry of Justice; previously Strategic Advisor, Deloittes and Permanent Secretary at DCMS

Sundaram, Preethi – Fawcett Society

Swain, Corinne – Fellow at Arup; previously Director and Head of Planning, Arup

Swinson, Jo – MP and Coalition Government Minister

Taverne, Suzanne – BBC Trustee; previously Managing Director, British Museum and Director of Operations, Imperial College

Thompson, Dianne – CEO, Camelot; Chancellor, Manchester Metropolitan University

Thomson, Peninah – Chief Executive, Mentoring Foundation; Founder, FTSE 100 Cross Company Mentoring Programme; previously Partner at Praesta

Tonge, Baroness Jennie – Peer; previously MP for Richmond

Towers, Julie – Managing Director, Recruitment Solutions, Penna

Vadera, Baroness Shriti – Consultant; previously member, Council of Economic Advisers at the Treasury and Minister, Department for Business, Innovation and Skills and Cabinet Office

Venables, Jean – Chief Executive, Association of Drainage Authorities; Owner, Crane Environmental; former President, Institution of Civil Engineers

Vinnicombe, Susan – Professor of Organisational Behaviour/Diversity and Director of the International Centre for Women Leaders, Cranfield University

Walker, Rowenna – Civil Engineer, Jacobs/Jacobs SKM

Warner, Lady Suzanne – Board Member, Environment Agency; previously Chair, Botanical Gardens Conservation International and Group Director, Cable and Wireless

Watts, Anne – Independent Advisor, Opportunity Now; previously Chair, Appointments Commission

Wells, Helen – Talent Director, Teamspirit; previously Director, Opportunity Now

Wilkin, Lesley – Managing Director, Hay UK and Ireland

Williams, Clarissa – Former Headteacher, Tolworth School; previously President, NASUWT

Young, Baroness Barbara – Chief Executive, Diabetes UK; previously Chief Executive, Environment Agency

We also interviewed six other women. We were unable to contact two of them to gain permission to use their names. Four others, whom we did contact, decided that they did not want us to reveal that they had been interviewed.

Men Interviewed

We discussed details of our research with a number of men and interviewed four men at length:

Craft, Edward – Solicitor and Chair of the Corporate Governance Expert Group of the Quoted Companies Alliance

Mackenzie, Andrew – CEO, BHP Billiton

Minter, Bill – Civil Engineer

Smith, James – Chair, Carbon Trust; previously Chair, Shell UK

To emphasise prominence, information provided by our interviewees is displayed throughout the book in double quotation marks. Any other quote is shown in single quotation marks.

Preface

This book is about women. So it also has to be about men. We have interviewed well over 100 women and only a handful of men. But the attitudes, behaviour and creations of men are on every page. Men founded our government, our large companies and our great institutions. They designed our society. That is why we have called our book, *Man-Made*. And men still control what they once created. That is the nature of the challenge faced by every woman with an ambition to be successful. She must decide how she can best fit into organisations and systems that were fashioned for the convenience of men. Or she can attempt the monumental task of reforming the system to fit the needs of women.

A plethora of news items suggest that, because there is some interest in the unequal chances in life faced by many women, equality will soon be achieved. As we demonstrate in this book, this is emphatically not the case. There have been improvements, as we acknowledge in the following chapters, but progress is still glacially slow.

Equality is about power. Having more women in top jobs helps to correct the massive imbalance of power in our society. And having more women with power means that matters of importance to all women are more likely to be addressed than if decisions about policies and priorities are made by men.

During our research for this project, we met Rebecca Gill, Policy Officer for the Young Women's Trust which works with women between the ages of 16 and 30. They typically have no qualifications, are unemployed or are in and out of low-paid work. Many of them became mothers very young. "They need a platform – a voice,"[1] Rebecca told us.

What they need is the voice of women with enough power and influence to give them hope as well as practical advice and help.

If we are going to force our society to face the reality of the very different career prospects, not only of the frustrated high flyers who seem to get stuck just below the topmost jobs but the huge number of women in low-paid, insecure and boring work, we need women at the top who can use their influence to challenge and change current inequalities.

Rather than concentrating on a 'deficit' model of women who, for whatever reasons, have not reached their potential, we decided to interview a very large number of successful women to see whether a pattern emerged to account for their success in this man-made society.

We listened to the life experiences of over 100 very busy women from different walks of life. They were generous with their time and the interviews were inspiring and sometimes humbling. We did not rely on checklists. We sent our potential interviewees a short summary of what our research was about and asked them to meet one of us face to face. Only one of the women we interviewed was accompanied by a colleague. The normal pattern was for one of us to meet the interviewee in private and on her own.

We did not prompt the discussion but instead asked each interviewee to tell us about her career and about as much of her life as she thought was relevant. So the women we interviewed set their own agenda and concentrated on the issues and happenings that were important to them. At the end of each interview we asked only one direct question: Do you regard yourself as a feminist? How they replied is analysed at the end of the book.

We were surprised and delighted by their brave, honest and open attitude. They have not only allowed us to quote their words but have been extremely encouraging about our enterprise.

There were a few disappointments. A very small number of the women we interviewed decided on reflection that they did not want us to mention their names. A bigger problem was that we were frustrated in our intention to interview the relevant Front Bench spokespersons and MPs from all the major political parties. Regrettably this was not possible. Although we were able to interview Labour and Liberal Democrat representatives, our many and sustained approaches to Conservative MPs and Ministers always produced one line refusals from their aides and assistants.

When we embarked on this project and as we read the extensive literature, we had in mind an outline of how it would be written, but we knew from the outset that the interviews we conducted would shape the final structure of the book.

Our aim is to show what can be achieved by some women with enough determination and drive to confront and overcome barriers. This is not the end of the story and another piece of work will be needed to ensure that the power of successful women is fully used to enable other women to achieve success. As one woman put it to us, "The objective should not be to hand out a limited number of life belts so that a few more women can float to the top; we need to build a raft with enough space for all woman-kind."

The interviews produced surprises, some unwelcome. We were both startled by the extent of apparently relentless low-level sexism still encountered by many of the women we spoke to: memorably described by one woman as "water torture". We were also alarmed by the sexual harassment that some of them had suffered. Some of the incidents were truly appalling.

A much happier revelation was the modesty of the women we talked to. Even the most well-known and high-flying of the women we interviewed were inclined to downplay their achievements and to stress how lucky they had been.

Unusually for a book about gender issues, *Man-Made* has been written by a woman and a man. We come from very different backgrounds and experiences. Eva Tutchell's professional life was in education: having spent years in the classroom as a secondary teacher, she then worked as an adviser on gender equality to children, teachers and local authorities. John Edmonds was for many years the General Secretary of the GMB Union, one of the largest trade unions in Britain. He had to deal daily with inequalities of many kinds and says that he has, "Seen just about every form of discrimination devised by man."

Two women writing a book together about gender would probably have many shared assumptions about the place of women in our society: the masculine language pervading our culture, the nagging lack of confidence felt – though often hidden – by even successful women, the need for women to be 'liked', the strong inclination to 'care' for others even to their own detriment, the intensely visceral need many women have to care for their children and the over-riding importance of 'appearance'. So a lot could be taken for granted. Without this shared experience, we felt the need to examine more and explain more, and we delve more deeply into these complex matters than most of the books we have read.

Our co-authorship also meant that we could look at the behaviour of men from different viewpoints and could estimate with some authority how men would react to measures intended to improve the life chances of women. Our conclusions are not always very comfortable but they are carefully considered and realistic.

However, though there were inevitable clashes of opinion which sprang mainly from our different experiences of life as a man and a woman – mirroring the central concerns of the book itself – we found a surprising degree of unanimity in our judgments and recommendations. We both learnt a lot.

The chapters in *Man-Made* have been written by both of us with the exception of the final chapter on Feminism which was written by Eva Tutchell alone.

In addition to the women and men whom we interviewed, we owe thanks to family, friends and colleagues who have helped and supported us in many ways:

Lin Edmonds and Derek Tutchell, for their interest and encouragement; Valerie Stead and Carole Elliott whose book was so useful to us and who took the time to read several of our chapters; Marianne Coleman who gave us generous advice based on her own experience in writing a book based on similar themes; Keith Ewing, Howard Gospel and Margaret Littlewood who made suggestions and commented on our ideas; Richard Ennals whose enthusiasm is so infectious and who introduced us to Francesca White, our supportive literary agent; Jim Flood for his invaluable practical advice; Kim Beat, Melissa Benn, Agnes Bolsø, Kathleen Bolton, Edward Craft, Jo Delaney, Jayne Grant, Barbara Imrie, Elisabeth Kelan, Liz Mackenzie, Liz Nichols, Helen O'Connell, Annie Pye, Lynne Segal, James Smith, Sue Vinnicombe and Jane Whitworth for engaging in conversations about our book over the past three years.

Special thanks to the irrepressible feminist campaigner Dale Spender for giving us permission to use the title *Man-Made*, echoing her own seminal work of 1980: *Man Made Language*.

Man-Made is dedicated to our grandchildren: Sophie, Maia, Jake and Joel and to Caitlin, Jack, Bethany and Harry in the hope that a book like this will no longer be necessary long before they reach our age.

The cover design is based on a drawing produced by Harry Rowland.

Chapter 1
The Illusion of Continuous Improvement

This book has its origins in the General Election of 2010. Not in the result but in the nature of the campaign: it was so unmistakably and disconcertingly male. Where were Harriet Harman and Theresa May and Yvette Cooper and Shirley Williams? No doubt they were all out campaigning but they never got into the limelight. All we saw on television were three male Party leaders and a few male acolytes. We bear no ill-will towards Sarah Brown but it cannot be right for the wife of the Prime Minister to be the only female face that appears regularly on our TV screens in the three weeks of a General Election campaign.

A Game for Men

After polling day the impression that national politics is a game played only by men became even stronger. David Cameron and Nick Clegg selected the Coalition Cabinet. It contained 19 men and only four women. Five other Ministers were also entitled to attend Cabinet meetings. They were all men. So the four women around the Cabinet table were outnumbered by six to one.

On the other side of the House of Commons, Gordon Brown resigned and the Labour Party organised an election to replace him as Party Leader. Harriet Harman decided not to stand. Yvette Cooper made the same decision and, in a bizarre twist, allowed her husband to make that announcement on her behalf. Eventually five candidates emerged: four men and only one woman. And the woman candidate, Diane Abbott, only got onto the ballot form after some backroom manoeuvring. When it became clear that she would not secure enough nominations from Labour MPs to reach the minimum constitutional requirement, two of the male candidates asked their supporters to switch their nominations to Abbott. It was only by this device that the Labour Party managed to avoid the embarrassment of an all-male leadership contest.

Thoroughly discouraged by this saga of male supremacy and condescension, we decided to write this book. We started by looking beyond national politics to see exactly what was happening in the rest of society. We knew that the management of private companies was dominated by men but the overwhelming extent of that domination was a shock. We looked at the professions and the professional institutions and found a similar pattern: some exceptional women have broken through but almost all the positions of power are held by men. Local government was not much different. Nowadays there are twice as many male Councillors as women, but, even more significantly, the person who holds the power as the Council Leader is nearly always a man. We hoped to find a different story in education but again we were disappointed. With the exception of Primary schools, men hold a large majority of the powerful positions. Charities and the Arts provided other unpleasant surprises. Women sit on the Committees and Boards but men occupy almost all the real positions of power.

Misconceptions

So what had happened to the comfortable assumption that the 'glass ceiling' has been shattered and gender equality is within touching distance? It turns out to be an illusion. And the difference between public perception and reality is much greater than we expected. It should not have been such a surprise. Neither of us is inexperienced in matters of gender and neither of us would normally be described as naïve. The female author of this book spent many years advising public authorities on equality issues and has first-hand experience of the determination that men show when defending their privileges. The male author led a large trade union for nearly 20 years and has seen at close quarters how badly some women are treated at work. Yet, in spite of scepticism born of hard experience, both of us believed that things were better than they proved to be. Like most of Britain, we accepted the optimistic view. And, like most of Britain, we were wrong.

There is a second misconception that reinforces this optimism. Even people who appreciate that there is a large imbalance of power between the sexes tend to believe that we are set on a path that will lead eventually and inexorably to gender equality. It is certainly true that some big battles have been won. Since the middle of the nineteenth century women have gained most of the rights that men previously kept for themselves. Women have won the right to own property, the right to vote and the right to sit in Parliament, equal access to education, the equal right to divorce, the right to control their fertility, the legal right to equal pay and the legal right to be treated equally at work. So perhaps it is understandable that people look back over the last century and see what seems like steady progress. The optimists are also comforted by the knowledge that the discourse about women's rights has changed. Apart from a few eccentric individuals like that crusty MEP, Godfrey Bloom,[1] the refusniks have all but disappeared from public life. Nowadays just about everyone says that *of course* women should have equal rights and *of course* women should have equal opportunities. What could be more reasonable than to assume that, although we are not quite there yet, it is only a matter of time before Britain achieves gender equality? We have a national consensus: just wait a little longer and all will be well.

Periods of Reform

Regrettably this warm and seductive prospect is based on a misreading of history. The progress towards gender equality only looks smooth and continuous if we wear rose-tinted glasses and take a cursory glance over our collective shoulder. What might look like a century and more of steady progress is more accurately described as two periods of considerable change followed by long periods of what the optimists will call consolidation but others might call stagnation. In the 1920s the vote was won and a degree of political equality was achieved. In the 1960s and 1970s new rights at work were secured and new standards were set for the way men were expected to describe and treat women. Outside these periods of exciting reform there have been very few important improvements. So has the last century been a period of continuous and inexorable progress? Unfortunately not.

The further disappointment is that the two periods of exciting reform did not, unfortunately, deliver as much as the campaigners expected. The most famous advance for women was of course the winning of the right to vote and the right to sit in Parliament. There were hopes that these stupendous reforms would transform politics but, in the event, change came very slowly. In 1919 Nancy Astor was the first woman to take her seat in Parliament. Twenty years later there were still only seven women MPs. These seven included such formidable women as Ellen Wilkinson and Irene Ward but the House of Commons looked much the same as it did in 1919. Even now, nearly a century after Nancy Astor's election victory, male MPs outnumber women by more than three to one.

The second period of change was prompted by the campaigns of the Women's Liberation Movement in the 1960s and 1970s. Two landmark Acts of Parliament were passed: to guarantee equal pay and to outlaw many forms of discrimination, especially at work. This legislation, and the debate that the proposals provoked, did enormous good in changing the discourse about women's rights and the place of women in society. However the two Acts of Parliament specifically promised to put an end to some of the worst examples of inequality and that has been the greatest disappointment. As we explain in Chapter 2, neither law has been properly enforced and the result has been a very unfortunate discrepancy between what the laws appeared to guarantee and what has actually been delivered. Notwithstanding the Equal Pay Act, there is still a substantial gap between the pay of men and women in Britain. In spite of the Sex Discrimination Act, discrimination on grounds of gender remains a problem in many workplaces.

The Women's Liberation Movement in the 1960s and 1970s had the wider objective of trying to change the way that women are treated, described and portrayed. Much good was done. Pictures of naked and semi-naked women are no longer displayed in most workplaces and sexual harassment is much less common than it was 30 years ago. But, as we explain in Chapter 5, that particular revolution stalled well before the desired changes were fully embedded in the public consciousness. Here too we are left with an unhappy mixture of good intentions and inadequate delivery. The law declares that rape is a very serious offence carrying heavy penalties but accusations of rape rarely get to court. Allegations of sexual harassment often lead to a demeaning examination of the victim's dress, behaviour and background. Pictures of scantily-clad women still appear in Britain's biggest-selling newspaper and the front covers of so-called 'lads mags' display photos of nude women in thousands of shops. Even more serious, easy access to hard-core internet porn is beginning to cause deep concern about the way in which boys regard women and the way in which girls regard themselves.

On examination the belief in some inexorable progress towards gender equality turns out to be a myth. Reforms have not come steadily. They have come in fits and starts and, significantly, progress has only been made when the campaign for reform has been backed by a powerful movement: the suffragettes in the early part of the twentieth century and the Women's Liberation Movement in the 1960s and 1970s. When those campaigns lost their vigour the momentum for reform dissipated. The gains that had been made were not followed by new improvements. Indeed, without the momentum provided by these two powerful campaigns, even the gains that had been secured had less effect than had been hoped and expected. And during those long periods in the last hundred years when there has been no powerful movement campaigning for women's rights, women have suffered significant reverses. The lesson of history is not that progress towards gender equality is steady and inexorable. The real lesson is that, without a powerful movement maintaining the pressure, improvements come very slowly, tend to be fragile and the position of women is liable to be eroded.

Reverses and Delays

Some of the reverses have been very damaging. New employment opportunities opened up for women during the two World Wars. Particularly during the Second World War, many male jobs were taken over by women. Women learned new skills, earned more money and began to have a clearer vision of independence. But after 1918 and particularly after 1945 all that changed. The men returned from the war and the women were displaced, often without much warning or notice. Indeed it is remarkable how quickly the old order was re-established and how little of a legacy remained after those brief periods of emancipation. In peace-time after 1945 women quickly went back to being housewives and little public recognition was given to the fact that many women wanted more in their lives than an obligation to look after husband, children and home.

A glance at the advertisements of the period shows the extent to which women were identified with the role of housewife. Women radiating contentment were seen at home cooking, cleaning and attending to their family's needs. Bessie Braddock, the most famous woman in the House of Commons at that time, was known as the MP who spoke up for British housewives. In the same era there were precious few politicians who spoke up for what were then called 'career women'. And woe betide a woman with children at school who wanted to work full time. The term 'latch key kids' was coined by the press to describe the off-spring of such a neglectful mother. Another quarter of a century passed before it became more or less respectable for a woman with children to have anything that looked like a career.

Anyone who believes in the illusion of steady progress should also give some thought to the timescale of improvement. The optimists in Britain will need to be patient. At our current rate of progress it will take until 2070 for gender equality to be reached on the Boards of Britain's 350 largest companies. And they are the leading group of companies; elsewhere things are moving even more slowly. In politics, the best estimate is that the House of Commons will not contain equal numbers of women and men until about 2080. These are depressing predictions. Unless we find the energy to generate another of those rare periods of rapid reform, we had better prepare our great granddaughters for disappointment: the next three generations of British women will face the dispiriting prospect of continuing inequality.

Women are sometimes startled by the slow pace of change that even apparently enlightened men are prepared to contemplate. Elin Hurvenes, who runs companies in Norway and Britain, had always been against positive discrimination on the grounds that special treatment would be demeaning to women. So she was against the proposal to require Norway's biggest companies to apply a quota to Board membership to ensure that at least 40 per cent of Board members are women. But the shock of listening to one of Norway's top entrepreneurs, a self-made billionaire whom she had previously admired, changed her mind. "We should let nature take its course," he said. "In a hundred years there will be as many women as men on company boards." Elin Hurvenes was not impressed. "That would be too late for me, my daughter and for any possible granddaughters."

In the event the more conservative forces were defeated and Norway decided to increase equality by introducing quotas for company Board membership. Other countries have used different policy instruments but most of the so-called advanced western countries and a good number of others have displayed greater urgency than Britain. As a result the UK has dropped down the rankings in the Global Gender Gap[2] Report compiled by the World Economic Forum (WEF). The Report measures the position of women in the economy and in respect of education, health and politics. The WEF's first league table was published in 2006 and at that time the UK was ranked ninth. In 2014 the UK was ranked 26th – behind a host of European countries and also behind the US, South Africa, Nicaragua, Rwanda, Burundi and the Philippines. The unpleasant conclusion is that British women are being left behind.

Men in Britain seem to be content with the slow rate of change. After all, any move towards greater gender equality will have to challenge cultural norms that have existed for hundreds of years and which are very comfortable for men. In Chapter 3 we show how the structure of many institutions and organisations in Britain were formed in the nineteenth century and reflect the way in which women were seen at that time. Men went out into the world and wielded the power while women stayed at home and provided the domestic support. Nowadays these notions seem very old-fashioned but it is surprising how persistent they remain as they flow down through the generations: grandparents teach parents and parents teach us. Our language reveals the strength of this legacy. People who chair meetings are still called Chairmen even if they happen to be women. In many selection meetings someone is likely to talk about, 'getting the right man for the job' even if some of the candidates are female.

This legacy from the distant past affects the way so many things are handled, both important and trivial. Recently the man largely responsible for appointing a new Director General of the BBC could not help using phrases that revealed to the world that, even before the appointment process had started, he expected the successful candidate to be a man. At about the same time a famous television presenter was cross about a technical hitch and told the viewers that the search was on for 'a man with a screwdriver'. One of the authors has suffered a frustrating half-hour trying to teach a male trade union official to break the in-grained habit of referring to all his colleagues as 'he' when some of those colleagues were self-evidently female.

If a man who makes such a revealing mistake is challenged, he will usually wave the criticism aside. The remark is only, 'a slip of the tongue' or 'just a figure of speech'. But of course it is nothing of the kind. Stereotypes have a strong hold on our expectations. Doctors are male and nurses are female. That is what history and experience has taught us. And any development that seems to challenge these comfortable assumptions is disconcerting and rather unwelcome. It is not surprising that men, who benefit so obviously from the legacy of centuries of male dominance, are not rushing to make early changes in the way society is organised.

A Focus on Power

The key question that we encountered as we researched gender equality concerned power and its distribution. While some women in Britain have become famous and many more had achieved positions of influence, very few women have managed to reach positions of real power. So we decided that this book should focus on the great imbalance of power that we found in all parts of our society. In the following chapters we seek an answer to the important and straightforward question: Why are so few women in positions of power in Britain?

It is ridiculously easy to identify the obstacles that face women who want to make a successful career. We wanted to go much further. We wanted to learn the secrets of success and the reasons for failure. Does the problem lie with the system or does the explanation lie in the women themselves? Some writers have suggested that women lack the necessary ambition or determination. Is there any truth in that allegation?

We could have examined the statistics and reviewed the existing research and left it at that. Instead we decided on an approach which we thought would produce more insights and a clearer picture. The best people to tell us what it takes to get to the top in modern Britain are those women who have made that journey. Successful women could not only tell us about any obstacles in the path of ambitious women but could also suggest how those obstacles might be bypassed or overcome.

Interviews

We set about the task of interviewing more than 100 successful women. We were given excellent access. Very few of the women we approached refused to be interviewed. We are very grateful for their willingness to help, for their trust and for their frankness. To provide a little balance and a wider perspective, we also interviewed some women who are not yet at the top and a few men.

After a time, a pattern began to emerge. Our first and enduring conclusion is that these successful women are exceptional people. We noticed an absence of any female equivalent of the time-serving, worthy and rather uninspiring man who will often occupy a senior position in many organisations. In current circumstances women have to be extremely able to get to the top in Britain. In Chapter 9 we try to unravel the secrets of their success.

Most of the women accepted as a fact of life that they would have had an easier, and in some cases an even more successful, career if they had been born a man. But there was a notable absence of rancour. They accepted life as they found it without much complaint. When they mentioned any apparent unfairness – which happened less often than we expected – they tended to do so with a wry smile and with practiced understatement. Successful women do not spend much time moaning about the difficulties that they have faced.

Made by Men

But difficulties there are. The first and the most subtle of the difficulties inspired the title of this book. In very many ways British society is man-made: fashioned by men for the convenience of men. The way most organisations operate – the rigid hierarchy of power, command and control management, the long hours with the melding of work and male-orientated social activities, the expectation of a career uninterrupted by children or family duties and the definition of leadership with its multitude of sporting and military metaphors – has been designed to make men feel secure and is guaranteed to make most women feel uncomfortable. Just how much of life has been arranged to suit men, and just how difficult it is for women to fit in without making themselves into clones of the men they see around them, is explored in Chapters 3 and 4.

Particularly irritating is the more or less universal expectation amongst men that people of importance will also be men. At the very least this can lead to great discourtesy. Stella Creasey MP tells the story about how, soon after she took her seat in the House of Commons, she was ordered out of a lift because it was reserved for the exclusive use of MPs. The middle-aged male politician who laid down the law to her could not conceive that a young woman like Stella Creasey might possibly be an MP.

Stella Creasey thinks that the mistake was significant but she was able to laugh it off. However, as we show in Chapter 5, sexism can also lead to a restriction in promotional opportunities and, most obviously, to pay discrimination. Many salary levels are secret so it is often difficult to get to the truth but many of the women we interviewed had more than a suspicion that they were paid less than the men doing similar jobs in their organisation. But, as with so many of the examples of unfairness we describe, their reaction tended to be a shrug of resignation followed by the admission that, "It was probably my own fault for not pushing hard enough for a salary increase."

Sexism also comes in much nastier forms. We were surprised at how many examples of sexual harassment we were told about, sometimes mentioned almost as a sad afterthought by women determined to put such unpleasant memories behind them. We were also told how difficult it is to challenge such behaviour. There are rarely adequate procedures, proof is difficult to demonstrate and the victim always seems to end up with damage to her reputation. A lot depends on the culture of the organisation. By and large the public services seem to have a better record than private companies, particularly those in the financial world. But we also found examples of overt sexism in unexpected places. In Chapter 5 we describe some of the disgraceful things that happen in British orchestras.

Subtle Pressures

All women are subject to the subtle pressures that arise directly from the nature of our culture. Although rarely acknowledged, they form a matrix of uncomfortable constraints. Girls and women are judged by their appearance to an extent that men, if they suffered similar scrutiny, would find intolerable. Men have, in the dark suit, a convenient uniform that will pass as satisfactory dress for most work and formal occasions. Women on the other hand have to find a style of dress and presentation that matches their personality and avoids the pitfalls of dowdiness, flamboyance and sexiness. And this has to be achieved in the full knowledge that a woman's appearance will be studied more intently than any man's and that every person she meets will draw conclusions about her personality and her competence from the clothes that she wears, the make-up she has chosen and the way her hair is styled. We examine the compelling importance of appearance in Chapter 6.

How to behave is an even more potent dilemma. Men know the behaviour that is expected from powerful men because they see examples of such men at the top of just about every organisation. But if a woman copies the behaviour of a typical alpha male she is liable to be greatly disliked. Male society has a list of unpleasant labels to describe such a woman: 'Hard bitch' is one that comes quickly to mind. On the other hand if she adopts the softer manner that men are taught to expect from women, she is liable to be dismissed as weak and lacking in those leadership qualities that men define in such overtly male terms. In Chapter 7 we explore how the expectations of family, colleagues and society inhibit women and how those pressures affect a woman as she tries to forge a successful career.

Maternity

Ambitious men sometimes claim that men and women face similar problems and that the differences are merely matters of degree. But even the most ardent defender of the male position would have to admit that in one very important respect the difficulties faced by women and men are qualitatively different. Our society has not yet found a way to reconcile the requirements of work and motherhood. Employment in this country, as in many others, is based on the expectation that careers will be continuous with no breaks. So every woman who wants a child faces what amounts to a crisis in her career as she grapples with an entanglement of dilemmas that have no equivalent in the lives of men. A woman must decide whether it is better to have children early or late, whether it is better to have children close together or with a gap, how long she dares take for maternity leave, whether to move down – because in the eyes of most employers, it is down – to part-time work, how to organise childcare, how to deal with child illnesses, how much support to expect from her partner or husband and how to rationalise her situation so that the career can be kept alive and the guilt, which she feels and which others will load on her, can be kept under control. As every woman knows, even this list is only a pale description of problems that, in reality, can build one upon the other until they form an obstacle that seems impossible to surmount. We have named Chapter 8 'The Maternal Wall' because maternity acts as a barrier in every woman's career. In some cases banging up against the maternal wall can kill a career or stop it dead.

Solutions

We never intended this book to be merely descriptive. We believe that the imbalance of power in Britain is wrong and that action needs to be taken to spread power much more evenly between the sexes. So the last part of our book discusses what can and should be done to remedy what we regard as a great unfairness in British society. Some people might call our proposals aspirational and so they are. But the irony of the current situation is that almost all our politicians and industrial leaders say that they support the aim of having more women at the top – in business, in politics, in the professions and in the Arts. Referring to the changes that the Government wants to see in private companies but also expressing the principle that is apparently supported across all sectors of British society, the Secretary of State for Business, Innovation and Science has said that:

> *Increasing the number of women on boards is not just an aspiration for greater equality; it is also an important issue for economic growth. Research shows that diverse boards make better decisions and are more effective.*[3]

We examine the commitment of our Governments to such statements in Chapter 10. However it is worth noting at the outset that the support that the British establishment gives to increasing the number of women in senior positions is based on a narrow argument: that organisations and the British economy will work better with more women in senior positions. This is an extraordinary piece of, mainly male, narrow-mindedness. In our view the greatest benefit is not any improvement in the quality of decision making or in the performance of our economic system but the benefit to the female half of our population. The opportunity to undertake rewarding and fulfilling work improves the quality of life for women as surely as it improves the quality of life for men.

Quality of Life

Some popular newspapers choose to forget how cramped were the lives of women in the 1950s and 1960s and continue to peddle the notion that women in the western world are happiest when they can stay at home and look after children and husband. The Editors should be introduced to Betty Friedan's book, *The Feminine Mystique*.[4] After talking in-depth to American housewives Friedan uncovered what she called, 'the problem that has no name':

> *Each suburban housewife struggled with it alone. As she made the beds, shopped for groceries, matched slip cover material, ate peanut butter sandwiches with her children, chauffeured Cub Scouts and Brownies, lay beside her husband at night, she was afraid even to ask of herself the silent question: 'Is this all?'*

The facile assumption that work prevents women from achieving contentment is contradicted by all the research carried out during the last 40 years. A notice should be hung in every news-room and in every politician's office reminding them that women have a greater sense of wellbeing if they work and more depression when they stay at home. After surveying the evidence, American researchers Rosalind Barnett and Karen Gareis[5] conclude that, 'In no studies did employed women have worse mental and physical health and a lower quality of life than non-employed women.'

The benefits from work are obvious and substantial. Work brings extra money into the home and gives the person who is in paid work a greater feeling of independence. Employment brings contact with work colleagues, leading to friendship and social support. If the work itself is satisfying, it brings intellectual stimulation and the personal fulfilment that comes from using talent and skills. It is obvious that not all jobs deliver all of these benefits.

Too many jobs are of such low quality that social contact with workmates and a pay cheque are all that can be counted as benefits. Indeed, the challenge for a modern society is to improve the quality of work, for men as well as women. Directing more women back to dependence on a male partner should be no part of any enlightened solution.

Barnet and Gareis do not pretend that there are no conflicts between the demands of work and the demands of domestic life. Time is usually in short supply and the emotional need to be with family members, young or old, often competes with the demands of the job or, more accurately, with demands made by employers. This again is a problem to be solved but the good news is that alleviating the problem is not as difficult as many people with limited imagination (or with a vested interest in the status quo) often suggest.

Implementation and Achievement

We agree with the consensus that something must be done to give women greater opportunity. However we would like to see future policy more firmly based on the needs of women rather than on the performance of organisations and the needs of business. But we are also aiming to do something which is much more unusual. We are interested in progress and implementation; we want to find the best way to achieve what most of the leaders of our country say they want. Sad to report, that happens to be a considerable innovation because, while the leaders of our society insist that *of course* women should have equal rights, *of course* women should have equal opportunities and *of course* there should be more women at the top, in practice, those leaders spend very little time searching for the workable policies that would achieve these laudable outcomes.

A redistribution of power in our society will only be effective if the opportunities available to women are genuinely equal and equivalent to the opportunities available to men. We are not much interested in the sort of changes that appear to offer equal rights but, because they fail to address the deeper problems of unfairness in our culture, produce lots of hope but little fulfilment. As we explain in Chapter 10, we are not interested in some specious numbers game in which women are levered into high-sounding positions but are kept away from the real power. Putting more women on company boards as Non-Executive Directors will not represent equality if the Executive Directors, who wield so much of the power, are almost all men.

Many men and rather too many women think that a solution will come by trying to deal with each difficulty or impediment in turn. Such a programme might produce some welcome improvements but, in the long run, we doubt whether it can reach beneath the symptoms of inequality and deal with the deeper causes. What we have found is that women face a complex of difficulties that are related and in some cases overlap. Appearance and behaviour are closely connected but each derives from the deeper problem of how our society regards women. If we are going to change perceptions we will have to complete the stalled revolution that began more than 40 years ago. Substantial changes will need to be made in how we educate our children, in how women are portrayed in all parts of the media and, even more controversially, in how we define manhood.

We will not achieve equality of opportunity at work unless we find an answer to what Brenda Hale, the only woman on the Supreme Court, has called, "the baby question." Better maternity provisions would be welcome but the deeper problem is that society has not yet accepted that work has to be redesigned so that women can have babies without detriment to their career. And if women are to be given the opportunity to return to their work in a reasonable time, that in turn means that the care of children cannot be left solely to the mother with the father contributing as much or as little help as he feels inclined.

Such matters involve enormous cultural change. In Chapter 10 we consider the possibility that gender equality can be achieved by a slow and steady process. We conclude that this sort of incremental change is too feeble and too open to manipulation to succeed within a reasonable timeframe. We then consider what needs to be done to achieve a substantial redistribution of power within a reasonable timescale – say in a single generation. We recommend ten reforms, involving not just considerable changes in the world of work but also more widely in our society. We accept that a programme with these radical intentions could only be carried through with great determination and through the exercise of considerable political will.

Lessons

In our last chapter, we return to the two lessons that the history of the last 100 years has taught us. The first is that big improvements in gender equality only come about when the changes are backed by a powerful movement of people willing to keep up the pressure until the reforms have been agreed. The second lesson is that the job is not done until those reforms have been carried through and the improvements have been fully implemented. An effective programme is about achieving a genuine change in the distribution of power. After the half completed victories of the 1970s, women should not be content with grand policy statements or with laws that promise much but deliver too little.

That last chapter is about whether women in Britain – and some of the men – are prepared to form a powerful movement to demand that the rhetoric of our political and industrial leaders is transformed into a workable programme of reform. We can find plenty of reasons for optimism in the many campaigns being waged to improve the status of women and to remove the many slights and insults that women are expected to tolerate. But it is not yet clear whether those campaigns can coalesce into a more powerful movement with a wide and radical agenda. That remains an open question but anyone who doubts whether such a campaign is necessary should look at the figures in the next chapter as we describe the extraordinary extent to which women are outnumbered by men in positions of power in just about every part of British society.

Chapter 2

Outnumbered

Brenda Hale sits in the Supreme Court and is now the Deputy President. She is the most senior woman Judge in the United Kingdom. Alongside her sit 11 male Judges. Eleven to one might seem like an oppressive ratio but Brenda Hale is used to being outnumbered by men. When she studied law at Cambridge she was one of only six women on a course of over 100. While at Manchester University she was one of very few women teachers of law in Britain. As she rose through the judicial system, at each level the number of women became fewer and fewer. In 2004 she became the first and only woman to be appointed to the House of Lords as a Lord (sic) of Appeal in Ordinary. She was then appointed to the Supreme Court.

A Shared Experience

Being outnumbered by men is an experience shared by almost all the successful women we interviewed. As they progress up the career ladder, on each rung they find fewer women and more men. For some women the experience started as early as their schooldays. Not long ago mathematics and the sciences were regarded as subjects that boys studied and which girls need not bother with. A girl who wanted to specialise in maths or science was under pressure to change her mind, like the barrister Adrienne Morgan who switched from science to arts because the science teaching at her Girls' grammar school was so inadequate. If a girl was lucky, like Jenny Tonge – now in the House of Lords – she might be allowed to traipse along to the local Boys' School for her science lessons. Helena Morrissey, now CEO of Newton Investments, was in a co-ed Comprehensive school with good maths and science teachers but she still remembers being the only girl in the A level maths class. The scientist Jocelyn Bell Burnell was affronted when all the boys at her school in Lurgan were sent to one room to study the natural sciences and all the girls were sent to another room for domestic science lessons. As she recalls, her parents 'read the riot act' to the school and Jocelyn was allowed to study physics with two other girls amongst a classroom full of boys.

The gender bias in science, engineering and related subjects continued into university. Joan Ruddock MP was one of only 160 women at Imperial College amongst over 3,000 men. Jean Venables, now a successful Civil Engineer, was one of only two women with 60 men on her engineering course. By the second year the other woman had pulled out and Jean Venables was left on her own. More recently at Brunel University, Clare Hierons, now Head of a charitable foundation, was in a group of seven women with over 30 men.

Women who went to university in the 20 years after 1960 usually found themselves heavily outnumbered even when studying arts subjects. Pauline Neville-Jones,[1] later to become the Chairman of the British Joint Intelligence Committee, recalls that, 'There were two women in my year out of a class of 20, but in other years there were none at all. There were very few of us around.' Susan Palmer, who went on to become a Director of Grant Thornton, recalls that in the history lectures at Cambridge there were 10 women and over 300 men. She and the other 'Girton girls' – as they called themselves – decided that, rather than hide, they would sit in the front row of the lecture theatre. Susan Palmer says that Cambridge provided her with a first lesson in how to cope with what became a lifetime experience of being surrounded by large numbers of men.

As they moved into work most successful women once again found that they were heavily outnumbered by men. Sue Vinnicombe, now a Professor at Cranfield University and adviser to the Davies Inquiry into women on Boards, became a graduate trainee at De la Rue where she was the only female among a large group of mainly Oxbridge graduates. When the company relocated to Basingstoke she moved to a post at Lancaster University. Again she was the only woman, this time with 42 men.

Some women also noticed a change of ethos. Not only was there a heavy preponderance of men in the senior positions but the atmosphere felt more macho than it had seemed at university. Together with another woman we interviewed, Shriti Vadera, who became a member of the Council of Economic Advisers at the UK Treasury and then a Minister in the Brown Government, secured a graduate trainee place with Warburg's, the merchant bank. The position was prestigious and the quality of candidates was very high; Nicola Horlick had become a graduate trainee at the Bank the year before. However the women trainees were outnumbered three to one by the men. The strong feeling of being in a minority was increased because the culture was so very male. "It was all there: the jokes, the banter, the lifestyle and the trick the men played of putting a jacket over their chair to pretend that they never went home."

Working in a heavily male environment has become so much like second nature for many successful women that it scarcely merits comment. When prompted, Rowenna Walker, who now works for the global engineering company, Jacobs SKM, explained that men always outnumber women by more than three to one on engineering projects and she is so used to working with large numbers of men that she admits to finding it "rather strange" if she is ever at any event where women are in the majority.

Women are sometimes told that there are benefits in being a woman in a man's world. When Clare Hierons was recruited by Romeike, the media services company, she was approached by a male colleague who told her that he knew why she had got the job. He explained rather ungraciously that, in his view, it was because the company wanted a woman manager who "could deal with women's issues". Clare Hierons says that she had a mental picture of being required to keep a calendar detailing the menstrual cycles of all the female staff.

As successful women rise into the topmost positions, they find that the number of women thins out even more. Sally Martin, now a Vice President at Shell Downstream, notes that at the moment there are three female Non-Executive Directors on the main Board and no women at all on the Executive Committee. There is often a similar pattern in the public sector. When Mary Evans joined Wandsworth Council in 2000 she discovered that most of the top 50 or so posts were filled by men. "There was just one other woman and me."

Pioneers

By going into jobs that were so male dominated, the women were breaking new ground. Thirty years ago very few occupations were regarded as normal for women to enter. One of the authors remembers the hierarchy of ambition that operated when she was in her teens. The very brightest girls at her girls' grammar school went to university, the next group were expected to go to teacher training college, the next trained as nurses and finally the others were urged to become secretaries. Even getting into university did not open up many new opportunities and women graduates often went on to become teachers, like one of the authors of this book. Jan Royall, Leader of the Opposition in the House of Lords, took a degree in French and Spanish at Westfield College, London and – not sure what to do next – took a bilingual secretarial course at South Bank Polytechnic. Another woman told us that her mother had encouraged her to become a bilingual secretary and work locally and was very surprised when her daughter moved to London to do a PhD and then joined the Civil Service.

Many women went on to become pioneers in their chosen profession, breaking through to become, like Brenda Hale, the first woman who has held a job that in the past had always been occupied by men. Susan Greenfield was the first woman to be head of the Royal Institution. Deirdre Hutton is the first woman to chair the Civil Aviation Authority. Suzanna Taverne is the first woman to be in charge of managing the British Museum. And, famously, Marin Alsop became the first woman to conduct the Last Night of the Proms, although when she made her closing speech she expressed some surprise that in the twenty-first century women were still having to record 'firsts'.

Being a pioneer is never easy. The first woman appointed to a job that has always been held by a man will be scrutinised by everyone around her. If she is to survive, she had better be very well qualified, very thick-skinned and have impeccable judgment. As Brenda Hale shrewdly observes, "Being first is very hard. Being second is much easier".

Unfortunately that second appointment is sometimes a long time coming. After an election that was fiercely contested and not altogether straightforward, solicitor Pamela Castle was the first woman to be become Chairman of the UK Environmental Lawyers' Association (UKELA). But a decade has now gone by and no other woman has chaired UKELA. The Institution of Civil Engineers (ICE) was founded nearly two centuries ago and has so far elected 150 Presidents; 149 of them have been men. In 2008 Jean Venables was elected as ICE's only woman President. She has not set a trend. Women make up less than 2 per cent of the Fellows (sic) of ICE and no other woman has followed her.[2]

Brenda Hale fears that something similar might happen in the Supreme Court. "I am disappointed that in the 10 years since I was appointed not one among the 13 subsequent appointments to this court has been a woman. Things are improving in the lower ranks of the Judiciary but regrettably not up here."

Barriers

Most of the women who achieved success in the last decade began their climb to the top in the 1970s and 1980s when discrimination and misogyny were both common and overt. Joan Ruddock became an MP in1987 and says that she felt that she had, "entered a world where I didn't fit". The atmosphere in Parliament was oppressive. "It felt like a cross between a public school and a working men's club." Early on Joan Ruddock spoke in a debate about the iniquities of strip searches in Northern Ireland. A Tory MP shouted out, 'I'd like to strip search you!' Joan Ruddock adds that no one protested at this outrageous remark and the MP concerned was not censured in public or in private. The House of Commons in the 1980s was no place for a woman who was faint-hearted.

Wendy Savage went to Cambridge to study chemistry but when she and two men decided to switch to medicine she hit an unexpected barrier. She discovered that women were only allowed to take up a tenth of the places on the medical degree course. So while her two male colleagues started their medical studies immediately, Wendy Savage had to wait for a year until she could be fitted in. Even when she qualified she was made to feel out of place. In what must be the most ridiculous example of narrow-mindedness that we heard during our research she assures us that, when she applied for a senior registrar post at a world famous London hospital, she was told by a senior consultant in all seriousness that, "There is no place in gynaecology and obstetrics for married women!" She adds that she was pleased to meet this man later in life after she had become a consultant gynaecologist.

In the 1980s stupidity, customary restrictions and informal rules meant that many employment opportunities were closed to women. Barbara Young, now CEO of Diabetes UK, recalls that when she applied for a job at Westminster Hospital she was told by the Chairman of the interview panel that, "We don't usually do women at Westminster."

Women employees were often regarded as a source of trouble. The scientist Jocelyn Bell Burnell[3] spent the summer after university working at the Jodrell Bank Observatory. She enjoyed it so much that she wanted to stay on to study for her PhD in radio astronomy. However she was warned by other students that Jodrell Bank would not take her on because of an incident that had occurred a few years earlier. Apparently a woman and a male colleague had, as Jocelyn Bell Burnell recalls, 'put the dormitory to a use for which it was not intended'. After this, Bernard Lovell decreed, 'No women!'

At job interviews women were regularly asked whether they were intending to get married. Jenny Tonge made the tactical mistake of telling the truth. She explained that she had just become engaged and was planning to marry the following year. She did not get the job and when she met one of her interviewers some years later he told her that the appointment panel were horrified by her answer.

The Civil Service operated very straightforward restrictions. Pauline Neville-Jones[4] explains that during her early days in the Foreign Office, 'We were second-class citizens, really ... There were quite a lot of things that women were considered unsuitable for.' Women who wanted to be diplomats had to stay single. 'There was the bar on marriage. That lasted until the mid-1970s. The situation was that you had to resign if you got engaged – if you were a woman that is!' Men on the other hand were encouraged to marry. Having a 'presentable wife' was regarded as a significant advantage for a male diplomat.

At the time, married women were regarded by most employers as having divided loyalties and the first pregnancy usually marked the end of a woman's career. In most occupations the expectation was that a woman would leave her job some time before the birth of her child and would not return. There were few exceptions. Mary Evans, who worked first as a teacher in Wiltshire and then as an officer in local government told us, "When I first started teaching, I didn't know of anyone who'd had children and then came back to work."

Because women, and particularly young women, were generally regarded as short-term employees, little attention was given to training or developing their skills. We were told of one big company that had a written policy that they would recruit boys after A levels but girls would be recruited at age 16 because their work was less demanding and they did not need the higher qualification. Mary Chadwick was recruited to the Management Development Programme of a large bank. However she was surprised to find that her male colleagues were being sent on training courses while she was not. Eventually she asked when she would be trained, and was told that she could go on a course when it "could be fitted in." It never was. Significantly she adds, "I didn't pick up on it as discrimination at the time. I thought that it was personal to me."

Men were regarded as much more likely to be reliable long-term employees than women. That assumption led to all sorts of unfairness. Deirdre Mackinlay trained as a midwife but when she became a junior manager in the 1980s she noticed that applications from women for the most senior jobs were given little attention. Men always seemed to get the top positions. Indeed, "Men who had retired from the army and the navy, with no clinical experience, were being recruited to be our managers in the NHS."

Pay and Discrimination

The most obvious area of discrimination was pay. Separate rates of pay for men and women were common until well into the 1970s. The fact that men were paid more was justified on the grounds that men had to be the breadwinners for a whole family while a woman was working for what, even in the 1980s, was often called 'pin money'. In 1975 the gap between the hourly earnings of men and women was nearly a third.

Pay differences between men and women proved difficult to eradicate. Eventually in the 1960s the campaigns mounted by the trade unions for equal pay for white collar workers in the public sector achieved some success. Equal pay was agreed for teachers in 1961 and for most white collar civil servants and local government officials in stages by 1962. However, only women doing exactly the same jobs as men benefitted and there were many exceptions.

Progress for women doing manual work was even slower. In 1968, women working in the upholstery section of Fords in Dagenham objected to new pay proposals that would have reduced their status. Their strike gained enormous publicity, particularly after Barbara Castle, the Minister, intervened. Although the strikers ended up with rather less than they deserved, the strike focused public and media attention on the unfairness of women's pay. Reflecting the change in public mood, the Equal Pay Act was passed in 1970 and took effect at the end of 1975. There were significant ambiguities in the Act but at least it established the principle in law that women should be paid the same as men for the same work and for work of equal value.

In 1975 the Sex Discrimination Act was passed with the intention of protecting women (and men) from discrimination on grounds of sex or marriage. The Act covered employment, education, training, the selling of goods and services and the sale of property. The Act also set up the Equal Opportunities Commission with the duty of promoting equality and ending discrimination. The Commission added an important element to the Equal Pay Act: the Commission could help women (and men) bring discrimination cases to Industrial Tribunals and to the courts.

Transition

Reflecting on the 1970s and 1980s, many of the women we interviewed describe it as a period of transition. Significant changes were taking place in society. The contraceptive pill came into general use during the sixties. Abortion was legalised in 1967. From the 1960s a new wave of feminist campaigners in the Women's Liberation Movement exposed and challenged the sexism that was such a well-established feature of British life. Their agenda was to eradicate discrimination in all areas of life and they won some notable successes. In a number of ways British life was transformed. Slowly the way women were regarded began to change. It became accepted for married women with children to have careers. More women went to university. More women thought that they had choices in life. The demeaning and offensive remarks, the patting, the touching and the swaggering macho behaviour that was alleged to define masculinity became somewhat less acceptable and less apparent.

The Women's Liberation Movement wanted to start a revolution and their campaigns certainly managed to change the way women were treated, the way women felt about themselves and the way the discourse about women's rights was conducted. Equality for women moved from being regarded as an eccentric demand put forward by strange women who wore dungarees and no make-up into a mainstream political position supported by every civilised person. That was the great success of Women's Liberation. Unfortunately there was also a significant failure. The transformation in cultural values was not accompanied by any substantial change in the balance of power in British society.

The Figures

The many reasons why equality has not been achieved are presented in this book. Some are controversial. But what is clear with the clarity of best crystal is that, in twenty-first century Britain, men continue to hold most of the positions of power and women do not. More than 30 years after the high point of the Women's Liberation Movement, the level of control that men continue to exercise on positions of power is extraordinary. Here are some of the figures:[5]

In Government:
>The Coalition Government is committed to equality for women. But more than three quarters of the Coalition Cabinet is male.

In Parliament:

In 2014 the Conservative Party is the largest Party in the House of Commons. Male Tory MPs outnumber female Tory MPs by more than five to one.

The Liberal Democrats do even worse. Only one in every eight LibDem MPs is a woman.

The Labour Party is the best of the main Parties but male Labour MPs still outnumber women by about two to one.

In the Civil Service:

There are 35 Permanent Secretaries or their equivalents at the top of the Civil Service. Only seven of these 35 are women. The Head of the Civil Service is a man.

Amongst all levels of senior management in the Civil Service, men outnumber women by more than two to one.

In the Judiciary:

Out of 12 Judges in the Supreme Court, only one is a woman.

In the Court of Appeal, only one of nine Judges is a woman.

In the High Court only one out of every six Judges is a woman.

In the Crown and County Courts only about a quarter of Judges are women but the highest proportion of women sit at the lowest level as Deputy District Judges.

However in the Magistrates Courts about half the Magistrates are women and almost half the Bench Chairmen (sic) are women.

In private companies:

The most powerful people in large Companies are the CEO and the Finance Director. In the 350 biggest Companies (the FTSE 350) there are 700 such positions. Only 31 of these posts are held by women and 669 (over 95 per cent) are held by men.

After an Inquiry and much exhortation, the proportion of women sitting on company Boards has reached about 20 per cent in the biggest 100 companies. That means there are still four men for every woman.

The situation in the next 250 companies by size is worse: more than six men for every woman. And the proportion in the next 800 companies – those small enough to escape the spotlight – is worse still.

In the trade unions:

> Half of the trade unions in the Trade Union Congress (TUC) are led by women, and the General Secretary of the TUC is a woman. However the three largest trade unions, which have in membership about half of all trade unionists in the UK, are all led by male General Secretaries.

In the media:

> Only one of the 20 national newspapers is edited by a woman, and women are similarly outnumbered amongst the editors of regional newspapers.
>
> Over three-quarters of the articles in national newspapers are written by men.
>
> Fewer than a quarter of accredited Westminster Lobby Correspondents are women.
>
> Over eight out of every ten people who appear on Radio 4's flagship Today programme are men.

In the police:

> Fewer than one in every seven Chief Constables is a woman.
>
> Only one in every six Superintendents is a woman.
>
> Only one in every seven elected Police Commissioners is a woman.

In the military:

> There is no woman holding the rank of General, Major General or Brigadier.
>
> The most senior rank held by women is the rank of Colonel and fewer than four in every 100 Colonels are women.

These statistics point to an unequivocal conclusion: the optimists we mentioned in Chapter 1 are wrong: men have an iron grip on positions of power in Britain. Men control the Government, Parliament, private companies, the media, the Judiciary, law enforcement, the military and important institutions. The balance of power in favour of men is not marginal or even substantial: it must accurately be described as overwhelming.

Many of these results are entirely predictable. Few people will be surprised to learn that men dominate the senior ranks in the police and the armed forces. In the same vein the male dominance of the House of Commons is well known. Indeed it is a sad and ridiculous truth that if you add together the Members of Parliament called David and Michael the total comes to the same number as there are women MPs in the Conservative Party.[6] Nevertheless, optimism persists. Many of the women we interviewed accepted that things were discouraging within their own sector but believed that things were more equal elsewhere. In particular, women in the private sector assumed that women are doing significantly better in the public sector. In strict statistical terms this is true: women certainly hold more important positions in the public sector than in private companies. However the public sector figures only look relatively good because the record of most private companies is so poor. There is scarcely any part of the public sector where women hold more positions of power than men. The NHS is fairly typical. About two-thirds of Chief Executives and two-thirds of the Chairs of NHS Trusts are men. And of course the Chief Executive of the NHS is a man.

The situation in local government is rather worse. Fewer than one in four local authority Chief Executives is a woman. At one time the number of elected women Councillors was rising steadily and there were even predictions of gender parity. That prospect has receded. Male Councillors outnumber female Councillors by about two to one. Perhaps more significant is the revelation that in local government, as in so much of private industry, the real positions of power are almost all held by men. Approximately seven out of every eight Council Leaders are men.

The situation in education is something of a surprise, even to people familiar with the sector. It is true that 71 per cent of the Head Teachers of Primary schools are women but this is a wholly exceptional statistic; women have not claimed a majority of headships elsewhere. Almost two-thirds of Secondary school Head Teachers are men. And in higher education only one in every seven University Vice Chancellors is a woman.

Some people that we interviewed suggested that women have done particularly well in the voluntary sector. This turns out to be another myth. If there ever was a time when women led a substantial proportion of major charities, that moment is past. In 2012, 74 of the 100 largest charities had a man as Chief Executive or Director. In that year, 83 of the 100 largest charities were chaired by a man. Perhaps even more surprising, over two-thirds of the Trustees of the 100 largest charities are men.

The Arts are often mentioned as a sector where women come into their own. Once again the research reveals that this claim has little substance. The only British professional orchestra with a female leader is the Northern Symphonia. There are 22 national theatre companies in the UK and only seven have a woman as Director. Even more surprising is that only three out of those 22 national theatre companies have a governing body that is chaired by a woman.

There are 50 principal national and regional museums and galleries in the UK. Only 14 have a Director who is a woman and only seven have a Chair of Trustees who is a woman. Amongst the Trustees of these organisations, men outnumber women by nearly three to one.

In television companies the picture is even more dismal. Not a single woman is the Chair or Chief Executive of a privately owned television company; male Directors outnumber women Directors by almost three to one.

Many of the statistics quoted in this chapter comes from 'Sex and Power',[7] the excellent reports produced for the Equality and Human Rights Commission. Taking account of the statistics from that report and all of the relevant surveys, including our own research, it is easy to summarise the position of women in Britain in the second decade of the twenty-first century:

> In general, women only hold about one in five of the important positions of power. There are few sectors where women hold as many as a third of the powerful positions and it is a great rarity for women to hold over 40 per cent.

In short, and with only a tiny number of exceptions, men heavily outnumber women wherever power is located and wherever power is exercised.

The Exceptions

However, the exceptions – although few in number – are worth considering. There are only two examples where women have achieved a position of power by what might be termed 'natural evolution': women hold a substantial majority of Primary school headships and women are also close to holding a majority of Chairs of Magistrates; men still hold more but the margin is narrow.

The other two notable exceptions have not resulted from evolution but from direct and determined action. The BBC Trust, unlike the Boards of other big media organisations, includes an equal number of men and women. This was achieved not by evolution but as a result of deliberate policy. More important is what happened in the Devolved Administrations. Both the Scottish Parliament and the Welsh Assembly were set up amid declarations that these new democratic institutions would not replicate the male hegemony of the House of Commons. As a result of determined action by the political parties in Scotland and Wales, women have achieved a better representation than in Westminster. Compared with the figure of 22 per cent of women MPs in the House of Commons, about 35 per cent of the Members of the Scottish Parliament are women and 42 per cent of Members of the Welsh Parliament are women. The rather better news is that, for a short time until Johann Lamont resigned, the Leaders of the three main Parties in Scotland were all women – a situation that was unique in the Western World.

Policy makers might learn important lessons from these exceptions. The circumstances where women have achieved power by natural evolution without direct action are very few in number and the occasions when direct action has been taken to achieve equality are also very few. So laissez-faire governs policy and Britain remains what Angela Eagle MP calls 'an 80:20 society': men hold 80 per cent of the positions of power and women hold only 20 per cent.

The Reasons Why

This book aims to explain why, after what seems like a significant change in public attitudes, after a general acceptance amongst Britain's leaders that we need greater equality and after two major statutes, this enormous imbalance of power continues. We start with the two ground-breaking pieces of legislation that were intended to end discrimination and open the way to greater equality.

The Equal Pay Act and the Sex Discrimination Act were enormously important in declaring that public policy supported equal rights for women. But unfortunately they had only limited success in their specific tasks of wiping out discrimination and delivering equality. As so many women have found, equality in law does not, of itself, guarantee equality in practice.

New laws, particularly laws that seek to establish new rights, need to be enforced and, as several of the lawyers we interviewed have explained, the enforcement of these two laws has been patchy, uncertain and incomplete. On the plus side Emma Howard Boyd, a Director at Jupiter Asset Management, told us how the behaviour of financial services companies in the City has changed significantly in recent years, in part due to a series of important and costly legal cases brought by individual women. We note that some of these women have become public figures as a result. Unfortunately this high level of publicity is part of the problem.

A woman who feels that she has suffered discrimination is able to take her case to a Tribunal. At first sight that seems wonderfully reasonable. In practice it usually results in a horrendous experience for the woman applicant. Tribunals were meant to provide informal justice in a relaxed atmosphere. That hope has never been fulfilled. Very quickly cases became adversarial contests between lawyers, many of whom – as barrister Adrienne Morgan pointed out to us – are used to practising in the criminal courts. To be successful, the woman applicant has to challenge her employer in public and that can be traumatic. The employer's lawyers will most likely disagree with her version of events, cross-question her about the details and suggest that she is either mistaken or telling lies.

Soon after the two Acts became law, local and national newspapers discovered that Tribunal cases could provide good human interest stories. So an applicant who takes a discrimination case is likely to find her plight publicised far and wide. A few comments about her appearance and her background will usually be added to perk up the journalist's copy. If the woman is supported by a trade union so much the better but after a few days in a Tribunal even the most resilient individual will feel lonely and isolated. Human Rights Barrister Helena Kennedy always warns women about the risks of taking discrimination cases. "You may be a victim of your success even if you win the case. Disclosure will make you vulnerable and you will pay the price. You may well be seen as a trouble maker by future employers. It might well be a pyrrhic victory." Most of the women who told us about cases of discrimination had reached a similar conclusion. They had decided that keeping quiet and moving on was a better option than the trauma of many hours spent under cross-examination in the witness box taking a case which, whatever the outcome, would raise doubts in the mind of any future employer.

Relying on the heroic and self-sacrificing actions of individual women to enforce major pieces of social legislation is ludicrous. The woman applicant is extremely vulnerable but the employer has a great deal of room to manoeuvre. The employer can brief the best lawyers while the applicant has to meet her own costs: there is no legal aid for Tribunal cases. If the case is likely to be difficult or embarrassing, the employer can always buy his way out of the situation by settling out of court, often with a confidentiality guarantee and at a relatively low figure. Pretty soon employers realised that, in practice, they had much more freedom of action than they expected.

Getting Round the Law

Many of the women whom we interviewed also explained that, because the pay levels of individuals are kept secret, it is easy to get round the law by concealing differences in pay between men and women. When Deborah Hargreaves moved jobs as a journalist on the *Financial Times*, she discovered that her less-experienced male replacement was going to earn £10,000 a year more than she had been paid. She went to see the Managing Editor to complain. 'That cannot be the case,' he said. When he eventually agreed to check, he found that she was right and agreed to increase her salary by the required amount. Deborah Hargreaves discovered the pay difference by accident and she suspects that a lot of women are "quietly paid less than the men they work with".

A mountain of research indicates that men are much more likely than women to go to their boss and argue for a pay rise. When employers want to recruit a particular man or appease a man who is making pay demands, all sorts of little tricks can be used. Men can be advanced through the salary grades more rapidly than women, or they can be offered extra bonuses or 'payments for outstanding performance' that their female colleagues rarely hear about. Lucy Neville Rolfe, who went on to become an Executive Director in Tesco, bears no grudges but reflects wryly that "I think that I was consistently paid less than I should have been until I got on the Board".

Some employers are just as canny, or just as casual, in implementing the Sex Discrimination Act. When Suzanna Taverne was the Finance Director for the Independent Group of newspapers, she encountered behaviour that was so unreasonable that she immediately took legal advice. She told the story as a warning to other ambitious women during a reunion at her College.

> *The Board ... hired a new Chief Executive ... from Mirror Group newspapers, where he had worked for Robert Maxwell. He was well versed in Maxwell's bullying techniques for getting rid of people – removing their desks, ignoring them and forcing them to litigate to prove constructive dismissal.*

> *Intent on cutting costs, one of the new Chief Executive's first acts was to sack me. I was eight and a half months pregnant and he certainly didn't want to waste money on maternity leave.*

Suzanna Taverne stuck it out and eventually the dispute was resolved because the Independent Group was taken over and all the Directors, herself included, were made redundant.

Some people might think that Suzanna Taverne's case is extreme but we heard enough other stories from women we interviewed (some of which are recounted elsewhere in this book) to realise that quite a number of senior managers make decisions about hiring, firing, pay levels and promotion without much regard for the law. Typically they decide what they want to do and expect their HR department or their lawyers to sort out any consequential difficulties. Very often they get away with it because they have great power, long pockets and because the emotional and financial cost to a complainant is so high. Suzanna Taverne accepts that she was helped by a particular turn of events. Otherwise she would have faced what she describes with notable understatement as a "long, testing legal wrangle".

Implications of Failure

The depressing reality is that the revolution that started in the 1970s and raised so many expectations about a major change in British society had little effect on the balance of power. The Equal Pay Act and the Sex Discrimination Act made grand declarations and carried many hopes but, in practice, the provisions could be circumvented with some ease. Unfortunately the period of rapid change in the 1970s was not followed by any continuing drive for reform. In the 1980s the Government of Margaret Thatcher had little sympathy with calls for greater gender equality; she spoke of the Women's Liberation Movement with withering contempt. The Thatcher Governments were a time of high unemployment and great economic upheaval. To many of the activists of the 1970s, the demand for equal rights seemed less urgent than the need to prevent cuts in jobs and pay.

By 1990, as a result of the relaxation of political pressure and the support of Governments, the men who held the top jobs in Britain were more secure in their power and privilege than at any time for a generation. The Labour Government that came to power 1997, while happy to address the issues of childcare and to introduce tax credits that helped many women, had no appetite for a challenge to male dominance in business and gave no particular priority to increasing the number of women in senior jobs in the public sector or even in politics.

The dismal figures that we have presented in this chapter are the result of 30 years of relative stagnation in the field of women's rights. Things are much worse than most people think and there is little sign that things will get much better in the near future. The optimists, of whom there are many, still seem to believe that we are on a path of sustained progress. And, to maintain that convenient fiction, many in Government and in the higher echelons of industry have adopted the cynical practice of applauding each small improvement and consistently ignoring the big picture – with its stark evidence of failure.

Expectations are now so depressed that companies and organisations with only a quarter of the seats on their governing bodies filled by women are apt to congratulate themselves on their success in achieving gender diversity. And because such organisations are generally regarded as progressive, there is little pressure on the rest to change their behaviour. Tokenism is enough. Organisations that have no ambitions to lead the way on gender issues point out smugly that they have a woman or two on their governing body and see no reason to appoint more women to senior positions.

This miserable reality has a depressing effect on the ambitions of campaigning organisations. Groups and individuals who support gender equality might be expected to be pressing for policies that secure an equal position for women wherever power is exercised. But in fact most reformers have set targets that fall well short of a 50/50 split. One well connected organisation campaigning for more women on company Boards is quite explicit about its limited objective: it calls itself the '30% Club'. To be a member, a company Chairman has to promise to use his best endeavours to change the gender balance on his Board so that women make up at least 30 per cent of Board membership. Lord Mervyn Davies, who is advising the Government on how to increase the number of women who sit on the Boards of the UK's biggest companies, has set his target even lower. He wants to achieve a target of 25 per cent by 2015. What is meant to happen if and when that 25 per cent target is achieved has not been made clear. But, for the time being, 25 per cent has been set as a definition of success.

Other organisations have followed Lord Davies and set similar targets. UK Sport and Sport England have decided that the governing bodies of all sports should be made up of 25 per cent of women members by 2017. This target setting, an obvious echo of the Davies process, was an attempt to reverse the decline in women members of sports governing bodies that has occurred since 2011. Is 25 per cent ambitious enough? Senior sporting administrator Debbie Jevans does not think so. 'Surely,' she argued in a recent article,[8] 'we have to be aiming at 50 per cent, to reflect the population.'

The imbalance of power in British society is so considerable that any improvement is to be welcomed. Nevertheless it is difficult to see how targets of 25 per cent or 30 per cent can be justified unless such targets are explicitly described as milestones on the road to equality. That is rarely the case. Very few men seem to acknowledge the self-evident fact stated by Debbie Jevans. In a country where there are roughly the same number of men and women of working age, any figure other than 50 per cent is – by its very nature – arbitrary.

Later in our book we consider how to create a society where power is shared more equally and where women are no longer heavily outnumbered in the top positions. First, we explore the reasons why there are so many men and so few women in those senior positions and why it is so difficult for large numbers of women to break through into the strongholds of male strength and power.

Chapter 3
Fashioned by Men

Until 2011 James Smith was the Chair of Shell UK. During his long career in senior management he often heard people talking about the importance of networks in business. "I never gave the issue much attention. I had done well enough in my career without having a network and I tended to wonder what all the fuss was about." But when James Smith retired he reflected on his time at Shell and experienced what might be called an epiphany moment. "I suddenly realised that I did not have to join some special network because Shell itself was my network. The Shell Company was created for men just like me."

Because it dealt in oil, the British part of Shell was formed later in the nineteenth century than the engineering and textile companies that made Britain into the workshop of the world. Marcus Samuel set up the Shell Transport and Trading Company as an offshoot of the general trading concern that his father had founded 70 years earlier. Samuel, father and son, were ambitious for wealth and success. Marcus Samuel, the son, became Lord Mayor of London, was first knighted and was then ennobled as Lord Bearsted, with a great estate in Kent. In fact Marcus Samuel was the very model of a nineteenth-century grandee: very rich, very powerful and, of course, stereotypically male.

The Natural Order

It is no surprise that Shell was founded by a man. Almost every company was. In the nineteenth century male supremacy was the natural order of things. Men were expected to control every part of public life: politics, business, the great institutions and, naturally, the military. By an irony of history there happened to be a woman on the throne, but the companies, the professions and the processes of government were created and fashioned by men. They were set up and operated in a manner that men found convenient and comfortable.

It would be unfair to say that the great men of the nineteenth century did not value women. Politicians from Wellington to Gladstone, industrialists from Wedgewood to Hunter, and scientists from Faraday to Huxley would have insisted, with comforting platitudes – and in Gladstone's case with an appropriate quotation from the Bible – that women had a vital role to perform in British society. However these great men and most of their contemporaries would have defined a woman's role as managing the household, rearing the children in a godly manner and supporting their menfolk in the public work for which men alone were destined. The almost unanimous view of the men who fashioned Britain in the nineteenth century was that women had no part to play in business, politics or public affairs.

What is now regarded as the subordination of women was taken for granted and reinforced by law. No woman had the vote and the right of women to own property was tightly restricted. A few progressive thinkers like John Stuart Mill challenged the justice of such laws. In his 1869 tract, *The Subjection of Women*, Mill argued that the 'legal subordination of one sex by another ... is wrong in itself, and ... one of the chief hindrances to human improvement'. But Mill's campaign to achieve equality before the law was generally regarded as eccentric and the notion that women might share power equally with men was dismissed as a foolish and dangerous reverie.

Nearly 150 years have passed since Mill's celebrated tract and most of the legal constraints on the rights of women have been removed. However to achieve equality requires more than the removal of barriers or even, as we saw in Chapter 2, the passing of new laws. What still remain in Britain are many of the organisational arrangements, a good deal of the language and a substantial residue of the customs and cultural attitudes that supported the male supremacy of that earlier time. Indeed, the detritus from that male heritage still litters Britain like leaves from some ancient tree that has outlived its time but refuses to die.

The Legacy

The Houses of Parliament are laid out in the style of an exclusive men's club, magnificent and indisputably male. Julie Elliott MP revealed that even the armchairs in the private areas are too big for most women to sit in with any comfort. Aspiring barristers have to attend a set number of dinners in an atmosphere that most outsiders would regard as reminiscent of the comfortably male events that wealthy men arranged for themselves a century and a half ago. As the distinguished neuroscientist Susan Greenfield found when she became Director of the Royal Institution, some of Britain's most prestigious organisations are apt to become rather tetchy if a man is not in charge. Some of the legacy from this distant period of uncontested male supremacy seems particularly bizarre. University teachers are routinely called Fellows even though many of them happen to be women. And their female students study for university degrees that label young women as Bachelors and Masters.

Soon after she started work with the subsidiary of a global bank, marketing expert Susan Palmer met two Directors of the parent company for lunch in the executive dining room. The meeting was lengthy and she asked to be shown to the ladies' room. Consternation followed. In that fine nineteenth-century building there were several lavatories for men but none for women. Eventually Susan Palmer was taken to the top floor and shown to the bathroom in the executive flat. It was not necessary to explain to her that the building was designed for the comfort of men.

The unhelpful heritage from that bygone age still affects the way companies and institutions are organised, where power is located and the way power is wielded. In particular the nineteenth century expectation that the men in our society should dedicate themselves to their public role while women handle domestic matters continues to have a tenacious grip on the popular consciousness and still affects the way modern men and women live their lives.

Hierarchy and Control

Every organisation has its own way of working but, buried beneath the particular practices of individual companies and institutions, rests a male culture that reflects the preferences of the men who made the rules and established the norms of behaviour. In the nineteenth century very many companies were run by the founder or the family of the founder. Ownership was concentrated and the man at the top asserted his right, as the owner, to make all the important decisions. Beneath the owner was typically a hierarchical structure with employees at all levels drawing whatever authority they had from the man at the top. As it happens, most men are comfortable with a hierarchical structure of this sort. Indeed, when boys of all ages play, that is the arrangement that they tend to adopt: playing in large groups with a leader and a hierarchy of side-kicks and followers. So, when family firms needed to raise more capital, and ownership came to be dispersed amongst shareholders, the men who took over the management of Britain's great enterprises made little attempt to change the comfortable structure of hierarchical management and top down control.

Nowadays top Executives in private companies often talk as if they have adopted a management style which is highly participative, with extensive consultation and collective decision making. That impression is misleading. People who work in companies led by a John Browne or a Stuart Rose or a Martin Sorrell are in no doubt where the power lies. Notwithstanding the modern day rhetoric, hierarchical management remains the normal model for the structure of large companies in Britain. Unfortunately, as Rhona Rapaport and her research colleagues have pointed out in a shrewd piece of analysis published a decade ago,[1] that hierarchical structure entails considerable disadvantages. The man at the top usually tries to control too much and much of the talent of other people in the company is wasted. Any initiative launched by the top man is given priority over other work, even if that other work is very important. Catching the eye of the top man is a good way to gain recognition, so individual success and self-promotion come to be regarded as more important than collective effort. The routine and unglamorous work of support staff, most of whom are usually women, rarely catches the attention of the top man and, as a consequence, the work of these female support staff is routinely undervalued.

Giving the man at the top enormous power can also lead to appalling excesses. Extreme examples of just how badly macho managers could behave were revealed during the banking crisis. Fred Goodwin of RBS was called 'Pacman' after the violent character in the early computer game. One of his favourite 'motivational' ploys was to put a cabbage on the desk of anyone who failed to achieve their target. HBOS, RBS's main rival, was increasingly controlled by two men called the 'bootstrap boys' who delighted in their upfront 'in your face' methods. Increasingly the battles between the leaders of these banks became less about commercial advantage and more about personal prestige. According to George Mathewson, the RBS Chairman, even the massive bonuses were not about personal wealth but about who could win what he called, 'bragging rights in a Soho wine bar'. Male arrogance drove the excesses. Throughout the whole period of outlandish behaviour, greed, excess and collapse, no woman held a senior position in either RBS or HBOS.

There are many other stories about the excessive ambitions of male Chief Executives. According to reports that followed news of the Co-op Group's massive loss in 2013, former CEO, 'Peter Marks, bought Somerfield with a hefty £1.6bn price tag because he wanted to be a big grocer, ranking alongside Morrisons … Marks also wanted to run a big bank. So he bought the Britannia building society and wanted to buy up Lloyds. The Britannia deal brought with it thousands of bad loans. The upshot was that the Co-op bank nearly went to the wall'.[2] In his report on the Co-op Bank, Sir Christopher Kelly said that Peter Marks and other senior Co-op managers 'were running the organisation ... as their personal empire'.[3]

Nevertheless, whatever the risks and failures, the strength of tradition ensures that most people still regard a hierarchical structure with a man at the top as the normal way to run a large organisation. And most people still seem to think that it has to be a man. The American academic, Virginia Schein, first used the phrase, 'Think manager, think male' to summarise the results of research she undertook in the 1970s.[4] She asked men and women to identify the qualities needed to be a successful manager and then asked them whether they thought these qualities were possessed by men or by women. The unambiguous result was that a majority of both sexes thought that men had the necessary qualities to manage a business and women did not.

When Schein repeated the research 20 years later, there had been a change. By the 1990s a greater number of British women had come to believe that women, as well as men, might have the necessary qualities to lead companies. But Schein found no corresponding shift in the opinion held by men. In the 1990s a large majority of British men insisted, just as strongly as their predecessors had in the 1970s, that it is only men who have the necessary qualities to be a successful manager; women do not have what it takes.

Leadership

According to Schein's research, most people think that leaders should be tough and decisive. References to leaders and leadership in company meetings and in the media are laden with metaphors drawn from sport and from the military. The picture of the leader as a male hero leading his men to victory against determined opposition is as popular as it is fanciful. In the modern world, successful leadership is not like that. Lesley Wilkin, the UK Managing Director of Hay – the Human Resources consultants – is ideally placed to describe what is really needed. She says that good leaders must be adept at "managing the complex relationships with the many stakeholders" of an organisation. This is not a new conclusion. Annie Pye, from the University of Exeter Business School's Centre for Leadership Studies says that over a century ago sociologists such as Georg Simmel were studying the importance of the social networks through which people operate. Annie Pye's own research continues to demonstrate that successful leaders operate "at the centre of a web of relationships".

This alternative view of leadership, which puts relationships at the heart of a leader's work, might appear quite feminine in character but the traditional picture of the tough and heroic leader retains a much stronger grip on the popular imagination. Unfortunately the extensive body of management literature is not much help in developing a more modern view. Elisabeth Kelan, now Professor of Leadership at Cranfield Business School,[5] has examined the recent work of the three of the most influential management gurus: Charles Handy, Daniel Pink and Tom Peters. Kelan finds that these three have done little to break away from the traditional model. Of course no guru wishes to sound old fashioned and all three writers are keen to declare that modern corporations need to utilise the stereotypical female characteristics of empathy and the ability to multitask. Handy suggests that employers 'want as many women as they can get', Pink wonders whether the next 100 years might be the 'feminine century' and Peters goes as far as to use the female pronoun throughout a section of his book which he dedicates to Oprah Winfrey and Martha Stewart. But those apparently progressive thoughts turn out to be window dressing for what soon emerges as a very traditional view. Instead of accepting women as valid leaders equal to men, the three gurus seem content to place women in a special category where their 'feminine' qualities can be put to best use by their employers. It is as if women leaders are being confined to a side room while the men carry on with the real business of running the show. Pink comes close to giving the game away by concluding that, 'In the future, women earning less pay than men ... and a stubborn glass ceiling might end up mattering far less than some think.'

Leadership continues to be fashioned by men in their own idealised image. The strong support that the British establishment gives to the traditional view was very evident from the manner in which the marriage of Prince William and Katherine Middleton was staged. It was a magnificent spectacle and was watched on television by well over ten million people in Britain and many more abroad. As is customary, Katherine Middleton wore a beautiful white dress. Prince William on the other hand wore military uniform. There is nothing particularly surprising in that decision, although most people do not get married in their work clothes. The curiosity is that William did not wear the rather dull grey-blue uniform of the RAF, the military service in which he worked. Instead, as the *Daily Mail* recorded, 'Prince William was married ... in red'. He had swapped the grey-blue of the RAF for the bright red tunic of a Guards Regiment. The impression created – and obviously not by accident – was of a military hero, displayed in a manner that reinforced the manly stereotype of yesteryear.

By his side Katherine Middleton looked very pretty and supportive but, in the scene that has been imprinted on the minds of so many television viewers, there was not the slightest suggestion that the woman who was marrying Britain's future King would be anything other than a decorative support to this impressive and heroic man of action. In a tableau straight out of the nineteenth century, the future roles of William and Katherine were declared to the world.

Men Appointing Men

Having created the stereotype, men reinforce it repeatedly, often without much thought. When the BBC ran into difficulties during 2012, the Chair of the BBC Trust was interviewed about how the new Director General would be appointed. After explaining the process Lord Patten added, 'He (sic) will need to be surrounded by competent managers.' Patten was obviously so used to assuming that the Director General would be a man that he felt no need to add, 'or she' even though at least one person on the shortlist was a woman. Two weeks later Patten was asked why Tony Hall, the successful candidate, had not been considered for an earlier vacancy. Patten explained that he had first approached Hall in the summer but Hall had declined because he thought that the Director General's job should be done 'by a younger man (sic)'.

In these unguarded moments Patten revealed an attitude that he and many men have deeply embedded in their psyche. The propensity of men to appoint men rather than women to important jobs, often without a second thought, is a phenomenon that causes great frustration to the women we interviewed. Deborah Hargreaves, a journalist who now heads the High Pay Centre, recalls sharing experiences with her sister who works in the Police. "We both agreed that wherever you work, the picture is the same: men always appoint men like themselves." That telling phrase – men always appoint men – was used repeatedly during our interviews. Deirdre Hutton, Chair of the Civil Aviation Authority, believes it happens because so many British men are bad at working and socialising with women. Margaret Littlewood, who taught gender studies at the Open University, makes a similar comment: "Men tend to reproduce what they are comfortable with." The legacy of the past ensures that successful men normally work with other successful men and rarely work with women. In the absence of a strong and sustained challenge to this convenient state of affairs, the pattern (or Patten) is carried through to the next generation.

The American academic, Barbara Reskin,[6] argues that, when men set about making a senior appointment, it does not occur to them that being male might have some effect on their judgement. Indeed she suggests that, just as white people in a white society do not think of themselves as white but just as normal, so in a predominantly male environment men do not think of themselves in terms of gender but as normal people going about their business. Because almost all leaders are male, the appointment of men into important jobs is regarded as the norm; and the appointment of a woman is regarded as an exception to a well-established practice. Men usually find good reasons to hesitate before making that exception. Are we sure that she really has the right qualities for the job? Will she fit in? How will her subordinates react? Will it be a risk? Will the appointment of a woman make us the subject of ridicule if she fails? Is it fair to disappoint the man who probably expects to get the job? After such hesitation, the temptation to revert to what is safe and normal becomes difficult to resist. A consensus view begins to emerge that the woman in question, although a strong candidate, might not be 'quite ready' for promotion. So, with some relief, they appoint the best man for the job.

Closed and Informal

At least a woman who applies for a senior job in a public authority or in a charity can reasonably expect that the post will be advertised and that there will be a formal assessment, interview and appointment procedure. The private sector, on the other hand, follows a practice that is much more informal. The official Review by Derek Higgs[7] in 2003 found that almost half of all the Non-Executive Directors surveyed for the Review had been recruited through personal friendships and contacts. Even more startling was the revelation that only a tiny 4 per cent of Non-Executive Directors had been appointed after a formal interview and only a miniscule 1 per cent had been appointed after answering an advertisement. Lord Mervyn Davies looked again at these figures in 2011 and confirmed that little had changed. This is the old boy network operating without restraint. It is amazing that these disturbing facts have attracted so little public attention and almost no comment from the political parties.

What normally happens in the private sector is that the existing Company Directors, almost all of them men, brief a firm of head-hunters about the sort of person they want. Head-hunters, who make a tidy living out of the current system, normally advise against advertising the vacancy. At a recent City-based conference a leading head-hunter was questioned about this aversion to the advertising of vacancies for Non-Executive Directors. The reply was revealing. 'If these jobs are advertised, companies will have to sift through hundreds of applications, many of them unsuitable.' The questioner pointed out that this is exactly what a good Human Resources department is trained to do.

So in the absence of an advertisement, the head-hunters consult their usual range of contacts and draw up a list of people whom they regard as suitable candidates. The existing Directors will then meet and the lucky person is selected, often after an informal lunch with the Chairman to make sure that the preferred candidate has no unfortunate social habits and will 'get on' with the other Board members. This system is so well-established and so familiar that it is rarely questioned by the participants, who no doubt regard it as open and fair. Yet, short of genetic engineering, it is difficult to imagine a system that is more likely to produce perfect clones of the existing Directors. Without an advertisement, many good candidates will be unaware that a vacancy exists. Because the existing Directors have the power to decide on the sort of person they want, the natural tendency of human beings to favour people like themselves (sociologists call it the 'similarity-attraction paradigm') will be given full rein: men of a particular background and experience will appoint men of a similar background and experience. The Directors will make the decision in closed session, so there is no guarantee that a reasonable spread of candidates, including those with unusual characteristics – like being a woman – are considered at any stage. After this extraordinarily limited process no one should be surprised that the person appointed is almost always a man.

The trouble with a closed and informal system of appointments is that there is no effective scrutiny and no sustained challenge. The comfort and convenience of the men who operate the system are given priority over principles like fairness and equality. The men who appoint other men will deny prejudice, of course, but by doing what comes naturally they tend to exclude women (and many other groups) because there is no protocol which ensures that they must be considered.

Jane Fuller had a distinguished career as a journalist with the *Financial Times*, including as Financial Editor. She is well-known and, by all accounts, well-respected for her knowledge of the Financial sector. After the banking crisis of 2008 there was abundant evidence that the big banks needed to 'refresh' their Boards by appointing Non-Executive Directors with a broader view and greater independence. Of course none of the vacancies were advertised so Jane Fuller could not apply in an open and transparent way. Nevertheless many outsiders might assume that Jane Fuller would have been approached repeatedly by the banks and by head-hunters acting on their behalf. Not so. When pressed, Jane Fuller says that she has not noticed "a sniff of interest". The head-hunters continued to suggest male insiders and male insiders continued to be appointed.

Pauline Neville-Jones, a former security Minister in the Coalition Government, has made a strong case for reform and modernisation. She suggests[8] that the informal approach to appointments and career development damages the private sector and makes a career in the public sector into a better bet for ambitious women. "I believe women profit from merit and performance assessments which exist in the public sector. But this culture is much less strong in the commercial world. I think there is a huge waste of talent in the private sector." As a human relations specialist in the Penna consultancy that works across the economy, Julie Towers is well-placed to make the comparison between the various sectors. She says that public sector appointments are much more open to scrutiny. Most organisations in the public sector audit themselves regularly to see if any part of their procedures is biased, however subtly. So while the pay is likely to be lower for senior positions in the public sector, the ethos and the opportunities for women might often be better.

A Man's Job

The assumption that it is natural for men to do all the important jobs might well be archaic, and perhaps even laughable, but women are surprised at how strongly that feeling is still held by men of all ages. Jan Royall, the Leader of the Opposition in the House of Lords, was baffled when so many young men whom she interviewed for quite junior jobs turned out to be "so bumptious, full of themselves, and strident". A similar judgement was made by a senior civil servant about the attitude of some of the men in the Treasury. "I was surprised that so many of these rather inexperienced young men were so certain of their right to be there and do these important jobs."

In occupations that have been traditionally filled by men, the certainty seems very strong. Corinne Swain, who works for a global engineering company, says that in the 1980s it was not uncommon, after giving her name on the phone, for it to be assumed that she was an unnamed secretary about to transfer the connection over to her boss – 'Colin' – because at that time everyone assumed that senior people in the engineering sector must be men. Chi Onwurah MP says that women who work in science and engineering still have to put up with a very male environment. Stella Paes, the Head of Science for the examination regulator AQA, has organised competitions for young scientists since the 1970s. "The young men always seem to be surprised that a woman is the organiser of a science competition. They always expect a man." She notes that, in this respect, the attitudes of young men have scarcely changed throughout 30 years.

In medicine the stereotypes operate even more strongly. Most people expect a doctor to be a man and a nurse to be a woman. The stereotypes have such a hold on our consciousness that an ingenious American constructed a riddle to demonstrate the point. Here it is:

> *A man and his son are driving in a car one day when they get into a fatal accident. The man is killed instantly. The boy is knocked unconscious but he is still alive. He is rushed to hospital and will need immediate surgery. The doctor enters the emergency room, looks at the boy and says, 'I can't operate on this boy, he is my son.'*

On first hearing almost no one can explain how the doctor, who was apparently killed in the crash, can be well enough to walk in to the emergency room.

In fact the explanation is very simple. It just requires the reader to remember that the boy in the story has two parents. The father was killed in the accident but the doctor who enters the emergency room is the boy's mother: not the stereotypical man but that notable rarity, a woman with a scalpel. Jane Butters is an example of that rarity; she is one of the very few female surgeons at her hospital in Surrey. Even other surgeons find it difficult to appreciate that she is really one of them. At a recent Royal College of Surgeons' dinner, an event which she has been attending for 20 years, she was assumed to be the wife of a surgeon rather than a surgeon herself.

Entitlement

It is not surprising that this long-standing and pervasive assumption of male primacy is accompanied by a very strong feeling of male entitlement. The most extreme example is evident in the Church of England as it struggles to come to terms with the appointment of women Bishops. According to Sally Barnes, who has campaigned tirelessly for the reform, a group of evangelical fundamentalists in the Church believe in the principle of 'headship', declaring that a woman should not have authority over a man and should not teach men. To support their case they make much of the fact that all the disciples of Jesus Christ were men. The Reverend Rose Hudson Wilkins has heard that argument many times and brushes it aside. "All the disciples were also Jews," she points out, "and on that basis every member of the existing clergy would be disqualified from the priesthood".

Other women we interviewed gave less extreme examples but the strongly held view is that many ambitious men see success and recognition as their entitlement. Helena Kennedy, the Human Rights Barrister, notes the tendency for men on their way up the career ladder to behave as if they are the centre of the universe, often becoming "more than a bit arrogant and narcissistic". Joan Ruddock has been an MP for 27 years and has been surprised to find how many men in the House of Commons seem to expect promotion adding, "The ex-public school boys are the worst. They have been brought up to expect that they will get to the top." Eleanor Mack, an economist and energy specialist, suggests that this feeling of entitlement extends right through a man's career. "I have noticed that many men don't seem to feel that they are tightly bound by the rules. They feel entitled to take a chance and explain afterwards."

A common complaint from women is that this male feeling of entitlement sometimes extends to taking credit for the work of their female colleagues. Women record with some irritation that a success achieved by a team which includes women mysteriously comes to be regarded as a triumph for one of the men. "Men are quick to boast about anything they are involved in," is the explanation used by several of the women we interviewed.

Maria Adebowale, the Founder and Director of the Living Space Project, voices a reflection that is so common amongst women that it has passed into folklore. She sat on a Committee chaired by a very prominent male environmentalist. Much to her irritation he regularly ignored her requests to speak at meetings. When she was eventually able to voice her opinion, she noticed that, "My and other women's comments seemed to be ignored until a man said something similar. Then the point was taken seriously".

Sometimes the expectation that the man should be given all the credit for work done by women can be spectacularly unjust. In a recent radio interview[9] the celebrated astrophysicist Jocelyn Bell Burnell, described how, while she was working for her PhD, she made the momentous discovery of the first pulsar. However her supervisor, Anthony Hewlish, not only claimed the credit but, in due course, accepted the Nobel Prize that was awarded for the discovery. Hewlish has never expressed regret for accepting the prize which he clearly thought was his due. Many people do not agree. The prize has been renamed 'The No Bell Nobel Prize' by Jocelyn Bell Burnell's supporters.

A Supportive Wife

The corollary of this inherited picture of male leadership and entitlement is the nineteenth-century assumption that a senior male figure who dedicates his life to business or public affairs should be supported by a wife who confines herself to the domestic sphere and frees him from the distractions of household and family.

After the Women's Liberation campaigns of the 1970s there was some expectation that it would be normal for two successful people to marry and for each to pursue their chosen career. That possibility seems to have receded. The pattern that is re-emerging, particularly in the commercial world, is of marriages and partnerships where one of the partners is expected to forfeit their career for the sake of the other. And because of the long-standing assumption that it is the woman who has the prime responsibility for looking after the home and the children, it is usually the woman who gives up work. Anna Dugdale, Chief Executive of a NHS Trust, notes that very few of her female friends are employed. "Some do voluntary work but most concentrate on supporting their husband and looking after their family."

Liz McMeikan is a successful businesswoman who has worked at very senior levels in the retail and hospitality industries. Her son boards at an independent school with the sons of other affluent and successful people. Recently the boys in his class were asked if any of their mothers worked. Out of 20 pupils only two other boys put their hands up. Liz explains, "Whatever is said in public about men and women having equal career opportunities, the fact is that the wives of successful men are expected to support their husband and not to pursue their own career. The man's career is given greater importance."

In her book, *The End of Men* – a title that promises rather more than the book delivers – Hanna Rosin[10] has noticed the same trend re-emerging in North America. In the corporate world, there is renewed pressure on the wives of high-flying men to give up their jobs. Indeed Rosin goes on to tell ambitious women that if they want to pursue their own career they would be well advised to marry a man from middle management who has little hope of getting to the top.

One very successful woman we interviewed felt that she had to leave a job she loved when her husband was promoted to a position several hundred miles away. When it was pointed out that the alternative was for her husband to turn down the promotion so that her career could flourish, she said rather disconsolately, "We did not discuss it very much. I suppose that he was further advanced in his career and he was earning more than me." The nineteenth-century assumption that the man is the breadwinner and his career comes first is still deeply embedded in British culture.

Sometimes the women who give up work and devote themselves to these domestic and supportive responsibilities, console themselves with the thought that, in time, they can return to their job and continue climbing to the top of the career ladder. Such optimism is rarely justified. British public life assumes that careers will follow the male model – linear, continuous and uninterrupted. Women wanting to return to work after a break find that they are heavily penalised for being away. One woman working in the finance sector managed to negotiate career breaks but what she calls "these stalling periods" meant that she was quite a bit older than men on equivalent managerial positions in the firm, a continuing disadvantage. Pamela Castle had a similar experience. After a period during which she concentrated on looking after her young children, she trained as a solicitor but found that she was treated with some caution by prospective employers because she was several years older than men who had been through their training at a younger age.

Long Hours

Most high-powered jobs have long and unpredictable hours. Men can usually cope with this pressure because they have wives to support them. But women explain that they find it very difficult to accommodate such heavy time commitments while carrying out their traditional family and domestic responsibilities. Kate Grussing, who set up the specialist executive search firm, Sapphire Partners, says that when she worked for McKinsey's, the famous consulting firm, six day working with plenty of late nights was nothing out of the ordinary. Maura McGowan, the Chair of the Bar Council, observes that it is very difficult to conduct a normal family life and to carry normal domestic responsibilities when practising criminal law. "The work tends to be uneven and you can be sent all over the country with little notice, working from 8am till 11pm one day and then 6am to 10pm the next. There's a lot of uncertainty and running around. Such uncertainty means proper child care can be prohibitively expensive, especially when paid out of dramatically reducing fees. It is a terrible shame that the progress of the last 30 years will be undone by economics."

While she was a senior civil servant setting up the Benefits Agency, Ann Robinson says that she did not notice the cumulative effect of working very long hours until she looked down at her feet and found she was wearing one blue and one black shoe.

The obvious question is whether the long hours culture, which makes life difficult for so many ambitious women, is an inevitable requirement of jobs at the top or whether it simply reflects a lifestyle that men are prepared and sometimes happy to accept. Edward Craft, a Partner at solicitors, Wedlake Bell, admits that, when he was in his twenties, working to tight deadlines and even working through the night seemed exciting and rewarding. Fifteen years later he now plans his work rather more carefully to avoid what he regards as inefficient practices. The tiredness that comes with very long hours can lead to poor judgement, and most people who have worked through the night remember with horror some of the decisions that they made in the early hours of the morning.

Men who are less enlightened than Edward Craft can often find more selfish reasons for staying late at work. The job may be demanding but the life of a Senior Executive in a powerful organisation can also be rewarding and glamorous. A Senior Executive is treated with respect, his opinions are given careful attention by colleagues and his instructions are rarely challenged by subordinates. An assistant is usually on hand to make travel arrangements and to handle those minor administrative problems that can take up so much time and which many men find so tedious. And the distinction between work and enjoyable social activities can often be happily blurred, especially when there are clients or investors to be entertained. For some men the option of working late can seem more attractive than going home to help put the children to bed and to hear stories from a domestic world that is much more mundane than the life he is accustomed to at work.

Whether long attendance hours are really necessary was tested by Patricia Vaz while she was an Executive at BT.[11] She explains that she often saw men staying at the office for very long hours not because there was urgent work to do but because it happened to be the custom and seemed to impress the boss. Patricia Vaz did not have that option because she needed to be home in the evening to look after her children. So she did a deal that allowed her to leave at a reasonable time on condition that she accepted extra duties. She was also irritated by the way company workshops always seemed to be organised to include a night away from home. "When a workshop was being planned, (the manager) would ask people to attend the night before ... to have a team building event in the hotel bar." Were these nights in the bar really necessary? Patricia Vaz did not think so and she refused to attend unless there was a formal discussion.

Patricia Vaz is a resilient character and it takes a strong person to stand out against an accepted way of working. However the likeliest outcome of any complaint by an individual, as Patricia Vaz found, is not a change in the system but the acceptance that the woman concerned can opt out. Being treated as a special case might be convenient as a short-term fix but, in the long run, it is the last thing that most ambitious women want for themselves. Women who are given permission not to attend meetings miss out on early notice of important issues and have to spend a lot of time catching up. A woman who is regarded as a special case tends not to be promoted because lodged in some man's mind is the impression that she has asked for special treatment in the past and might be difficult again in the future.

Unattractive to Women

Men rarely appreciate just how deeply unattractive this male culture – with its manly leader, hierarchical structure, top down management control and long working hours – is to women. We heard a good few stories of "male autocrats throwing their weight around", as one woman described it to us. Occasionally the stories get out into the press but most women seem more inclined to keep quiet and look for another job. Emma Howard Boyd, a Partner at Jupiter Investments, says that for many years she took it for granted that the rules of company life were made by men and that women had no choice but to work within them. Gradually she changed her mind and she now believes that the strongly male culture of many organisations must be replaced. However she accepts that changing such deeply embedded attitudes and practices is very difficult and that, for many women, the realistic choice might be just to move on.

The extent of the underlying dissatisfaction with male culture is not always obvious because, once they have decided to change jobs, most women want to leave with the minimum of fuss and with the best possible chance of getting a good reference. In exit interviews women are inclined to cite family pressures as the main reason for leaving. To discover whether there were deeper reasons, Elisabeth Kelan conducted follow-up interviews with women who had left one large organisation.[12] Speaking in confidence some months after their resignation, many of the women explained that, whatever the domestic and other pressures, in reality the main reason why they had left was because they disliked the oppressive male culture in the firm. The suggestion that they were giving up full-time work for a period to spend more time with their family was a convenient fiction to avoid an awkward interview with the boss. Most of the women had either taken up another full-time job or were actively seeking full-time employment in a more congenial workplace.

Work in New Media

This quiet flight of women from workplaces with a culture that is determinedly male reveals a great deal about the nature of twentieth-century Britain. Writers like Charles Leadbetter[13] have taken a more optimistic tone. Leadbetter suggests that the newer industries, particularly in the media sector, are more open and more democratic, allowing the workers a greater degree of independence and control. If this were true it would be very welcome. Unfortunately the evidence suggests that, while the processes might have changed, many of the customs and attitudes that support the primacy of men still persist.

Rosalind Gill of the London School of Economics[14] was commissioned by the EU Commission to examine employment in new media companies in five European Union (EU) countries including the UK. She found that there is a significant gap between the earnings of men and women. Because of this difference many of the women could not afford to rent a studio or office close to the centres of new media activity. They had to work at home and this meant that they were less visible to potential clients and had greater difficulty in winning new contracts.

Perhaps Gill's most depressing conclusion was about attitudes. The informality of the sector, with few of the rules that condition behaviour and with little systematic evaluation of work or open competition in the awarding of contracts, means that personal recommendation is all-important. Women are excluded from many of the most valuable networks and tended to hear of contract opportunities later than the men. One woman commented bitterly, "Give me a formal hierarchy any day over the fake democracy and pseudo-equality of this job." The depressing picture was completed when Gill recorded that none of the women she had interviewed or had completed her questionnaires were mothers. At the conclusion of her research Gill asks the telling question: is this childlessness the result of choice or dictated by necessity?

Customs, Processes and Attitudes

During the last 30 years so many welcome opportunities have opened up for women that it is easy to disregard how much remains of the male primacy that was taken for granted 150 years ago. Some of the evidence is obvious and well-known. The Cabinet and the House of Commons is overwhelmingly male. Most of the biggest companies in Britain are run by men with Boards that are overwhelmingly male. A woman cannot become a priest in the Catholic Church and has yet to become a Bishop in the Church of England. Freemasons, one of the most powerful membership organisations in Britain, is exclusively male. Most of our most important sporting bodies are either exclusively or overwhelming male; this number includes the Boards of almost every Premiership Football Club. Few of Britain's great institutions contain many women and very few have women in senior positions.

All that is bad enough but it is far from being the whole story. As so often with matters of gender, it is what goes on below the surface and out of view which is even more significant and more worrying. The customs, the processes and the attitudes that have persisted since the nineteenth century still produce comfort and entitlement for men and disadvantage for women. Nowadays everyone likes to show a commitment to fairness and each perceived breach of the ill-defined principle of sexual equality is discussed and, with greater or lesser conviction, is regretted. But the normal reaction is significant. Many men try to insist that each example of unfairness is unusual or temporary or trivial. And many women are loath to draw any general conclusions and are inclined to say that life is too short to make a fuss every time a woman is treated worse than she should be. So the customs, the processes and the attitudes that are so convenient for men and so damaging to women are allowed to survive for another decade, or for another generation, or perhaps for much longer.

Equality will not come until the men and women of Britain decide that it is not enough to deal with each example of unfairness in isolation. The achievement of sexual equality requires a careful look beneath the surface at those customs, processes and attitudes that have been inherited from a previous and very unfair society. Moral and political courage is needed to jettison the remnants of that unworthy culture which continues to deliver unfair advantage to men and to deny equal opportunity to women.

Chapter 4
Fitting In

Soon after leaving university, Dianne Thompson, now CEO of Camelot, applied for a job in the ICI Paints division. There were very few women managers in ICI and Dianne Thompson was made to feel even more of an exception when she was told at interview that she needed to perform 10 per cent better than a man if she wanted to be treated equally. She got the job but admits that in her early twenties that demand for exceptional effort worried her. She kept asking herself, "Am I doing enough?"

Every successful woman we interviewed was very conscious of the need to work hard. To fit into organisations that normally have men in all the senior positions, women have, as Anne Marie Carrie put it, "to prove ourselves more often than we should". This feeling seems to pervade all sectors and all occupations. Early on in her career the lawyer Adrienne Morgan was taken aside by one of the Partners and congratulated on how well she was doing. Then he added, "You should know that you will always have to be better than the men." Pauline Neville-Jones[1] says that women in the Civil Service all knew that they would be judged harshly. 'To make average progress, women had to be rather better than average.' The Reverend Rose Hudson Wilkin, now Chaplain to the Speaker of the House of Commons, uses a similar phrase about her work in the Church of England, "I am constantly aware that to make progress I have to be ten times better than my male colleagues." Working harder, and proving themselves better than the men is the price women feel they have to pay if they are to break into the male domain of business and professional success.

Modesty

Unfortunately women soon find that being capable and working hard does not guarantee a stellar career. They also have to make sure that other people, especially the powers that be, know how well they are doing. But most women are reluctant to give much attention to self-promotion. We were told many times that the quality of a person's work "should speak for itself". And so it should – in an ideal world. However, in the world that men have designed, telling others about your successes is regarded as routine: it is an expected part of the culture and, if women do not play that game, they are likely to be over-looked. It is one of the first lessons that ambitious women need to learn.

Not all women do. Liz McMeiken says that she knows from hard experience that she has to be more outspoken about her own achievements but finds that most women are extraordinarily modest. Compared with those written by men, the CVs of women are typically candid and downbeat about their successes. After interviewing hundreds of men and women for senior jobs, Julie Towers has concluded that women tend to undervalue and undersell their experience and underestimate their ability to cope with jobs that they have not yet undertaken.

A head-hunter summed up the difference. "Many men look at a job advert and say, 'I can do that' even if there are a number of requirements that they do not meet. Women seem to search for the one requirement that they are uncertain about and then assume that a single deficiency will rule them out. If there are 18 requirements and a woman has 17, I find myself spending all my time talking about the solitary requirement that she thinks she cannot meet."

Women often need to be told that they are good enough to apply for a more senior job. Anna Dugdale worked as the Finance Director in a hospital Trust but says that she did not think about promotion until a male member of the Board surprised her by saying that he thought she would make a good Chief Executive. Hilary Cotton taught at the Civil Service Training Unit and regularly asked the women who attended the courses, "What is holding you back from getting a more senior job?" The answer was very often, "No one suggested that I should apply." A senior civil servant told us of her own experience that demonstrated the difference between the approach taken by a man and a woman. On one occasion, she had decided not to apply for a promotion because she had recently applied and failed. Many years later, and after several further promotions, a senior colleague would constantly tease her about this, telling people that she had been too busy to fill in the application form.

This constraining modesty continues even after an application has been made. Teresa Graham, Chair of Salix Finance and leader of the 'Women of the Year' initiative, says that, because women dislike boasting, they are reluctant to promote themselves enthusiastically to a prospective employer. Eleanor Mack told us that, in her experience, men apply for a job on the basis of what they think they can do, even if it involves some exaggeration. Women, on the other hand, tend to talk only about the things that they have already done. This analysis helps to explain the conclusions from a study by the consultants McKinsey[2] in 2011. They found that in the US men tend to be promoted on an assessment of their potential but women are promoted on the basis of their past achievements.

Even when a prestigious job is within grasp, women are often cautious about the move. Lesley Wilkin's boss at Hay left the company and she was urged to apply for the vacancy. However she was convinced that she did not have sufficient experience, particularly in one important aspect of the work. Eventually she agreed to apply because she thought that "the process will be useful experience". After interview the job was formally offered to her but she turned it down because, "I was not ready for it". Her colleagues were amazed and so was her husband. "A man would never have done that," was his verdict.

Other women told us that they had been reluctant to take on a task unless they were sure that they were completely ready. Sarah Anderson had gained a considerable reputation as a spokesperson for small companies. As a result she was approached by William Sargent, then Second Permanent Secretary at the Business Department, to undertake a review of existing regulations. She told him that she thought that she was not experienced enough to make a success of such a complex task. Sargent had to work very hard to persuade her that she had exactly the qualities that the task demanded. He was right. The resulting report that bears her name is generally regarded as a very accomplished piece of work.

Attitudes to Work

As we tried to unravel the reasons for this degree of modesty, we found a substantial difference between what men usually look for in a job and what women want. Susan Greenfield put it most succinctly: "Women apply for jobs because of something they want to *do*, while men apply because of what they want to *be*." This generalisation might seem a harsh judgment on men's career ambitions but it is supported by findings from a good deal of research.

In 1999 Jane Sturges[3] studied the attitudes and aspirations of managers in the telecommunications sector. She found that women valued job satisfaction and personal fulfilment more highly than men and in particular more highly than young men. Women saw promotion and pay increases as a means of achieving greater satisfaction and not as ends in themselves. When she came to categorise the interviewees, Sturges labelled nearly half the men she interviewed as "climbers" – people who valued salary and status very highly. Not one of the women was categorised in this group.

More recent research in 2008 by Nelarine Cornelius and Denise Skinner[4] came to similar conclusions. The study was based on interviews with men and women in senior Human Resource posts throughout the private, public and consultancy sectors. All the participants said they wanted to improve their knowledge and undertake challenging work, but there was a clear difference between the priorities of the women and the men. The women were more likely to talk about the challenges of the work while the men were more likely to talk about their status.

This greater concern for the nature of the job and the satisfaction that it gives might explain why quite a lot of successful women express reservations about working in parts of the private sector. Teresa Graham explains that many women dislike the narrow focus on profit and share price. Most women, she says, prefer to work for organisations with wider objectives. Lesley Wilkin also makes a contrast between public and private sector work. In her opinion public sector work requires more subtlety: there are more stakeholders, success is harder to define and certainly more difficult to measure than in the private sector. After working in the NHS and in the voluntary sector, Barbara Young spent some time on the Board of a private utility company as a Non-Executive Director. She says that the experience demonstrated to her that managers in the private sector focus overwhelmingly on profit and shareholder value. "It's almost all about the bottom line. Perhaps that's the way it has to be."

The Issue of Status

In our research we tried to understand just how strongly men and women feel about job satisfaction and status and whether the differences really are as marked as Sturges, Cornelius and Skinner suggest. In fact our research reinforces the results of the academic work: we were struck by how little importance most successful women seem to attach to status. We record in Chapter 3 and elsewhere that women are reluctant to press for salary increases. But the issue goes far beyond money. Most successful women have a clear idea of what they want from a job. Many of the women we spoke to talked about job satisfaction, some talked about the need for a job to pose a challenge. Lynne Berry said that hard work was fine but there also had to be enjoyment and a sense of fun in any job that attracted her. Not one woman we interviewed mentioned status as a reason for applying for a job.

At a conference we both attended, a recruitment specialist said, to knowing laughter, that in her experience men think about being promoted to a more important position almost all of the time, while women concentrate on the job in hand and the possibility of promotion rarely seems to cross their mind. During her career in Shell, Sally Martin says that she refused to give time and effort to what she describes as "just chasing promotion". Instead she insists, "I will judge the job on its merits, not on the basis of whether it will help me to get higher up."

After Kate Grussing left JPMorgan, she received a number of job offers, including a very lucrative offer from a private equity firm. She turned it down. "I decided that working for a very rich man just making money was not a very satisfying way of spending my time." Kate Grussing has a very supportive husband but it must have taken a lot of strength and maturity to walk away from such a well-paid job without having another option lined up.

Shriti Vadera moved out of a very senior and well-paid job in the finance sector to work for the Treasury. She admitted that, because the job was worthwhile, "I gave little attention to the money aspect". That turned out to be a considerable understatement because she subsequently found that her new salary was less than a tenth of the salary she would have been paid in the private sector. But, as she told us this story, she gave a little shrug and added that it did not really matter because, "I would have accepted the offer anyway."

A number of other women had moved to lower-status jobs because they thought that the work would be more interesting. Deborah Hargreaves was the Editor of the Monday edition of the *Financial Times* when a vacancy came up for the paper's EU correspondent. The Brussels job was at a much lower level in the paper's hierarchy but Deborah Hargreaves was keen to get it. Men working at the *Financial Times* expressed surprise that an Editor would even consider applying for a job that carried so much less power and status. Deborah Hargreaves explained, "I was not really bothered about the status because the Brussels job was the one that I had always wanted."

We found many examples of women who left prestigious and well-paid jobs because they were not getting the personal satisfaction they wanted. When Ruth Bushyager worked in the Cabinet Office she remembers looking out of the window at the cleaners tidying up Trafalgar Square and thinking, with some despair, that at least they could see some immediate benefit from what they were doing. She took a day off, had a good think and made up her mind to leave. Another woman, this time working in the private sector, resigned from a very senior position in the finance sector because, "I felt that the company had lost its way." She took a job with less responsibility but more satisfaction. She freely admits that this was a step down in career terms but said that she felt it was right for her at the time.

It is sometimes suggested that men are so concerned about the status of their job because, in our society, a man is almost completely defined by his employment. For men, success in work equates to success in life. For women, what constitutes success is more complex. Of course women are defined to some extent by their work but they also tend to be defined by their partner, by their children and especially, as we discuss in Chapter 6, by their appearance. Perhaps men feel that they have to be brash and aggressive as they strive for promotion and career success because, for them, the stakes are so high. Perhaps women can afford to be more cautious and more choosey about the work they do because they are able to take a less desperate and more rounded view of career success and its importance in their life.

However this analysis does not help a woman to make a successful career. Attitudes of modesty and caution are not in tune with the culture of the business, professional and political worlds where men have made the rules. In western society, people are used to the noisy assertiveness of business and political leaders and expect any candidate for a top job to behave in that way. When a woman displays caution, men are apt to believe that she is indecisive. When a woman shows little interest in increasing her status, men tend to conclude that she lacks ambition. Caution and modesty might seem admirable characteristics, but in our society they are not regarded as the valuable attributes of potential leaders. Instead they register as disqualifications for high position. In these, and in many other ways, ambitious women find themselves at odds with the prevailing culture of business and public affairs. As Lynne Segal[5] says,"Women usually find themselves working against the grain of the organisations that employ them."

The Stereotype Game

The same applies to so many of the other attributes, real or imagined, that we think of as feminine. Women soon discover that what might be called the 'stereotype game' works only one way, and that is against them.

Men are expected to be decisive and, when they reach decisions quickly, they are applauded. A woman is expected to be communal but, when she is soft spoken and collegiate, she is given little credit because 'that is the way women go about things'. A man who 'leads from the front' is much admired; a woman who consults her colleagues to ensure that a decision has widespread support tends to be the subject of impatient criticism: 'She takes an awful long time to make up her mind!' District Judge Susannah Jones told us that in her experience a man who takes time off to attend events at his children's school is praised as a good father but a woman who does exactly the same finds that people start muttering about how she should get her priorities right.

One Human Resources specialist explained, with an expression of regret, that the experience in multitasking and crisis management that almost every woman gains by running a home and coping with day to day problems is given no weight whatsoever when it comes to choosing someone for a management position. Another told us about a woman who had run a large and successful scout troop for several years but that skill and experience was given no value by potential employers. "As far as they were concerned it was just a case of a women looking after kids, and that is what women do." The different way these matters are regarded was given particular point when we heard a former civil servant praising John Prescott. 'He is very good with children, you know.' A man gets credit for such things but when a woman is good with children, it never gets a mention because being good with children is what is expected of every woman.

Advice

So with different attitudes, different aspirations and a different skill-set from the men who made the rules, how are women to fit in? Plenty of advice is available: a large number of self-help books have been written to tell women how to overcome the obstacles and get to the top. Two recent books have attracted a good deal of attention. Lois P Frankel's, *Nice Girls Don't Get the Corner Office*,[6] is written by a management specialist and gives generalised advice. Sheryl Sandberg's *Lean In: Women Work and the Will to Lead*[7] is written by a very successful businesswoman and draws on her own experience to suggest how the problems faced by women can be overcome.[8]

Frankel offers 101 pieces of advice to ambitious women. Some of the advice is straightforward and sensible – stop thinking that other people know more than you, avoid expressing yourself tentatively on every occasion and realise that working hard will not, in itself, bring promotion. But Frankel's book, like so much of the advice offered to women, gives a confusing view of what a successful woman should be like. After saying that a woman should not 'behave like a man', Frankel goes on to tell women to employ the same self-serving tricks that she believes men use to get to the top. She advises women to avoid difficult tasks – let someone else take the risk. Do not share valuable information with colleagues – keep it to yourself to use for future advantage. Try never to take sole responsibility for a task – you do not want to take all the blame if something goes wrong.

Frankel's advice is narrowly focused and determinedly amoral. She tells women to do whatever is necessary to get up the career ladder. There is little concern for friendship, teamwork, business ethics or, most extraordinary of all, job satisfaction. This is the rub. There is little joy or pleasure to be had from the recommendations in this book. Frankel's advice might help some women to get to the top but we can say for certain that most women will not enjoy the journey.

Sheryl Sandberg's book is different in style and tone. It is very readable and has an honesty that adds to its charm. She wrote the book while Chief Operating Officer of Facebook, after a glittering career with Google. This represents success in any terms but Sandberg writes with modesty and a full recognition of her own advantages. She admits, with self-deprecating asides, that she still falls into the traps that she warns other women to avoid. Her chapter on how wrongheaded it is to talk in terms of 'having it all' when many women are worried to distraction about 'losing it all' is well-judged and confronts the guilt that she acknowledges is part of the experience of every woman. Although she chides women for their lack of ambition she understands how difficult it is for women 'to play by the rules that others (she means men) created'.

Sandberg's book has attracted more criticism than she expected from women writers. Some of it is unfair. She is never complacent and no one who reads her book can doubt that she wishes for a better world where women do not have to go through the extraordinary contortions that are necessary to get to the top. But what has upset many critics is that most of her advice, although gently and sympathetically delivered, is telling women how they should change. Sandberg knows that the system is heavily weighted against women but, apart from a few references to the need for more flexible working, she proposes nothing that would make an unfair system more equal. Sandberg's book, like Frankel's, is pragmatic to a fault. Both authors know that women face unfairness but, instead of trying to fix that unfairness, Sandberg and Frankel go no further than suggesting that women should accept the world as it is and try to make the best of it.

Role Models

Unfortunately even some of the sensible advice offered by Frankel, Sandberg and others is, in practice, rather difficult to follow. Almost everybody tells women that having role models will help. Role models perform two useful functions. The fact that women occupy the top jobs in any organisation is a great encouragement to women. An Institute of Management Survey in 2001[9] found that women were much more optimistic about promotion if they could see senior women at the top of their company. Dianne Thompson believes that people have great difficulty in visualising a woman in a job that has always been done by a man. "Seeing a woman in a top job is the only way to convince people that it is possible." Sally Barnes believes that the problem of visualising women in senior positions has been a major reason for the continued resistance to women Bishops in some parts of the Anglican Church. Although there are role models for women Bishops across the world, she believes that full acceptance will only come in Britain when people no longer have to use their imagination but can actually see women acting as Bishops on a day to day basis within their own communities.

A second advantage is that observing role models can give guidance to women on style and behaviour. Most women we interviewed would have welcomed that opportunity but women who started their careers in the in the 1960s and 1970s faced not just a shortage of female role models but a total absence. Susan Palmer said that there was no opportunity to find a relevant role model at any stage in her career: she was usually the most senior woman in every company she worked for. Mary Marsh had the same experience. When reflecting on her own career in education and with the NSPCC, she said, "I had no role models. I had to make it up as I went along." Sarah Anderson was grateful for the magnificent training provided by Grand Met and by Compass but she could find no role models that meant much to her. Her senior colleagues were all male, older than her, with wives, mortgages and a different outlook on life.

We hoped that women who started their careers in the 1980s and 1990s might report a better experience. Unfortunately the evidence suggests that suitable role models are still a rarity. Eleanor Mack has frequently been advised to find a woman whose career she might emulate. She can see the advantages but, because there are so few women at the top of her organisation, she found the advice impossible to follow. On one occasion when the suggestion was made, she explained the problem and asked her colleague to suggest a name. After a pause, the colleague suggested Margaret Thatcher. Eleanor Mack thinks that this answer demonstrates the extent of the problem.

Without the guidance that comes from observing how others cope, women have to decide whether to try to develop their own style or copy the incumbent men. Very experienced women like Deirdre Hutton thought that, however difficult it is, every woman has to find their own approach based on her own talents and her personality. But this is hard work. Young women seem to need to see how women perform in senior women positions. Indeed, research by Penelope Lockwood[10] in 2006 found that female role models are more important to young women than male role models are to young men. Nearly two-thirds of the young women who took part in the study selected a female role model and said that the gender of the role model was important to them. When asked why, most of the women said that it was because the female role model was "like me". Lockwood also found that reading an article about a successful woman in their own occupation increased a woman's self-esteem. Men, on the other hand, did not change their opinion of themselves if they read an article about a successful man.

Having a single role model is not enough. Val Singh, Sue Vinnicombe and Kim James[11] found that young women seem to gain most if they have a wide range of people with admirable qualities that they can select from and emulate, not attempting to copy one person but adopting what might be called a smorgasbord approach.

Singh and her colleagues also confirmed that having female role models in their own organisation was important to the young women they studied. This research echoed what Helen Wells told us when she was Director of Opportunity Now. "Of course it is difficult for young women to find the right approach. They often have almost no one above them in the hierarchy to copy. And those women who have reached the top sometimes have had to adopt a very masculine approach to succeed."

In fact Singh, Vinnicombe and James went rather further. They reported that women who are unable to find female role models in their own organisations tend to suppress their own feminine qualities and take on more masculine modes of behaviour. The researchers could not conclusively explain why this happened but suggest that, in the absence of female role models, the young women might just be copying the behaviour of the men who occupied the top jobs.

Copying Men

Singh, Vinnicombe and James were understandably tentative but their explanation seems very plausible. In an organisation with only men at the top, some women are bound to think that the best way to do well is to behave like those men. Many of the women we interviewed say that they had seen women copy successful men and the result was often extremely unfortunate. Suzanne Warner said that she had worked at various times for four women bosses and three of them appeared more hard-edged and masculine than the men around them – trying too hard, never appearing relaxed and obviously under enormous pressure. When she joined a merchant bank, one interviewee noted that there were only three senior women, "all very driven and scary".

The pressure seems to be greatest on women who are on their own, surrounded by men. Jean Venables recalls that the first woman on the Council of the Institution of Civil Engineers had been brought up to believe that women should choose between marriage and a career and should not expect both. When Jean Venables, a young married woman, was first elected to the Council the incumbent woman found it very challenging. Lucy Neville-Rolfe says that when she first joined Tesco, she found that the sole woman on the Tesco Board was regarded as the toughest person in senior management. Sue Vinnicombe believes that the process happens unconsciously. She remembers a woman on one of her training courses who seemed to have no idea just how much her colleagues resented her harsh and unpleasant manner; she was horrified when she was told what the other course members thought of her.

Most women we interviewed said that they viewed women who imitate men as warnings about how *not* to behave. But Julie Towers is honest and brave enough to admit that, when she started out, she fell into the trap herself. She invariably wore a black trouser suit and adopted a sharp and unsympathetic style, "Trying to copy the alpha male." On one occasion she heard that a woman had been advised not to take a work–life balance problem to her, "because she is the worst person you can go to". With greater confidence and support from others she felt able to be herself, to adopt her own style of dress and to show the gentler and caring side of her personality. Julie Towers thinks that a lot of women make a similar journey.

Other women have found more congenial ways to emulate the men around them. Rowenna Walker feels that she has a natural self-confidence but adds that one of the reasons why she is comfortable working in a male environment is because she likes football and rugby. Another engineer said that early on in her career she was quite happy to be "one of the lads". Jane Fuller is keenly interested in sport and finds that knowledge is very valuable in talking to senior men, both as an ice-breaker and as a way of building good relationships. When one woman civil servant got her first job at the Department for Transport, she enjoyed the company of the "techie" men. She immersed herself so completely in the details of transport that, like many of her male colleagues, she became a train spotter.

Male Networks

Nevertheless, however well they adjust to the culture of an organisation and however hard they try to fit in, most women are conscious that men have all sorts of informal networks which are difficult to penetrate. Heather Hancock explained how these male networks can unthinkingly operate in large consultancies or professional firms. Building relationships can, for example, involve entertaining clients at sports events and other traditionally male-orientated activities. Many men are keen to go as a group: women tend to be less interested and may not always feel welcome. Bonding takes place on such occasions, friendships are made and all sort of gossip is exchanged. Many women, particularly if they have children, find it difficult to be away at weekends and often do not want to extend a long working week by going on to a bar or a restaurant in the evening. Heather Hancock sums it up in a few rueful words. "At the end of the week many of the boys want to play, but I just want to go home!"

Judy McKnight, who led the trade union that represents probation officers, told us what happened every Monday morning in the Civil Service union where she began her career as a trade union official. "Although this was meant to be a meeting to discuss work issues, the first half hour was invariably spent discussing rugby, golf and football. I wasn't interested in sport so I kept quiet but on one occasion one of my colleagues eventually turned to me and said, apparently to try to bring me into the conversation, 'Did you play tennis this weekend, Judy?'"

The process of creating and maintaining male networks starts early. We heard about one organisation where most of the men joined the sports club. At first the women took this at face value and thought that the members were just interested in sport. But it slowly dawned on them that the club was really a mutual-assistance group for the men: "It was full of alpha males helping each other to get on." The all-male Committee of the Club seemed to be the first to know about everything that was going on in the organisation and would plan activities that never seemed to include women.

The existence of powerful male networks is now so well recognised that women are sometimes advised that the best way to get onto the inside track is by joining one of those male networks. For a woman, this is neither easy nor particularly sensible. Male networks are designed to serve the needs of men. The chatter tends to be about stereotypically male issues and most of the men do not want that to change. The meeting places are often where women can be observed and commented on, not always in complimentary terms. Much of the conversation takes the form of banter about problems the men have solved, difficulties they have avoided and successes they have achieved. Male mickey-taking within well-understood limits forms a large part of the conversation. Many women find the unspoken rules mysterious and off-putting.

Researchers[12] have studied what happens when a woman tries to break into this particularly male world. A number of tests have to be passed. The first is to sit quietly through discussions about sport or cars or male achievements which are of little intrinsic interest. The woman will have to field questions which tend to be phrased in ways that challenge her to disagree. Then one of the men will offer her a subtle invitation to distance herself from the rest of her gender by accepting that women, as a whole, do not have an aptitude for certain tasks at which men are claimed to excel. At some point there is usually someone who starts telling a sexually explicit joke to see how she reacts. And if she does not react, she might well be asked to confirm that she does not object to the joke or to the language. If she passes all these tests, she might be accepted, for the time being, as 'one of the lads'. But no back-sliding will be permitted and she will be expected to demonstrate her laddishness at regular intervals. It is not a happy choice. Being on the outside means being short of allies and late with the gossip but, for most women, the price of admittance to male groups and networks usually turns out to be disconcerting, humiliating and rather too high.

Women-Only Networks

An alternative piece of advice proposes that women form their own networks to match the advantages gained by the men. Some of the women we interviewed were doubtful about this approach. "After all," said one very experienced woman working in the private sector, "Men are in the senior positions, so setting up a group that excludes them won't help women to get any closer to the action." Maggie Baxter pointed out that, because of their domestic responsibilities, many women are under greater time pressure than most men. "Networking is only useful if the meetings are for a good purpose. Otherwise it's a lot of hard work for very little reward." We even heard of a case where a group of women got so fed up with being excluded from an influential network that they formed a club with exactly the same name as the male club. It was a good try but unfortunately the men failed to notice the irony, ignored the competition and carried on regardless.

The women who expressed greater enthusiasm for women-only networks mostly had a different model in mind. They were not looking to set up and maintain networks that competed for power and influence with the better-placed male networks. Instead they see the value of women-only networks as a means of providing support for women in a working environment that is often pressurised and uncomfortable. Most of these networks are informal. Helen Charlton says she uses hers to "keep in touch with people who have had similar experience to me". We were told of a few that have been set up within individual companies but they tend to be vulnerable as company structures change or as the most enthusiastic women move on. We also heard from Corinne Swain of a women's support group that seemed to be doing well until the men complained that they were not allowed to join. It was not clear whether the men felt threatened by a women-only organisation or wanted to display some deep commitment to gender equality. The network survived and successfully adapted with a wider remit. It does good work but of course it is no longer a support group just for women.

The most robust groups are more spontaneous and span several organisations. Eleanor Mack met a group of able women on a cross-sector training course. They have kept in touch as a mutual support network. Maura McGowan belongs to a group of barristers and judges that meet socially about four times a year for dinner and more often in smaller groups. A few years ago Barbara Young was part of an expert group set up by King's Fund, the health service think tank. The seven members got on so well that they still meet regularly and they chat through issues either individually or as a group. Barbara Young calls this her "peer support group".

More formal women-only support networks have also been set up for particular professions and occupations. Marianne Coleman[13] describes the work of five of the most important in her book *Women at the Top, Challenges, Choices and Change*. These women-only support networks can be of great value. For women in the law there is the Temple Women's Forum, which is designed to bring people together and offer guidance and help but principally encouragement. The highest accolade was awarded by Dianne Thompson to WACL (Women in Advertising and Communications in London). This professional network was a great help to her when she first moved south and she has seen many other women being given similar help. "The philosophy is to give total support in dealing with all kinds of problems – at work or home or in matters of health." WACL has a regular session when senior women are asked to give a single piece of advice to colleagues. Much of the advice is very down to earth. One speaker explains how to avoid breaking down when subjected to fierce criticism: "Try quietly whistling to yourself." Dianne Thompson believes that the key to WACL's success is the breadth of support that if provides.

WACL was set up nearly 100 years ago and is robust but many formal networks that have been set up in the last 20 years seem to be rather fragile. In fact two of the five featured by Coleman appear to have gone out of existence since she published her book in 2011. Of course formal networks need servicing and that can take a lot of time, which for most women is in short supply. But Coleman also found that women have mixed feelings about the value of formal networks. A few women scorned the very idea that they need the support of other women. "I've made it here myself and don't need a group like this," was the comment from one younger woman. Other women were, at best, ambivalent. One criticism was that the formal networks could too clubby, spending too much time on gossip and not enough on important issues. Some said that the networks tended to be too strong on entitlement rather than on what women really deserved. Others thought that women-only networks might be seen as anti-men. More profoundly, some argued that a women-only network is wrong in principle because it perpetuates the idea that people of one gender should meet and act on their own. Men had started that practice and women should not copy something that is so obviously unacceptable.

The dilemma of what to do about networks is a sharp illustration of the problems faced by women trying to fit into male-dominated organisations. Male networks bring advantages to men by giving them access to power and information. Women cannot easily join those male networks and therefore miss out on power and miss out on information. If women set up their own women-only networks, they gain the support of other women – and that is valuable – but, by its very nature, a woman-only network will not provide access to the power and information held by the men.

Mentors

Without suitable role models and having to cope outside the more powerful networks, women are regularly told that they need to find a mentor who knows the ropes and can help an ambitious woman to fit in and build a successful career. Julie Towers works for Penna, which supports mentoring and provides executive coaching, and she emphasised the value of mentors both from her professional and her personal experience. She had several mentors during her career and they had helped her greatly. Other women talked with enthusiasm about the mentors who had helped them. Anne Marie Carrie gave the names of three people, including a high-profile sporting coach, whom she had relied on for good advice. Maggie Baxter, Chair of Trustees of Rosa, spoke of two people "who believed in me and made me think out my values". Liz McMeikan says that she has been given good advice by several mentors during her career. Barbara Young says that she has a mentor "who can be brutal" but whose advice she values.

These mentoring arrangements obviously worked well but research into the value of mentoring suggests that the advantages might be patchy rather than general. Catalyst[14] looked at mentoring in the US and found that American businesswomen are mentored and coached far more than men, but this has not led to any great increase in the number of women in senior positions. Peninah Thomson, the Chief Executive of The Mentoring Foundation, believes that the problem is not in the concept of mentoring but because many mentoring systems are badly designed. Her own research shows that the greatest benefit is when the mentor is a very senior person from an outside organisation. This gives the mentor a useful detachment and avoids the complaint of favouritism that can arise if a woman is mentored by a top person in her own firm.

The FTSE 100 Cross-Company Mentoring Programme grew out of this research. The mentors are encouraged to take a continuing interest in the careers of the women they mentor, and from time to time behave much like sponsors. Peninah Thomson feels that the seniority of the mentors is important not only because the advice is likely to be of high quality but also because the women are given individual attention by someone who has already achieved significant professional success. That helps to build self-confidence.

Mentoring seems to bring clear benefits to some women but, regrettably, the central problem remains. Just as there are too few women to act as suitable role models, so there are too few senior women to act as mentors. Almost all of the mentors named by the women we interviewed are men and all but two of the 60 or so mentors provided by the Mentoring Foundation's Executive Programme at the moment are men: Alison Carnwarth and Sarah Hogg are the exceptions. Optimists might hope that a male mentor can be an advantage because he can give an insight into the world of male success. It also seems that the men gain from the experience. Peninah Thomson says that several of the male mentors have told her that the discussions they have with the women whom they are mentoring has increased their understanding of the difficulties faced by women in business.

Getting rid of male ignorance is very useful but relying on men to mentor women has obvious drawbacks. A man is not in a good position to advise women on those crucial issues of appearance, style, behaviour and maternity that we discuss in later chapters. Moreover in handling career choices and in resolving problems, men are likely to suggest methods and approaches that have worked for them as men and might not work as well for women. There is also another problem that was mentioned to us several times. Helena Kennedy put it delicately: "The relationship between an older male mentor and a younger woman can quickly become the subject of speculation." Kate Grussing told us that she had found quite a lot of men "feel uncomfortable about agreeing to mentor women because of the likelihood of gossip. Single and attractive women have to be aware of an unspoken suspicion about why senior men would have a strong interest in their career". Young women also face the problem of exactly how they are meant to approach a senior male Executive without putting him off or having their motives misunderstood.

Outsiders

This accumulation of problems not only makes it difficult for women to fit in, but it also tends to make them feel like outsiders. Many of the women we interviewed remembered a moment when that feeling struck them very strongly: one woman walking into the Directors' dining room of a large bank with the room full of male colleagues already seated and swivelling their heads to look at her; Suzanna Taverne being told by a head-hunter that she, a highly experienced manager approaching 40 years of age, might well be appointed as Managing Director of the British Museum because Trustees would see her as "a slip of a girl" who would not challenge their decisions; a lawyer discovering that the law firm who had recruited her would never use her skills properly because the Partners and their major clients so obviously preferred to work with men; Ann Robinson going to speak at the Civil Service College and finding that the class full of men, all younger and junior to her, had apparently decided that they would spend the whole session interrupting her and disagreeing with everything she said.

The Massachusetts-based Executive coach Denise Cormier[15] examined this feeling of being an outsider in an article published in 2007. She made a shrewd distinction. Cormier noticed that much of the advice to ambitious women and to their employers focuses on how women can be given a greater feeling of inclusion. In Cormier's view, that is not sufficient. The aim should not be inclusion, it should be integration. Integration means that organisations do not just have to open their doors to women, but they need to change their nature to reflect the priorities and aspirations of women alongside the priorities and aspirations of men.

Cormier's argument is that a lack of concern for integration is responsible for the large number of women leaving senior positions in US corporations. She says that the flight of talented women is now so extensive that it amounts to what she calls an "opt out revolution". Cormier is talking of a phenomenon that is quite different in scale from the tendency, which we described in Chapter 3, of individual women leaving companies that have an unpleasantly macho style of leadership. Cormier thinks that the flight of senior women from the corporate sector is a systemic problem that will do great damage to the US economy and to American women.

Attrition

The trend in the UK is less well defined because drop-out rates are rarely recorded. But there is some evidence that UK business and the professions face a similar attrition of talented women. The Association of Women Solicitors has published figures which show that the drop-out rate for women is twice that of men. Many British companies tell a sad tale about their graduate intake. Even if they try to recruit a similar number of men and women as management trainees that situation does not last long. After five years, so many of the women have left that men typically outnumber women by two to one. And the imbalance gets greater with each following year. Jill May told us from her experience at UBS that the attrition of women graduates and women in the earlier stages of their careers means there is no 'bench' of reasonably senior women ready to take on the top jobs when a vacancy occurs. Rowenna Walker described something similar that was happening in engineering. "Companies might start by recruiting women to make up a third or even more of their graduate Engineer intake but after ten years the proportion of those women who have reached senior engineering level is usually down to a tenth." Rowenna Walker says the fall is caused by a combination of attrition and of women not being promoted from lower-level positions. The Bar Council has regretted publicly that the drop-out rate for women barristers after ten to 12 years of service is still too high and Maura McGowan says that retention of women barristers in Chambers "was, and is, a problem".

The difficulty of fitting in and of sustaining success in organisations that were still not comfortable for women had prompted a number of the women we interviewed to consider a change of direction to make their life easier. Some had decided to leave Executive positions and 'go plural': use their experience to build a portfolio of Non-Executive Board positions. Some advocated the increased flexibility and control that comes from self-employment. Others had moved from the private into the public sector. A few told us that they were prepared to accept the difficulties of their present senior positions but had decided not to compete for jobs at the very top. Women who lead very large organisations face such enormous exposure and scrutiny that the pressure is much greater on them than on men.

A few women compared their careers with the careers of men they worked with. "Men have so much less hassle," was one conclusion. Another said that, had she been a man, she knew she would have been promoted earlier and further. A third resented the fact that she had to keep proving what she could do when, had she been a man with a similar CV, it would have been taken for granted that she was competent. Three women said that they would have been more successful if they had had a wife to support them – in each case no joke was intended. Another said that she did not realise how hard it was until her company was taken over by a Swedish firm. "Within a week the women felt more relaxed. For the first time men and women were really treated the same – just like normal employees."

The argument put forward in this book is that we need to redesign our society on the assumption that work should be integrated into the rest of life and that, where there is a conflict, work should not automatically be given priority over the other objectives of a civilised and rewarding existence. Women should no longer have to face the uncomfortable task of fitting into a world that gives priority to the needs and aspirations of men and very little importance to the needs and aspirations of women. Society needs to be restructured so that work takes its proper place alongside other imperatives and is fashioned to balance the needs of both genders. Such changes will certainly ensure that many more women achieve positions of power. But, even more important, it will give every woman – ambitious or not, high-flying or not, in whatever family or lifestyle – a better chance of using her talents, fulfilling her potential and achieving her own particular kind of happiness.

Chapter 5

Sexism and Discrimination

Women in Britain are better regarded and better treated than they were 30 years ago. Women no longer face the blatant misogyny that they had to suffer in the 1980s and which we describe in Chapter 2. Unfortunately the sexism, although to some extent transformed, has not disappeared. In the words of the Human Rights Barrister, Helena Kennedy, "A lot has happened but not enough has changed." The sexism and discrimination of the twenty-first century is less obvious and more subtle than it used to be but the effect on the lives of women is damaging and persistent.

Deirdre Hutton is the Chair of the Civil Aviation Authority and has extensive experience of many other organisations. She says that her working life has been full of examples of casual discourtesy and snubs by men; they were mostly unaware of the offence they were causing. This devastating judgment is delivered in a matter of fact tone and without rancour. "You just get used to it," she says. "You cannot make a fuss about each incident because so many of them are petty and it is very easy to get a reputation for having a thin skin."

Uncomfortable Mistakes

Deirdre Hutton explains that in her experience many men are still surprised to find a woman in a senior position: they take it for granted that any women they meet will be in support roles. She recalls that, as Deputy Chair of an important regulatory body, she hosted a visit by a group of very senior UK individuals. She lined up the welcoming party with some of her male colleagues on one side of her and some on the other. When the leader of the visiting group arrived, he shook hands with all the men to one side of Deirdre Hutton, nodded to her and shook hands with the men on her other side. Once the pattern had been established the other members of this august group did the same, shaking hands with all the men and nodding to her. Deidre Hutton realised that her important visitors thought that she was one of the support staff. "When I called everyone to order and started chairing the meeting, there was a good deal of embarrassment and shuffling of feet."

A surprising number of the *women we interviewed* told us of similar experiences. At a conference one of the principal speakers had a coffee cup pushed into her hand by a man asking for a refill. Many other women say they have been given a coffee cup or an empty wine glass. One Company Director found herself at a complete loss when a man handed her his coat. Frances O'Grady, the General Secretary of the TUC, says with a grin that she has often been mistaken for a waitress. Chi Onwurah MP wryly notes that people often think that she is someone's secretary. Maria Adebowale, Director of The Living Space Project, is also black and she explains, "It's certainly happened to me. I think it's something to do with an unconscious belief for some people that women, and women of colour in particular, can only do certain jobs."

Most women are so used to these uncomfortable mistakes that, like Deirdre Hutton, they shrug them off. The academic Elisabeth Kelan keeps her business card at the ready so that she can thrust it into the hand of any man who thinks she is there to serve the canapés. Heather Hancock says that she responds with her impressive "frosty stare". Helen Wells who led the lobbying organisation 'Opportunity Now' offers practical advice. "I warn women not to wear black and white, because the sorry truth is that I've heard far too many stories from women who have been mistaken for one of the caterers."

The mistakes made by these men, although laughable, are very revealing. The women we interviewed seemed more amused than affronted but several of them pointed out that men almost never have a similar experience. Although some men claim that equality between the sexes has been achieved, many men still have to be reminded that the women they meet might hold a powerful position.

NHS Trust Chief Executive Anna Dugdale says that, when she is away from her place of work, men often ask her, "And what do you do?" When she replies that she "works at the hospital", their first assumption is that she must be a nurse. The second guess is usually that she is a secretary. Anna Dugdale says that when she explains that she is the Chief Executive, the man usually expresses surprise. "And then – if I am lucky – we have a proper conversation."

The figures in Chapter 2 demonstrate that very few women hold positions of power in Britain. So it might be understandable for men to feel a little disconcerted when they meet a woman who is more important than they are.

But many of the women we interviewed are certain that the male reaction signifies rather more than a moment of surprise at encountering a rarity. Lesley Wilkin remembers hosting a dinner for her company and sitting between guests who were husband and wife. During the conversation Lesley Wilkin thought that she had made it quite clear that she was the Managing Director but the man had obviously not understood. He eventually asked the question that must have been troubling him for some time, 'So who is in charge here?' Before Lesley Wilkin had time to answer, the man's wife – obviously burdened with fewer preconceptions than her husband – muttered, 'She is, you fool!'

In the Background

When a woman challenges for a position normally held by a man, the male assumption about the natural order of things often surfaces. We were told of an occasion when a woman stood for election to a senior position in a prestigious institution. She polled the same number of votes as a man. The normal practice in such cases is for a run-off ballot to be held between the top two candidates. However the Chairman of the Institution decided on a different approach. He ignored the votes cast for the woman and chose the man. It was not until a great fuss was made that a compromise was eventually reached. The Chairman gave no explanation for his behaviour but many people – and most women – concluded that the Chairman preferred not to have a woman in such a senior position.

The unspoken assumption that the appropriate role for women is in the background supporting men lies behind much of the sexism of twenty-first century Britain. It can lead to everything from minor unpleasantness to serious forms of discrimination and worse. Many of the women we interviewed expressed their irritation that when a man and a woman are together, the man gets most of the attention. Deborah Bull, the celebrated ballet dancer who became Creative Director of the Royal Opera House, told us, "It comes as a jolt when I meet people in the 'outside world' and if I'm with a man they automatically address him, even though we are there as equals or I am the more senior partner." When we interviewed the MP, Julie Elliott, she had recently attended a reception for Backbenchers at a very prestigious location. While waiting to go into the reception she stood talking to a male colleague. When she got to the head of the queue, the usher reached past her and took the man's invitation, ignoring her. "He must have done it so many times that he didn't realise what he was doing. When I indicated how rude he had been, he was mortified."

Most of the women we interviewed acknowledged that much of this male behaviour is not intended to be unpleasant. The objective is not to snub or to insult; the man is just doing what comes naturally. But, whatever the explanation, when the deeply held conviction that men have a higher status than women is taken into the workplace, it can lead to great unfairness in pay, in career development and in promotion.

The Gender Pay Gap

Pay comparisons, like most statistical constructs, are always open to challenge. However the evidence that most women are paid less than most men is so overwhelming that the debate is no longer about whether a gender pay gap exists – it surely does – but about the size of the gap and whether it can be justified.

In Chapter 2 we note that just before the Equal Pay Act took effect in 1975 the gender pay gap was massive. We also reached the disappointing conclusion that the Act has not eliminated the problem of pay discrimination. The law itself is defective and the process of enforcement is ludicrously inadequate.

Nowadays the size of the gender pay gap is calculated by the Office of National Statistics (ONS). In December 2013 the ONS announced that in the previous year:

> *The gender pay gap ... for full-time employees increased to 10.0% from 9.5%.*

The announcement caused a ripple of media interest because it is very unusual for the gender pay gap to widen. In most of the previous years the official figures had shown that the pay gap was gradually shrinking. The trend had appeared so strong that there were even predictions that the gap would soon disappear.

However many people, and not just women, were surprised by the figure of 10 per cent for a different reason. They wondered why is it so small. After all, other published figures showed that the gap between the average pay of men and women is more than £10,000 a year, which represents much more than 10 per cent.

The answer lies in the way the ONS calculates the figures. The pay of men and women can be compared in a host of different ways but the ONS believes that the most valid comparison is between the hourly earnings of men and women who are full-time employees, excluding overtime. This is the calculation that produces the published figure of 10 per cent.

The professional and statistical skill of the ONS is unquestioned. Nevertheless, and although we can be sure that this is not the intention, the ONS's preferred method of calculation has the effect of minimising the size of the gender pay gap and tends to disregard some important elements of discrimination in employment. Three features of the ONS's calculation are particularly contentious.

In the first place, ONS prefers to *exclude overtime* from the comparisons. ONS explains this by saying that, 'Including overtime can skew the results because men work relatively more overtime than women.' Absolutely true: on average, men earn three times more from overtime pay than women. But this large difference in overtime pay is not some statistical quirk. It occurs because women are typically given less opportunity to work paid overtime than men. So excluding overtime pay from the calculation ignores a significant element of actual and potential discrimination.

Second, ONS bases its preferred comparison on the hourly pay of *full-time workers* and does not include the pay of part-timers. ONS explains this by referring to the fact that there are many more women working part time than men. Absolutely true but once again the implications are very important. Part-time workers still tend to be paid less per hour than full-time workers even when they are undertaking work of similar value, and focusing exclusively on the pay of full-time workers ignores the pay discrimination against part-timers, most of whom are women.

Third, ONS prefers to base its comparisons on *median earnings* (the midway point in the list of the pay levels reported) rather than on what most people refer to as 'average earnings' but statisticians call the 'mean' (calculated by adding everyone's earnings together and dividing by the total number of workers). This is no doubt impeccable as a piece of statistical presentation but once again it ignores an important element of pay discrimination. If averages were to be used, it would mean that the calculation would include the pay of very high earners, almost all of whom are men. This would inflate the male earnings figures considerably and show a much wider gender pay gap.

To demonstrate just how important the method of calculation is, we quote two illustrative figures:

If the hourly rates of part-timers are included in the calculation:

- the gender pay gap in 2013 for all employees (full time and part time) based on median hourly earnings (excluding overtime) would have been shown to be 19.1 per cent.

This is nearly twice as high as the ONS's preferred calculation of 10.0 per cent.

If we include all employees (full time and part time), include overtime pay and base the calculation on average earnings (the mean) rather than on median earnings:

- the gender pay gap in 2013 based on the average total weekly earnings of all employees would have been shown to be 36.2 per cent.

This is well over three times as high as the ONS's preferred calculation of 10.0 per cent.

This book is not the place to argue which of these figures – 10.0 per cent, 19.1 per cent or 36.2 per cent – gives the best impression of the gender pay gap in Britain. However the important message is that, depending on how it is calculated, the pay gap is either wide or very wide. Even the lowest figure represents a gap of about £160 a month or nearly £2,000 a year. The highest figure represents a pay gap of about £850 a month or over £10,000 a year.

Some people complain that many gender pay comparisons are invalid because men and women have different levels of skill and carry different levels of responsibility. The Chartered Management Institute (CMI) addressed this issue directly by comparing the pay of men and women at similar levels on the career ladder. According to the CMI's 2013 National Management Salary Survey,[1] the gender pay gap on average is about 25 per cent. If bonuses are added the gap widens to more than 30 per cent. Indeed in 2014 the CMI calculated that the gender pay gap is so wide that women managers would have to work until they reach 80 before their lifetime earnings match men who have retired at 65.

The differences are substantial and discussion of the gender pay gap understandably focuses on the financial consequences. However, the wider implications are also important. Job applicants are often asked to declare their current earnings and money talks. A higher-paid man can easily be regarded as being worth more to the prospective employer than a lower-paid woman, even if they are currently in similar jobs. Even if the woman is successful, she is likely to be offered a lower starting rate than the higher-paid male applicant. In Chapter 8 we note that, after the birth of children, caring responsibilities force many couples to decide whose career should be allowed to progress and whose career should be put on hold. The natural inclination is for the family to hold onto the higher salary and in most cases it is the man who earns more. So the age-old prejudice that a man's career is more important is reinforced and the woman is left having to play catch-up. This is why Harriet Harman says that pay differences not only cost women large sums of money but they also sustain much that is unfair in British society. The gender pay gap, she says, "acts as a drag anchor on change".

Getting beyond the general position and finding the details of pay rates for men and women in a particular organisation is surprisingly difficult. In modern companies information about other people's pay is not readily available and it takes a considerable effort to get the information and to make the comparisons. One woman in the finance sector suspects that she and her female colleagues have long been paid less than the men who work alongside them but she explained, "The pay system is so complex and secret that it is impossible for any of us to be sure."

Nevertheless, some of the women we interviewed were conscious of pay differences and a few resented them strongly. During her career in a series of mainly male workplaces, one young woman kept finding that she was paid less than the men. On two occasions the discrepancy was corrected after she complained but on a third occasion the unfairness was not put right until she threatened to resign. In Chapter 2 we also recorded how Deborah Hargreaves had successfully complained when she discovered that the man who followed her into a job at the *Financial Times* was being paid thousands of pounds more than her. Confronting the boss and requiring the injustice to be corrected worked well for both of these women. However their reaction is not typical of the attitude of most of the successful women we interviewed.

More common than a determination to ensure equality of pay is a general feeling that, although the men are probably getting more money, it is not something to get very upset about. Sally Martin, a Vice President in Shell Downstream, says that she appreciates a good salary but she will only do a job if she enjoys it and if it is clear that the company values her work. Once that enjoyment or that sense of being valued goes, she will consider doing something else. She says that enjoyment and personal fulfilment are very much more important to her than chasing increases in pay.

Distasteful to Ask

Several women told us explicitly that, if they were paid less than men, it was probably their own fault for not pressing their case hard enough. A senior civil servant explained that, following an extensive reorganisation of her department, she was asked to take on substantial additional responsibility. She acknowledges that many men faced with the same request would have negotiated an increase in pay but she did not. She says that she was flattered to be asked, did not really think about asking for extra pay and in any case would have found this, "distasteful".

There is a good deal of research which shows that this attitude is fairly typical of successful women. Most are happy to press for better pay for their staff or to support pay applications from their colleagues but they do not want to negotiate pay increases for themselves. The figures from research in the US[2] are striking. Fifty-seven per cent of male managers negotiate their own salary but only 7 per cent of female managers do so. We have found no equivalent figures for the UK but it is perhaps significant that out of more than a hundred women we interviewed only one woman told us that she had successfully negotiated an increase in the starting salary for a new job.

American researchers have worked hard to understand why women in the US hold back from pay applications while men submit them as a matter of course. Experiments conducted by Hannah Bowles[3] and colleagues at Harvard were especially revealing. Over 200 adults were asked to act as senior managers and decide whether to accept an internal candidate for a vacancy. The experiment involved applications on paper and the participants did not meet the candidates. The result was that women candidates who asked for more pay than was on offer were heavily penalised by both men and women. This reaction was registered whether the woman candidate made the request politely or aggressively. The male candidates who asked for higher pay were not penalised at all.

In a further experiment, videos of the requests for extra pay were also watched. Once again the male participants penalised women who asked for more pay but applied no penalty to the men who asked. However the reaction of the women participants was different. The women participants penalised everyone – both men and women – who asked for more pay.

In the last experiment over 300 adults were tested on their willingness to initiate pay negotiations on their own behalf. The men showed themselves to be very willing. Women were also willing but only when their boss was a woman.

If their boss happened to be a man, the women were much more reluctant. The research did not establish a single clear-cut reason for this difference but the female participants mentioned a general nervousness and the fear of a backlash if they asked a male boss for a pay rise.

All in all the researchers conclude that women who press for pay rises are likely to face much greater resistance and many more difficulties than men. Bowles and her colleagues sum up their main conclusion in the title of their article: *Sometimes it does hurt to ask.*

Conclusions from experimental research of this type must always be treated with caution. The circumstances are artificially created and there is no guarantee that people will react in the same way in a real life situation. Moreover the experiments were conducted in the US and we know of no similar experiments in the UK. Nevertheless the conclusions are consistent with other research about how men and women are viewed which we explore in greater detail in Chapters 6 and 7. Men are expected to be assertive and, when they make demands, they are not penalised for doing what people expect. Women, on the other hand, are expected to be less challenging. When a woman acts assertively – like a man is expected to behave – she is criticised and penalised. At the very least the experiments ought to give pause to those management gurus, both male and female, who advise women to be more aggressive in asking for pay rises. The cultural pressures on women in western society are heavier and more complex than many of these gurus seem to appreciate.

Appointment and Promotion

In contrast to their attitude to discrimination on pay, the reaction of most of the women we interviewed to any perceived unfairness in career development and promotion was much more unforgiving. Of course there is no suggestion that every woman suffers discrimination. Twelve of the women we interviewed volunteered their belief that they had never suffered discrimination in appointment or promotion. However, over twice as many women told us that they had seen instances where men had been pushed forward and women had been held back. And any apparent discrimination against women in these crucial matters of career development is strongly resented.

Kate Grussing worked in JPMorgan, the investment bank. Because her work was appraised so highly, she expected to be promoted to be a Managing Director of one of the bank's divisions. However she failed to gain that promotion on four occasions. Each time she received favourable comments about her work and after each rejection she was given more responsibility. On one occasion she moved roles and businesses internally to respond to the suggestion that she lacked experience in a particular area of work. But the promotion was still elusive. Kate's frustration was particularly acute because women and men in the bank repeatedly told her that she was an important role model and people outside the company assumed that she had long ago been promoted to be a Managing Director.

Another woman who worked for an investment bank lost status when her bank was taken over and she was assimilated into the enlarged organisation at a lower level. At first she had no complaints as male Directors were treated in a similar manner and, like the men, she expected to regain her earlier position fairly quickly. But in her case this did not happen. She accepted the position because she was given a plausible explanation. However, somewhat later she found that the rules that were quoted to prevent her promotion had been relaxed for some of the men.

Both of these difficulties occurred in the banking sector and recent research suggests that this is a problem area for women. In 2007 and 2008 Ruth Sealey[4] from Cranfield University interviewed 33 senior women Executives in six large City investment banks to discover whether they thought that the banks operated as a meritocracy in which women could succeed as easily as men.

Sealey recorded a significant change in attitude as the women moved through their careers. Early on, the general view was that if they learnt company culture – the so-called rules of the game – they would achieve equality with the men. Some women thought that they would do well if they copied the men. One, 'pretended to be more like the guys'. Another said, 'I didn't want to be seen as a woman, even.' However, at a later stage in their careers most of the women were much more sceptical about whether women were really treated as the equals of men. They felt that women's leadership styles were not valued, that women did not get the best assignments and that women were rarely interviewed for Executive Directorships. Women felt that they were being given an obvious and demoralising message. Half of the 33 were so disenchanted that they had considered leaving.

Most appointment and promotion decisions are taken behind closed doors and, as several women acknowledged, it is often difficult to be certain that sexual discrimination had any part to play. One woman explained to us that she was very disappointed when she was turned down for promotion that went instead to a man. However after weeks of uncertainty when the possibility of sexual discrimination was very much in her mind, she was given a reasonable explanation and a reassurance that she would be considered again in the near future. The promise was kept and a couple of years later she was promoted.

However in some instances there can be no doubt that discrimination has been at work. One woman told us of the time when she sat on an appointment panel of a large international company. The European Sales Director said that they should reject a woman's application because "the girl will be off in six months to have babies and we will be back to square one". All the men accepted this argument and a man was appointed.

Race and Class

Gender is not the only reason why some of the women we interviewed were vulnerable to discrimination. Reverend Rose Hudson Wilkin is black and feels she has been hampered in her work by racial as well as sexual prejudice. In Chapter 4, we quoted her as saying, "I am constantly aware that I have to be ten times more able than my male colleagues." When we spoke to her, she added that she feels that she also has to be ten times more able than her "white female colleagues".

It is difficult to disentangle the disadvantage that comes from being black from the disadvantage that comes from being a woman. Recognising that there is a significant minority population in the London Diocese, Rose Hudson Wilkin stood for election for one of the ten clergy places from the Diocese of London on the General Synod. She received seven votes out of a possible 400. This was not just personally hurtful, she thought it was "disrespectful for the thousands of minority ethnic people who worship in our Churches".

Even Rose Hudson Wilkin's appointment as Chaplain to the Speaker of the House of Commons did not go smoothly. The Church of England recommended a white male to the Speaker. John Bercow preferred to appoint Rose Hudson Wilkin. For a very long time the Chaplain to the Speaker has also been appointed as Rector of St Margaret's, the parliamentary church which is controlled by Westminster Abbey. Rose Hudson Wilkin was not appointed to be the Rector of St Margaret's. That appointment went to a white male.

The founder of the urban place-making company, The Living Space Project, Maria Adebowale, is also black. She is often asked where she comes from. When she says West Yorkshire, the question is usually pressed further: 'Yes, but where do you really come from?' Maria Adebowale thinks that when this question is asked "it's often because the questioner equates you with being an outsider and they need some kind of evidence to prove it. Not having that evidence flummoxes them".

Class prejudice attracts much less public condemnation than prejudice based on race or sex. Maria Adebowale says that it upsets her as much as other prejudices. It bothers her that, for instance, "people think it's OK to call someone a 'chav'".

Pamela Castle told us that, although she had been to a grammar school, her working class upbringing was very different from the public school background of many of the men she worked with. She had also taken a career break which meant that she was older than her colleagues. And of course she is a woman. In her opinion the disadvantages of class, age and gender reinforce each other. There were many occasions when she felt that she was treated differently from the younger, upper class men. Other women who identified themselves as coming from a working class background told us of similar experiences. They coped but the notion of reinforcement is important. Some men also suffer disadvantage because of class or race or age. But for women there are more layers of prejudice and more difficulty in pinning down the reason for being at a disadvantage, or seeming to be an outsider or just feeling that others are being better treated.

Ushered Away from Power

Nowadays, because discrimination of all kinds is generally more subtle than it used to be, it is often surrounded by uncertainty. Jill May told us that UBS recruited nearly as many women graduates as men but the women who stayed with the bank for the long term seemed to go into the support departments, like HR, legal and corporate responsibility whereas men moved into the high-profile and more powerful 'client facing' jobs. She has never been sure whether this is because the women were being ushered into the support functions where arguably work–life balance might be thought to be easier or whether the male managers in the client facing roles tended to promote and recruit in their own image. Whatever the reason, she believes that the outcome was unsatisfactory.

The same pattern can be observed in many British companies. Some departments and some Directorships are regarded as more important than others. The Chief Executive sits at the top of the hierarchy. Next in line comes the Finance Director. Then comes an important group that includes Operations and Marketing. Lower down the pecking order comes Strategy, Public Affairs and Human Resources. The bottom place usually goes to the Director for Social Responsibility. Below the level of Executive Director, there is a similar ranking for senior managers: finance and so-called client facing jobs are regarded as having more status than jobs in the support functions. So anyone who works in a support function has a much reduced chance of becoming a Chief Executive or getting into one of the top flight jobs. And it is the men who tend to be found in the important and high-status areas and the women who seem to be found in the support functions.

Bill Minter, who has worked in senior positions for one of the UK's major civil engineering contractors, explained how the segregation of roles comes about in that sector. After a few years out on the sites, qualified women tend to move into office-based jobs, in Design, Estimating, Quality Management and Human Resources. These jobs can lead to senior positions but rarely to the very top. This segregation is a result of the rugged and sometimes macho style of management out on the sites and the fact that civil engineering contractors require site managers to work anywhere in Britain, which damages social life. There is little overt pressure on women to move into the support functions but neither are there policies in place to make work on the sites any more congenial for women. So the men travel and the women work in the office.

Eleanor Mack said that she has also seen the apparent segregation of roles and the perpetuation of a culture that does not advance many women. Formerly there was only one woman on the main Board and she was in charge of Communications, which was not regarded by the organisation as one of the key roles. Eleanor Mack says that many of the most able and ambitious women in the company seem to be encouraged into support positions rather than into those leading operational areas which provide experience that is critical for a career at the top of the business.

The tendency to usher women away from positions of power do not just happen in industry. Brenda Dean, who was General Secretary of the paper and printing trade union, SOGAT, told us of two attempts by her predecessor, Bill Keyes, to entice her away from her position as a powerful local official into an advisory role. As a local official she was in a good position to seek election to the top job when Keyes retired but in an advisory job she would be out of the running. One of the jobs she was offered must have been created especially for her because, after she turned it down, the post was never filled. Her assessment of Keyes is that he was happy to have women in senior advisory positions and was keen to promote women to this level, but he could not entertain the thought of a woman becoming the union's General Secretary.

The women and the man who explained the segregation to us were not decrying the importance of the support and advisory functions. We interviewed six women who have made very successful careers in Human Resources, either for major companies or in leading consultancies. But when FTSE 350 companies, or head-hunters working on their behalf, want to recruit a new CEO or a new Chair(man) they rarely give much attention to the claims of people who have a successful career in a support function. Whether the segregation appears to be the result of the most powerful jobs being uncongenial to most women, as in civil engineering, or more obviously the result of some manipulation by people at the top, the outcome puts ambitious women at a serious disadvantage compared with men. No doubt many benign explanations can be found for this process but a cynic will notice that a segregation of jobs with women in lower-status positions supporting men who hold most of the power, looks very like a more subtle version of the sexism that, two generations ago, prevented women from even applying for the most important positions in industry and the public sector.

The process of segregation even has an effect on the appointment of Board members who are Non-Executive Directors. Sue Vinnicombe's team at Cranfield University have been tracking Board appointments in Britain's largest companies. On the basis of this research, she concludes that, even when recruiting Non-Executive Directors, large companies rarely search outside the mainstream departments, and they very often specify that a candidate must have high-level Finance experience. Sue Vinnicombe believes that this restrictive approach is wrong-headed and it certainly reduces the number of women who are regarded as qualified to sit as Non-Executives on Boards. Evidence from the reconstruction of company Boards in Norway suggests that it might be in the national interest to look not only to women who specialise in the so-called support functions, but to women who work in the academic world, in the voluntary sector and even in the Arts. Arne Selvik,[5] a Norwegian who has served on a variety of Boards across Europe and in Japan, insists that, in his experience, "Professionals from outside the business world may be difficult to deal with, but they certainly play the role of the Devil's Advocate … on company Boards … very well."

Patronised

Segregation of jobs reinforces the notion, which is so deeply embedded in the British psyche, that men do the important work and the women are there to help. The difference in the perceived status of men and women in Britain has a host of unpleasant consequences. It shows itself in the way many men patronise women, often without apparently realising what they are doing. "It is a constant irritant, like water torture," says Helen Wells. "You have no alternative but to get used to it." The women we interviewed gave us a long list of examples. Liz Nelson, who chairs Fly UK, says that she recently ran two successful meetings but, at the third, one of the men suggested quite seriously that she should not only act as Chair but also take the minutes. Liz Nelson thinks that it is "inconceivable that they would have suggested that idea to a man".

Dianne Thompson, now CEO of Camelot, ran a large tool-making company and attended the annual lunch of the trade association. The Chairman of the association was keen to point out that she was the only woman CEO present and asked her to stand up so everyone could see her properly. "It was not intended maliciously but he should have realised that it was embarrassing and patronising to be picked out like that and he should not have done it."

Some men hold to the patronising view that a husband is in control of everything that a wife does, even when a woman has built her own successful career. Businesswoman Sarah Anderson chaired an important Committee of the CBI. One day she was walking to the Chelsea Flower Show with her husband when she saw Digby Jones, the Director General of the CBI, coming towards them. She waited until Jones finished speaking on his mobile phone and introduced him to her husband. Jones launched into a little homily, thanking her husband 'for allowing (sic) Sarah to spend so much time with us at the CBI'. Both Sarah Anderson and her husband were surprised.

Melissa Benn told us of a rather more public discourtesy when she took part in a radio debate at Bristol University on education policy. She was the only woman on a panel of four and John Humphrys of the 'Today' programme fame was in the Chair. At the end of a lively discussion, Humphrys asked everyone to stay in their seats while he recorded the introductions for each of the panellists. He then described the three male panellists in suitably respectful terms, reciting their qualifications, status and experience. But when it came to the only female on the panel, he simply said, 'Melissa Benn is the daughter of

Tony Benn who recently received an honorary degree from this University. When Melissa was 11, she won a place to the fee-paying St Paul's Girls School but her parents decided to send her to Holland Park comprehensive instead.' Melissa Benn is a renowned campaigner on education issues; she has written important books and numerous articles on the subject. She is now in her fifties and thought she was old enough to be identified as an individual in her own right and not just by reference to her father. And she was angry enough to say so.

Humphrys was taken aback. He said, 'All right then, what do you want me to say?' Melissa Benn wrote him a few lines and he dutifully read them out with his own intro, 'Melissa Benn, daughter of Tony, is ...' Afterwards he apologised for the few additional words: 'Sorry I had to add that – your Dad is national treasure after all.' However he made no mention of the original discourtesy and it is not clear whether he realised how patronising it had been to describe the men on the panel in terms of their own achievements while referring to the woman merely as the daughter of a famous man.

Men often justify behaviour that women regard as patronising by insisting that they are just being courteous. The trouble is that making an unusual fuss of a woman tends to inhibit the development of the sort of relaxed personal relations that most work colleagues prefer. Susan Palmer, as the only senior woman in a large financial services company, says that she was sometimes treated "as a sort of mascot". The men behaved in a kindly fashion and she got used to it but she was constantly reminded of the exceptional nature of her position.

Only a Joke

The behaviour of male colleagues can sometimes be much nastier. Several of the women we interviewed said that they knew they were the subject of comments about their gender and appearance. Some of the comments were masquerading as jokes but many seemed deliberately unkind and a few seemed intended to intimidate. Michaela Bergman is now a senior official in the European Bank for Reconstruction and Development. She talked about one overseas posting much earlier in her career where she was heavily outnumbered by the men. "There was a lot of heavy drinking and unsympathetic behaviour. A few of the men also seemed to take delight in talking about me behind my back and calling me names, some of which had nasty sexual overtones. It went on for many months and was very unpleasant."

Offensive comments about women that are made in a jokey manner are particularly difficult to deal with. To take offence invites the joker to claim that the woman has no sense of humour. To keep quiet tempts the joker to work even harder to get a reaction. And to join in usually encourages the joker to extend his performance. A woman faced with this situation is understandably uneasy because she knows, and research has demonstrated, that sexist humour is usually a camouflage for something more serious. Jokes and remarks that put women down invite anyone listening to agree that women are in some way inferior to men or that aspects of women's behaviour are laughable. And jokes and offensive remarks can quickly move from the general to the particular. Women find themselves being asked questions that range from the irritating, 'I bet you have trouble reading a map', to the frankly insulting, 'So who wears the trousers in your house?'

When the jokes or remarks refer to the appearance of women or become overtly sexual in nature, the situation can become even more sinister and threatening. Research by Louise Fitzgerald[6] and colleagues at the University of Illinois has shown that there is an overlap between what she calls gender harassment, including jokes and disparaging remarks about the appearance or sexuality of women in general, and unwanted sexual attention directed at a particular woman. A man who makes sexual remarks about women is usually looking for a reaction from any woman who is present. If a woman reacts in any way, with embarrassment or disdain or even outright disgust, the man can often convince himself that her reaction shows that she must be interested in him and would welcome closer contact.

Sexual harassment

We were surprised at how many women told us that they had been subjected to unwelcome sexual attention from work colleagues. One woman named a man who is a well-known public figure. "He makes his views about women very clear. He either dismisses women as empty-headed and not worth talking to or regards them as targets for his predatory sexual behaviour. If I have the misfortune to sit next to him, I have to keep removing his hand from my leg."

Maura McGowan, the Chair of the Bar Council, recently wrote that, in her early years as a barrister, "Not only were we expected to make the tea, but we also had to do it looking backwards to avoid being pinched in the process." During our interview with her she explained that, "Most of the harassment was more jokey than sinister, an irritant rather than a threat." However, she went on to recount one incident that had occurred more than 30 years ago. A senior barrister told her privately, "There are two things I'd like to do with you before I retire. One is to make sure you value yourself and the other is to … "

The manner in which Maura McGowan recalled such an unpleasant incident is typical of the way several of our interviews developed. Examples of sexual harassment were usually only called to mind when the memory was specifically prompted. One very senior official from the public sector told us early in the interview that she had encountered no difficulties because of her gender. Much later she explained that she had left one job because she had been sexually harassed by her boss. At this point she told us that, in all, she had been the subject of serious sexual harassment on three occasions, twice by her boss at the time and once by a colleague. She had not reported any of the incidents because she felt that bringing a case like that would have dominated her life for a long time into the future. Her way of dealing with the incidents was to make her feelings clear to the men concerned, take the first opportunity to change jobs and then put the whole thing out of her mind. She added that, "You have to keep a sense of proportion in such matters."

Barbara Young is quite certain that her gender has not been a disadvantage during her career but she adds that sexual harassment has certainly been part of her experience. After taking up an appointment in the NHS she visited the clinician who was the Chairman of the Medical Committee. He was reassuring in a very patronising way about what he called 'the medical side of things', saying that he and his colleagues would sort all that out. He then put his hand on her thigh and left it there. Barbara Young told him that, providing he removed his hand and was never as patronising as that again, they would get on splendidly.

Many of the incidents were so disturbing because they were unexpected. We were told that one woman was at first startled and then shocked when the man next to her at a dinner of the British Retail Consortium put his arm round her shoulders and then started stroking her thigh. She was so uncertain about what to do at a high-profile occasion that she got up and went home. She then tried to put the incident out of her mind and made no subsequent complaint. Looking back she regrets that she did not make a fuss about what he had done.

Taking action is very brave and it rarely leads to a happy outcome for the victim. We were told one story which illustrates the difficulties. In a large company a senior manager was repeatedly behaving inappropriately towards women. Eventually a woman reported him, there was an investigation and he was sacked. He took legal action against the company and the woman was worried for months that she would have to give evidence in court. The company eventually reached a settlement but that cleared the way for the man to get a job in another company. The woman who complained has run into him a few times since and on one occasion she was, to her horror, allocated an aeroplane seat next to him. She got it changed very quickly.

The reaction of her work colleagues surprised her. Most of the women thought that she should have kept quiet and some said as much. She still does not understand their reaction. Some seemed upset by the investigation, some appeared to have been asked unsettling questions by their husbands and it is possible that some of her colleagues felt a little guilty that they had put up with the unpleasantness for so long. But, whatever the reasons, the whole episode and its aftermath caused her great distress.

Part of the Culture

Some men claim that things have changed and that sexual harassment rarely happens nowadays. This is a comforting piece of nonsense. There are still workplaces where sexual harassment is part of the culture. And the worst behaviour is not always where people most expect. We were shocked and discouraged by evidence that sexual harassment seems to be endemic in some of Britain's most celebrated orchestras. Several orchestral players told us of their experiences. The first thing that is noticeable is that the women in many orchestras are much younger than the men. When a woman is employed some of the men say openly, 'We booked her because she's really good looking.' The common assumption is that a woman has to be 'a babe or a slapper' to get anywhere in the orchestral world. Sexual harassment is often overt. Some senior men exploit the unequal power balance and the women victims are too frightened to talk publicly about it because it is 'career suicide'. This atmosphere in the industry also infects the Schools of Music. When women students tried to complain about the behaviour of the professor at Chetham's who has now been convicted for grotesque behaviour, they were told to ignore it.

We heard some nasty stories. During a performance one woman had to put up with the sight of a pornographic magazine that a brass player displayed on his music stand beside her. Apparently this is quite a common 'joke'. Two women had to tolerate pornographic films being shown on the orchestra's coach. No heed was paid to their protests. The situation is so bad that the pianist James Rhodes[7] wrote in a recent article about music in Britain that, "Sexism … is everywhere … Women have to cope … with an industry that has an ingrained sense of entitled chauvinism that is cause for alarm and shame in equal measure."

Sexual harassment seems to be so much part of the experience of women at work that some told us that they have reviewed the way they dress and present themselves to ensure that they are not creating an impression that can be regarded as in any way provocative or sexy. One senior figure from the charity sector goes even further. "I have a rule that I never go out to lunch with a man on my own." The extraordinary pressure on women to ensure that their appearance suits their own personality and also meets the demanding expectations of society is explored in Chapter 6.

Academic researchers have tried to explain why some men feel that it is acceptable to harass and assault women. A few researchers have explored the deeper question of why men in particular and society in general seem to be so tolerant of this abusive behaviour. In *The Social Psychology of Gender*, Laurie Rudman and Peter Glick[8] advance the theory that men have not resolved the tension between two quite different desires in their relationships with women. The researchers suggest that, on the one hand, men want dominance and control and, on the other, men seek an intimate and interdependent relationship. In a sentence of notable understatement, Rudman and Glick suggest that these two desires are often in conflict.

Rudman and Glick's analysis is compelling but it should be emphasised that, for some men, the desire to exercise dominance and control over women is almost certainly connected with failures in their private lives. Academic research suggests that a man who uses his power to disparage, harass and abuse women is much less likely to have a satisfactory intimate and sexual relationship with a woman compared with a man who treats women more like equals. The man who is a failure in his personal relationships with women looks for ways to get his own back on the sex who have not treated him in the way that he believes they should.

Other men seem to believe that by exercising power over women they can demonstrate their manliness and their attractiveness. A man seeks to show that he is 'a real man' and apparently believes that once he can display his masculine superiority, women will throw themselves at his feet. This is a common theme of popular fiction. Many film scripts and thousands of books have been written on the assumption that a hero with monumental self-confidence and a steely disdain will surely win the lady. In real life this allure, such as it is, rarely works for very long but it still forms part of the illusion of masculinity that retains such a hold on the popular imagination.

The more dangerous illusion is that an intimate relationship can be forced on a woman. From this source come all those vile suggestions that women who dress or behave in a manner that a man might regard as sexy are not only inviting a sexual approach but should be blamed for any violence done to them. 'She is gagging for it' is still a sentence heard in male gatherings, particularly after a few drinks. Even in polite company the thought is still not far beneath the surface. 'It was a terrible thing that happened to her, but what did she expect, going out late at night dressed like that.' Almost every rapist justifies his actions in similar terms.

Nothing To Do with Me

Abuse seems to arise from an imbalance of power. From time to time some men patronise women, treat them as inferiors, joke about them, humiliate them, grope them and assault them because they can. As recent court cases have demonstrated, men can get away with abuse because they have a powerful position and because the penalties that individual women can suffer if they protest are enormous. But these male abusers also escape punishment because other men behave as if the members of their sex who behave badly are nothing to do with them. Most men do not appreciate, or do not want to believe, that these problems need to be resolved by all men, acting together to create a better and less threatening model of masculinity.

Most men insist that the obnoxious behaviour of some other males is categorically different from the way they themselves treat women. Under pressure, they usually explain how well they get on with their partner or wife and how equal the relationship is. But questions always hang in the air. Do these self-consciously virtuous men never laugh at a sexist joke, do they always contradict a man who suggests that women are useless at something or other and do they always assume that the victim of sexual abuse is blameless? Over 40 years ago, Sheila Rowbotham[9] exposed and ridiculed male double-think. Addressing women, Rowbotham says, 'Men will often admit that other women are oppressed but not you. Well it was true in the past but not now. Well yes they are in Liverpool but not in London or wherever you live ...'. The unspoken message is that men always insist that the nastiness comes from other males and that they themselves would never collude.

A telling example of male double-think came to light when Richard Scudamore, the Director of the Premier Football League, was exposed as writing sexist emails to a friend and colleague. One of Scudamore's duties is to promote women's football yet he wrote about 'big titted broads', referred to women as 'gash' and recorded his opinion that women with children behave irrationally. Nevertheless a number of men came forward to defend him. They said that these were private emails (but sent from his office email address), he was 'only joking' and he 'is certainly not sexist'. The favourite defence, even used by some women, was that these sort of 'jokey remarks' would have been all right had they been used in a pub so it was not too serious when they appeared in private emails. The feminist Bea Campbell answered these points gently but firmly. The emails reveal what Scudamore has "in his head" and they show, deep down, how he really thinks of women.

Rachel Huxley, Chief Executive of the Environment City Trust in Peterborough, believes that Britain currently sets the threshold of sexist behaviour far too high. She thinks particularly of a friend with two young sons. He tries to give his sons a view of women infused with humanity and respect but knows that all around them are images of women as sex objects. Photos of bare breasted women have appeared on page 3 of Britain's best-selling newspaper for over 40 years and so-called 'lads mags' still display sexual images of women on their front covers in newsagents and supermarkets.

Chi Onwurah MP drew our attention to the difference between the way civil rights have been developed to prevent racial discrimination and the much feebler attempts to protect the civil rights of women. What constitutes racism is increasingly well defined but what constitutes sexism is a matter of continuing argument. We have been told of several senior managers who feel that it is acceptable to comment on the figure and legs of their female staff. Had they made similar comments about the skin colour of a black or Asian employee they would have been plunged straight into a discrimination case.

The worth of women's contribution to our national life is routinely undervalued. The Bank of England decided that all the images of British . achievement on our banknotes shall be male and the then Governor, Mervyn King, did not seem to realise that this might cause offence. When two women led a campaign to change the Bank's decision[10] they were abused on every social network. A sense of balance is important. This chapter has dealt with the sexist behaviour of many men towards women. Not all men behave in this way or want to preserve an unfair status quo. Some men profoundly wish for a more equal balance of power between the sexes and long for the transformation in society that this change would bring. Unfortunately and for the time being these men are outnumbered by men who want to preserve the power of men and, more significantly, by men who cannot see that there is a problem to resolve.

Misogyny

Brenda Hale, the Deputy President of the Supreme Court, admitted to us that she, like many others, is sometimes accused of understating the problem. She said that she was shocked when, after giving a recent lecture, she was challenged by a very successful woman barrister because she had not mentioned what the barrister called 'the misogyny at the Bar'. We conclude this chapter with two personal experiences that illustrates the misogyny that still exists in Britain.

One of the authors of this book went to speak at a meeting in the Midlands and, while waiting for the meeting to start, chatted to one of the organisers. This man explained that he used to work in the oil industry and mentioned a woman Director of the oil company. The author remarked that having a woman in such a senior position at that time – the 1980s – was unusual. The man explained that she was 'very lucky'. She had been in charge of health and safety, which was a 'non-job' but, 'luckily for her', the Piper Alpha accident had happened and 'suddenly health and safety people were very important'. After attempting to put aside thoughts about the scores of men who died on Piper Alpha, the author asked how well she did the Director's job. 'She was hard as nails – an absolute bitch,' was the answer. Beginning to show some irritation, the author asked this man what he would have said about a male Director who had been as tough as she had been. The reply came with a smile of triumph, 'I would have called him a son-of-a-bitch.'

The second incident occurred when, as part of the research for this book, both authors attended a meeting held in the City to discuss women on company Boards. In the question and answer session one of the participants referred to a senior woman manager whom she much admired. Andrew Hilton, the Director of the organisation running the meeting, agreed that the senior woman manager was very impressive. Indeed, to indicate the extent of his admiration, he added, 'She even pees standing up!' The audience went very quiet for a moment and then the meeting resumed. Andrew Hilton appeared not to notice any change in the atmosphere.

Chapter 6

How Women are Seen

A woman must continually watch herself. She is almost continually accompanied by her own image of herself ... from earliest childhood she has been taught and persuaded to survey herself constantly ... women watch themselves being looked at.

In 1972 John Berger[1] published *Ways of Seeing* based on his seminal television series of the same name. In his book he describes how women are seen by others and by themselves. His thesis is that women are judged against an idealised, unattainable image. They see themselves through the eyes of others with varying degrees of dissatisfaction and these negative feelings become a constant feature of their daily lives.

We heard echoes of Berger in interview after interview. Most of the women we have interviewed spoke about the overwhelming importance of appearance. Almost without exception they were aware of the significance of the way they presented themselves, in their hair and clothes and make up. They know that the impact they make on others, on colleagues, bosses and adversaries, is influenced by how they are perceived physically.

Pink for a Girl

A false image of the ideal female is presented to little girls when they are very young. Anyone who doubts this should try buying birth congratulation cards which do not contain openly sexist images and texts. It is virtually impossible to buy cards for baby girls which do not show a pretty child often with curls (usually blonde) dressed in pink with words that indicate that this baby will be smiling, pretty, compliant and docile: no trouble. The cards for boys are of course blue. The words in the boys' cards imply that this is a child you will notice: he is sturdy, striving and noisy. The characters of these children are already defined by day one: boys will be boisterous and messy; girls will be passive and sweet.

What boys and girls wear helps to emphasise their differences. It would take a brave parent who would dress their baby boy in pink. His masculinity would be in question. He may be mistaken for a girl. Although few baby girls are in fact dressed in blue, being taken for a boy would not be shocking in the same way. The only explanation for this discrepancy is the potency of the power conferred on men in our society.

Obviously most children do not conform readily to these stereotypes but much research tells us that, on the whole, we do treat children differently according to their sex. Baby girls are cradled more than boys, who are bounced up and down. Even those of us who offered our children toys which gave them an opportunity to break away from received expectations found that once they were playing with other children, the traditional patterns of desire and behaviour surfaced. I think with rueful amusement of the cartoon from the 1980s by feminist Jackie Fleming of a little girl sitting beneath a Christmas tree disconsolately holding a train set with the wish bubble above her head, 'I'd kill for a Barbie.'

It is of course true that most little girls now wear a variety of clothes in different colours and styles. Their movements are no longer restricted by frilly dresses. However the image of the ideal female adult is still dangled tantalisingly before them from an early age. Many of the clothes available in shops for even quite young girls tend to be mini versions of their mothers' outfits, sometimes with unsuitable sexual overtones. Most shocking was the sight of a thong for sale in the swimwear section for six year olds.

'The Glass Slipper' Effect

Pretty soon, little girls are brought up to aspire to being a princess. This message is conveyed through numerous fairy tales, romantic fiction, television and films. Cars even carry a sticker on their rear window declaring, 'Princess on board.'

Laura Bates's[2] *Everyday Sexism* tells us of 'the bombardment of media messages' bulldozing young girls towards what she memorably terms 'pretty pink pliancy' enumerating the proliferation of magazines aimed at young girls with titles like 'Tinker Bell', 'Princess Kingdom' or 'Fairy Princess'. There is no subtlety about it. The constant publicity surrounding the Duchess of Cambridge – a real princess – particularly during her marriage, has centred on her appearance. At her wedding not only she but her mother and her sister were minutely scrutinised, often to the point of prurience, by the world's media: their hair, their clothes, their make-up and their figures were freely commented on. A headline in a tabloid newspaper went so far as to describe her sister Pippa as 'the rear of the year'. A week after her baby was born, Catherine was subjected to disgraceful articles advising her on losing 'the baby bump'. She is referred to in newspaper articles with intrusively chummy intimacy as Kate whose main function is to smile constantly and never get fat.

The Need to be Thin

Added to the question of style in clothes is of course the need to be thin and, in the case of some models, skeletally thin. Much has been written about the problems this causes for girls and women, sometimes resulting in disordered eating.

It is hard to pin down exactly when being thin became a feminine ideal. Carol Dyhouse,[3] in her book *Glamour: Women, History, Feminism* dates our modern notions of glamour to before the First World War. 'Glamour is, and probably always has been about fantasy, desire and longing,' she writes. If she is correct then by their very nature these aspirations are almost bound to be unfulfilled, leaving women dissatisfied and a prey to the kind of advertising which promises unattainable goals. For many women this longing means always wanting to be thinner than they are.

Some of the earlier illustrations in Dyhouse's book are of extremely slim women, particularly in the 1930s. Diana Dors and Joan Collins in the 1950s show more 'curves' but they are the exception before we return to Jean Shrimpton in the 1960s and then to the big shoulder pads but tiny waists of the 1980s.

According to Brit Harper and Marika Triggerman[4] in *The Effect of Thin Ideal Media Images on Women's Self-Objectification, Mood, and Body Image*: 'Exposure to idealised magazine advertisements have a small but constant effect on women's wellbeing.'

Subjected to close scrutiny the models in magazines are unhealthily thin and we know that most survive on a starvation diet. Sadly, although aware of this fact and knowing that a few models have even died of malnutrition, many women find it difficult to resist the message of the advertisements and are beset by feelings of unhappiness with their appearance. Intelligent women will admit to the fact that their dissatisfaction is being artificially provoked, fuelled and maintained. Yet they still feel incapable of escaping its grip.

Nobody could argue with Susie Orbach's[5] seminal (and sensible) *Fat is a feminist issue* in which she insists that women should free themselves from the trap of obsession with their looks and therefore of food. However most of us who have read and totally agree intellectually with her book still find ourselves being drawn back emotionally to the old familiar, though uncomfortable, feelings of dissatisfaction with our bodies. In *Never Too Thin*, Eva Szekely[6] refers to a commentator who charges women with being 'natural narcissists'. Szekely points out the reasons: women are taught to be this way through 'ads, popular books, television programmes, movies, newspapers … which have been instrumental in fostering women's preoccupation with their appearance in general and more recently with their weight in particular'.

How Do I Look? is based on Jill Dawson's[7] many interviews with teenage girls and young women. This is 'Hannah' aged 18: 'It's not that I *want* to be the ideal woman. I'd simply like to be able to walk down a street and not even think about it.'

Helen, 23, says, 'It's not that I'm particularly unhappy with the shape of my body or with my image. It's just that I worry all the time about what people think about me, what impression they are getting. When I think of what the "ideal" look is for a girl, I always imagine it as someone looking happy, and that is the one thing I know I *don't* look.'

Muslim sixth former, Yasmin, is the only young woman interviewed by Dawson who is happy with her appearance: she wears the traditional shalwar kameez, a short tunic over long trousers. She can wear bright colours if she chooses. 'I feel there are a lot more important things in life than looking good … I am happy with the way I look, because it's the look that most suits who I am inside.'

Although published over 20 years ago it is unlikely that results would be very different if Dawson's interviews were carried out today. Indeed Facebook and Twitter seem to have increased the pressure on girls and young women by amplifying every unpleasant and critical comment. It is not surprising that some young women feel humiliated and hunted when a nasty remark is circulated to a vast audience. As we know, the effects have sometimes been fatal.

Here is a typical quote from Laura Bates's[8] book again: 'I'm fifteen and feel like girls of my age are under a lot of pressure that boys are not under. I know I am smart, I know I am kind and funny, and I know that everybody around me keeps telling me that I can be whatever I want to be. I know all this but I just don't feel that way. I always feel like if I don't look a certain way, if boys don't think I'm "sexy" or "hot" then I've failed and it doesn't matter if I am a doctor or writer, I'll still feel like nothing.'

Effect of Parents

Some women we have interviewed remember with continuing sadness comments by their parents about their appearance. One woman felt that she was a disappointment to her father, who wanted her to be sporty and teased her about being too fat. She is not the only person who referred to painful parental comments. Another recalls her mother's criticism of her appearance, "She told me that I was plain and chubby: that is my paranoia."

In a recent radio programme Jenny Murray's[9] confession about the effect of her mother's 'daily criticism' (sic) of her appearance, even after she became well known, was painful to listen to. She realised after her mother had died that what she had been trying to tell her was, 'I should try to look my best' and, 'Looks as well as brains are needed if you want to go far.' However, the memory of the unsolicited and hurtful comments still clearly make her flinch.

For gynaecologist and campaigner Wendy Savage, on the other hand, how she looks is not really a concern. "Well I don't understand those women who want plastic surgery," she said, continuing cheerfully, "I've always been flat-chested, and in fact my father used to make disparaging remarks about it!"

Don't Look Sexy

Some women told us how difficult it is to find the right style and appearance. A few are tempted to copy men. Suzanne Warner observed that, "I was always struck by how women who behaved like men also dressed like men, often in tailored trouser suits, or in tailored skirts suits in dark colours. I know the arguments about this but, for whatever reason, they had accepted the dress code of the man's world. They were not dressing on their own terms." Women search for a style that suits their personality and fits in with what is expected at work. A handful said that from time to time they had gained advantage by flirting or behaving in a sexually provocative way. But this approach was very exceptional. The consensus view was that sexy dress and behaviour is a great mistake and should be avoided. As one woman put it: "I have been chased around enough office tables to teach me that lesson." Helena Kennedy warned a successful and ambitious young female barrister that her provocative clothes not only gave rise to sniggering among her male colleagues but were preventing her application to become a QC from being taken seriously.

In *Dancing on the Ceiling: A Study of Women Managers in Education*, Valerie Hall[10] found that women Head Teachers paid close attention to how they dressed, moved and used body language. They had the problem of 'desexualising and remaining feminine. Their appearance needs to exemplify self-control not rigidity, adventurousness but not flamboyance'.

Barrister Adrienne Morgan spoke of "successful young female solicitors who conform to a stereotype: slim, wearing platinum rings with a single diamond, suits and high heels" – daunting to those who feel that their appearance falls short of this demanding image.

Mary Evans, Deputy Director of Children's Services in Wandsworth says she enjoys choosing clothes to wear to work but thinks that a few women dress inappropriately. "I struggle with large cleavages and think – oh, please put it away."

However, finding the dividing line between looking attractive and looking sexy is not something that can be left to chance. Norwegian academic Agnes Bolsø writes about the unspoken sexual signals and tensions in the workplace. She feels that, although these signals often go unacknowledged, they explain much of the behaviour when men and women sit in a meeting together.

In a recent book Catherine Hakim,[11] openly advocates using what she terms 'erotic capital' – advising women to use their femininity and sex appeal to get ahead at work: 'honey money' she calls it. Though it is difficult to believe that an academic from the London School of Economics could peddle such potentially inflammatory suggestions, Hakim got a lot of publicity when she floated her ideas. She seemed unaware of the potentially dangerous position women might find themselves in by flaunting their sexuality in the workplace. Hakim is sometimes referred to as a feminist but many women think that she is undermining the work that women have done to show that they are not sex symbols but strong, competent and serious with clear goals.

Don't be Drab

But if sexy is to be avoided, women also find that they can face significant criticism for appearing to be at all drab. Neuroscientist Professor Susan Greenfield told us the story of a 15-year-old schoolgirl whose class had been addressed by an eminent female scientist as part of a series she had organised to encourage girls to take up science as a career. "Well if that's what women scientists look like you can count me out," said the indignant 15 year old.

It often seems as if women cannot win. Susan Greenfield's own appearance was a target of destructive articles by journalists who showed more interest in her miniskirts and her long blonde hair than in her international reputation as a neuroscientist. She believes that her appearance incited prejudice because "it is seen as deviant and therefore not acceptable". Her former colleague, scientist Ellie Dommett, now lecturing in psychology at The Open University says wryly, "Lab coats cover a multitude of sins," but adds that when she is giving a talk to young women she does dress up (always with her trademark dangerously high heels), "otherwise they are turned off by the conventional image of drab women scientists".

These two women are serious scientists with a proven academic record of research and yet, rather than being assessed by their achievements, they find themselves spending time and effort on what should be a superficial concern: how they and their female colleagues look. No male scientist has to bother about such matters. His biggest sartorial dilemma will be whether or not to wear a tie.

As J.K. Rowling[12] said in a recent radio interview, 'It must be so nice to be a man and just think "which of my three suits will I wear today?"'

When renowned astronomer Jocelyn Bell Burnell[13] discovered the pulsar, the *Daily Mail* described her success as 'girl discovers little green men'. She remembers that, 'All they were interested in were my "vital statistics" – bust, waist and hip measurements.'

More recently, according to another entry in Laura Bates's blog,[14] *The Guardian* wrote the following about Home Secretary Theresa May: 'As she expounded her tough stance on immigration she stood in shoes worthy of the front row of Paris fashion week.'

Far from being drab, Anne Marie Carrie, former Chief Executive of Barnardo's told us, "I've always been meticulous about my wardrobe. I think carefully about what I wear. I don't believe in power dressing but dress appropriate to the audience." She finds out the corporate colours of the companies whom she persuades to donate to Barnardo's and wears those colours in promotional videos and to Board meetings. "I think they notice," she says "even subliminally!"

Former Head Teacher and National Association of Schoolmasters Union of Women Teachers (NASUWT) President Clarissa Williams says, "Looking good and suited is important for self-confidence. We don't do it for ourselves. We look smart for the children and as a head teacher I want the students to know that I thought they were worth making the effort for."

In a typically down to earth and refreshing remark, Glenys Kinnock, former Foreign Office Minister, now in the House of Lords says, "I've always liked clothes but I don't wear business suits. You don't have to be all trussed up."

Contradictory Pressures

One sportswoman described the conflict between the demands of sport and the current culture which gives such importance to a woman's appearance. "As a sportswoman the emphasis is on how you play and not how you look. Yet young sportswomen are surrounded by messages that they should look soft, pretty and submissive." Jessica Ennis-Hill is able to cope with these conflicting pressures. No one could doubt her spectacular sporting prowess and achievement, but it was her attractive face and her smile that helped her to become the poster girl for the 2012 Olympics Games.

Other sportswomen find different ways to handle stereotypical expectations of their appearance. Laura Trott,[15] who won an Olympic Gold medal in London when only 20 says, 'People think female athletes are tomboys, but I'm a girly girl. I like pink, I do my nails.' However she resists the idea that she should become some sort of sex symbol. In a newspaper interview in March 2014 Trott[16] says that she had been asked to attend the 'Sexiest Woman in the World' awards, 'but I don't want to be associated with that whole thing. I am 21 and I want girls to look up to me as a sportswoman. I want people to see my achievements before anything else'.

Jamaican gold medallist in the World Championships in Moscow 2013, Shelley-Ann Fraser Price's pony tail is dyed bright pink and tied with a yellow and black spotted bow. She wears ear rings and a necklace when she is running. Fellow medallist Murielle Ahouri wears bright lipstick and blows kisses to the crowd before her races. Both clearly delight in their femininity but when they are racing it is their ability on the track that we focus on.

But all these sporting champions are still judged by men on their appearance, not just whether they are good at their sport but crucially whether they are also beautiful. And a successful sportswoman who is not thought by some men to be sufficiently attractive finds that the focus of comment quickly shifts from sporting prowess to personal appearance. Marion Bartoli won the Wimbledon Singles title in 2013. Reflecting on her success, the BBC commentator, John Inverdale, added the irrelevant comment, 'She's never going to be a looker.' After some angry criticism, Inverdale gave a rather perfunctory apology and said that his comments were 'misinterpreted' and 'never intended to be taken seriously'. Culture secretary Maria Miller MP and many others were not satisfied with Inverdale's response but clearly the powers-that-be at the BBC saw nothing wrong and no action was taken against him. Some months later Inverdale found himself in the same commentary team as Bartoli. Under this embarrassing pressure he explained that when he commented on Bartoli's appearance he was suffering from hay fever (sic).

Faced with these heavy, often contradictory and destructive pressures, most women search for a way to look both feminine and smart. It requires continual attention. Judy McKnight, former General Secretary of the Probation Officers' union told us that she "always had a manicure and a haircut before the TUC Conference" and thought a lot about what she should wear. "Your appearance is an important part of who you are." But Mary Evans thinks that the pressure is increasing. "There is a preponderance of stereotyped images of airbrushed beauty now. I think there was a broader range when I was younger."

One woman gave us an example of how the need to look good can get out of proportion. She was giving a television interview that was very important to her company, so the pressure to set the right tone was considerable. When the interview was over her first question to a colleague was not whether she had got her points across but, "Did I look alright?"

Tanya Savkin, Senior Analyst at Moody's Investors Service, in answer to the question, "Does it really matter how women dresses?" said emphatically: "Yes definitely. If I have to give a presentation, the first thing I do is look in a mirror." And if they make a wrong judgment about how they should dress, it may affect the way they behave. Melanie Dawes speaks for many women we interviewed in saying that she buys good quality clothes but, "If I don't think I look good, I tend to take a lower profile that day."

To some women, giving so much attention to appearance may often be a creative, even enjoyable experience. As Barbara Young told us, "I thought that, if I am an exception, I might as well make the most of it and stand out."

Academic Carole Elliott reminded us, however, that women pay a price for the demands made by society. "Women's concern for their appearance has a disruptive effect on their lives. It takes up an awful lot of brain space." And the psychological consequences of constantly having to "manipulate the social repercussions of their appearance" can provoke feelings of anxiety, of worthlessness and even shame. These feelings inevitably affect women's behaviour.

Anxiety and Shame

In a significant piece of research carried out in the USA in 1998 – *That swimsuit becomes you* – Barbara Fredrickson[17] argues that self-objectification (seeing ourselves through the eyes of others) can actually alter cognitive reactions. 'Part of being human,' she says, 'is to wonder what others think of us … such thinking, through internalising other's appraisals, can determine our very sense of self.'

In her experiment, male and female undergraduates were asked to take part in a maths test wearing their own choice of clothing: they were informed in advance that there would be no record of their gender. Mathematics was chosen because it is an area where men traditionally score higher than women. At this stage the men and women performed equally well.

The GMAT (the heavily maths-based Graduate Admissions Test) was then undertaken by the students, some wearing sweaters and others in swimsuits. The tests were done individually: participants sitting on their own in cubicles with full-length mirrors.

The men wearing sweaters simply said they felt 'a bit silly' and their test scores were not affected. The women felt 'ashamed, guilty and silly' in sweaters. They scored worse than the men.

The men took a light hearted approach to wearing swimsuits and their scores were again unaffected. However, the women wearing swimsuits felt, without exception, 'disgust, disgrace, revulsion' and scored significantly worse than the men. Fredrickson's conclusion is that wearing swimsuits doubly reminded the women of their sex and, she maintains, 'the shame that women feel about their bodies is experienced as chronic and largely uncontrollable'. The response of these young women was not rational and it is surely alarming that negative emotions about their physical appearance could affect their intellectual ability to this extent. Some of the men in this experiment again admitted to 'feeling a bit silly' but none felt the intensity of the woman's reactions.

The women were reacting to impossibly perfect images of the female body by which they are daily bombarded and the impact of this eroded their confidence to such an extent that they underperformed.

Fredrickson goes on to suggest that part of the reason for the women's revulsion (some even felt anger) at seeing themselves in swimsuits takes on a moral dimension, in that not having a 'perfect' body contravenes societal rules about body shape and they felt extra guilt about not complying. How often do we hear women on diets saying, 'I'm going to be *good* today'?

Keeping Women in Their Place

When Joan Ruddock was elected into the House of Commons in 1987, women MPs were not allowed to wear trousers, although she and the late Jo Richardson MP defied this ruling. She recalls an occasion during a very hot summer when she was wearing a modest summer dress, carrying a jacket over her arm and was told very sharply by an usher, "Put your jacket on madam."

One piece of advice we were given was that a woman has to decide "whether she is being true to her view of herself and developing her own style". Perhaps easier said than done. Through whose eyes are we looking, after all? If we do not like what we see, being true to oneself is likely to lead to anxiety and dissatisfaction. One woman who did not want to be named went further. She thinks that the obsession with the way women look is an instance of the way our culture is male controlled. "The fact that men feel able to comment on a woman's appearance is a way of keeping women in their place."

Many women have found their appearance unashamedly commented upon when passing a group of men. Whether the comments are complimentary or not they are unwelcome. Some women in the 1970s and 1980s attempted to retaliate by responding with remarks about the appearance of the men but the tactic backfired, encouraging the men to make even more comments. In any event most women said that answering in kind made them feel felt uncomfortable rather than liberated.

As every woman knows, this is not a habit that has died. We were told of a typical example concerning a group of women in their sixties who had dressed up to go for a meal recently. As they passed a group of men in the bar of the pub, one of them made lewd remarks. He was in fact dealt with effectively by the most assertive of the women but there is something seriously wrong in our society when men feel that they can make rude remarks about the appearance of women who happen to be nearby. We have discussed in Chapter 5 why some men feel they have the right to behave in this objectionable manner. The reasons why some men find it possible and even necessary to pass judgement on the way women look are complex but we conclude that this kind of male behaviour must surely be connected to feelings of potency, if not power.

How Serious is the Issue of Women's Appearance?

To those who would dismiss concerns about appearance as superficial or frivolous, Kat Banyard[18] of UK Feminista gives a powerful riposte: 'Women are constantly judged by their appearance ... Women's bodies are denigrated as inanimate objects to be publicly scrutinised, judged, maintained and manipulated for the benefit of others. They are shared public property.' Reminding us of John Berger's 1970s insights Kat Banyard argues that, 'The rituals women go through are necessary because the sense of self hinges on the gaze of others ... women wake up each morning knowing that their appearance will be crucial currency for getting through the day.'

Supreme Court Judge Brenda Hale says, "Women's experiences are so different because they are looked at physically. Men relate to us as women before we are lawyers and that includes the way we dress and whether we are considered attractive."

In *The End of Men*, Hanna Rosin[19] describes Marissa Mayer, the highest-ranking woman at Google as 'tall and blond with Holly Golightly good looks and a great sense of style'. As an umbrella statement on the ideal 'look' for high-level women Executives in the USA this is hard to beat. Indeed some of the women we interviewed talked about the 'American look' of big hair and padded shoulders, not popular with businesswomen in Britain.

Relief at Getting Older

The need to give so much thought to presentation is wearisome at the very least. So it is not surprising that for some women there is relief in getting older. Julie Towers says that she now feels able to be "more herself and not to have to play a part. Appearance for me is much less important than it used to be". Professor Jane Miller[20] goes further. In her book, *Crazy Age* she expresses relief that being older brings 'a new invisibility in which I bask, which allows me to walk the streets and gaze at the world without attracting the least attention. And there is pleasure to be had from that ... Old age confers a delicious privacy in public places'.

On the other hand, feminist academic Lynne Segal[21] in her book *Out of Time* rejects the notion that invisibility brings relief. In the chapter entitled 'Flags of Resistance' and beneath the heading 'Defying Chronological Age' she writes, '"You haven't changed at all" are words I love to hear when meeting people I have not seen for a while. Guiltily, I cherish the thought that I don't look my age, and like to believe my friends and acquaintances when they flatter. So do all of my friends, I notice, and I've learned to offer these reassuring words myself.'

For many women, grey hair, considered distinguished on older men, is rejected as unacceptable. The majority of successful women dye their hair, some even in startling colours. Indeed the fact that the graphic, sexually explicit insults suffered by academic and TV presenter Mary Beard focused on her shoulder-length grey hair, is evidence of general intolerance to women allowing their age to show in public.

A young businesswoman told us a chilling story of witnessing a senior female colleague approach a woman with a few grey hairs which she touched saying, "You need to get rid of these for a start."

"Some men in orchestras talk as if women players are booked for glamour rather than for proficiency," says professional viola player, Katherine Chibah. "In one world famous British orchestra there is never a woman over the age of 35 whereas the average age for men is much older."

There does seem to be a general current obsession with youth and youthful looks for both men and women. Rising numbers of people are using plastic surgery or botox to remove or disguise 'blemishes' or the signs of ageing. But it is surely indicative of the pressures on women that 90 per cent of those opting for this kind of surgery are female.

So much of a woman's identity and feelings of self-worth depend on how they feel they look. They take to heart the arbitrary standards decreed by others (often swayed by commercial interests), apply them to their own appearance and view themselves critically.

Getting it Wrong

Sometimes a misjudgement about appearance can make an awful situation worse. Sharon Shoesmith was the Director of Children's Services in Haringey when a child died. Her personal misery was compounded by the press who hounded her. She presented herself as "a consummate professional": well dressed, articulate and knowledgeable. But she drew negative reactions from journalists who used this self-presentation to portray her as a heartless bureaucrat.

It is not the intention of this chapter to rehearse all the many and persuasive arguments about how women come to be in thrall to misconceptions about their size and shape but to reiterate the undeniable fact that negative perceptions about their appearance are, for the majority of even the most successful women, a daily obstacle to be faced and overcome.

Valerie Hall[22] describes these tensions as 'Florence Nightingale meets John Wayne'. Some of us wish it were no more complicated than that. Film star good looks, immaculate dress sense, an impression of eternal youth and an ever-ready smile might be added to the list of requirements that society seems to demand of a successful woman.

Two Women Presented as Role Models by the Press

Two images show how successful women are portrayed by the media. They were both presented in 2013 by *The Guardian*, a newspaper with a policy of treating women in an equal and even-handed manner. Beneath the headline 'Burberry chief executive becomes first woman to top FTSE 100 pay league' is a photo of Angela Ahrendts[23] speaking at the World Business Forum in New York two years earlier. She is sitting on a very high chair, facing the reader directly, wearing a black suit and knee-length shiny black boots with very high heels. Only her shoulder-length blonde hair softens the rather hard-edged image. The impression is of a strong, capable, daunting, female Chief Executive. It is unlikely that this image is arrived at by accident. Careful thought has gone into how she presents herself to her audience and the media. Were the two men who wrote this article responsible for choosing this particular photo (taken by a man) to accompany this article? One wonders why they chose this photo (taken two years before) from the many they must have had at their disposal. Indeed, later articles about Ahrendts, when moving on from Burberry, show a very different and more sympathetic image of a smiling and warm woman: no more need for the aggressive symbolism that accompanied her success in a male-dominated world.

In the same newspaper on the same day is a picture of the actor Gillian Anderson in the popular television series 'The Fall', where she plays Stella Gibson, a senior detective. She is described as, 'Steely, but with an underlying softness. A woman to make men weak.' Like Angela Ahrendts, she is blonde, tall, slim and the clothes she wears in the series are both business-like but consciously sexy. Her blouses are silk, deliberately outlining her shape, and her style is cool, often brusque and uncompromising, though slightly vulnerable.

Her manner puts both her male and female colleagues at a disadvantage because it is confusing. On the one hand she appears alluring: standing too close to male colleagues, while at the same time delivering caustic comments which undermine their professional judgements and challenge their masculinity.

While her terse way of speaking is clearly considered appropriate for a police chief, the camera constantly focuses on what are described as 'her flawless features' and long legs. The double message is unsettling because what is being admired is her contemptuous manner coupled with a clashing seductive quality. Stella Gibson seems to represent a very male view of the perfect female boss, from whom most women would probably recoil. We are talking about a fictional character here but no apologies need be given. Drama has a powerful impact on our opinions and there was widespread coverage in the press approving of Stella Gibson as the ideal, cool feminist boss – a sad and stereotypical reaction to a confused and unsympathetic woman who is a dangerous role model. In essence this character is constituted by melding the vulnerable princess with a caricature of the cold businesswoman: the worst of all possible combinations.

Body Image is Political

The meanings that have been assigned to women's bodies are culturally defined. If we are serious about our intention to see more women in positions of power, changes have to take place which radically challenge the perceptions we now hold.

Resolving the tensions between women's feelings about how they look and the reactions of others – men and women – to their appearance is far from straightforward. This issue is affected by social, psychological, sexual and political practices. "Body image is political," says MP Jo Swinson, whose policy paper *Real Women* was published in 2009 and received what she describes as "extraordinary media attention". She was inundated with emails from all over the country which have fuelled her campaign to get some advertisements banned as well as being instrumental in her decision to join some eating disorders groups.

Campaigns like hers and UK Feminista's 'Lose the Lads Mags', which has successfully persuaded The Co-op, Tesco and other retailers to remove offensive magazines portraying women as sexual objects from their shelves, are beginning to sink into the public consciousness.

Two articles in *The Observer*[24] gave an insight on how women see their bodies. First, pop singer Lily Allen revealed to journalist Eva Wiseman how close she came to having extensive plastic surgery to get rid of her 'mummy tummy'. 'Nobody's immune to the pressure to look thin,' she says. Visiting a Harley Street surgeon for advice on liposuction, she came out having been advised that she should reshape her entire body – thighs, belly, ankles (sic!), knees and back. The idea would be laughable if it were not so monstrous!

In the same issue of the newspaper, Tracy Mcveigh speaks to seven teenage girls, aged between 16 and 18 about 'sexism, feminism and twerking'. Although they understand the pressures pop stars are under, the teenage girls express their own strongly held and generally sensible views on the music industry. They go on to discuss the pressure on boys to use weights to achieve the ideal male body, the inadequate reporting on women's sports on television as well as, rather disconcertingly, their own views on feminism. Seventeen-year-old Rachel Macpherson says, 'You can be a feminist and take off your clothes.' She also says that, 'Famous women hide when they are pregnant because they can't bear not to have perfect bodies.'

Sixteen-year-old Genevieve Koputsoumnais blames schools. 'There is this emphasis on not being racist or homophobic at school. But no one explains why you shouldn't be sexist.'

Eighteen-year-old Holly Kinsell ends the discussion on a somewhat despondent note: 'This won't be the last time these things are talked about. It will be talked about for generations. Until there is equality.'

We have to hope that her timescale is wrong, but in general the range of their discussion should give us cause for optimism. The young women are aware of the way that the media can manipulate us all and they take for granted that it can be resisted. But they also know that resistance is hard.

What is needed is for girls like these and their male counterparts to have the courage to take action so solutions are found in the first part of this century and debate does not last for the generations that Holly Kinsell predicts.

Dissatisfaction with our appearance has a cumulative, corrosive effect on our self-esteem. How we see ourselves and how others see us influences the way we behave, and that is the subject of our next chapter.

Chapter 7

How Women
are Expected to Behave

'Women have come through the concrete wall, shattered the glass ceiling and are now negotiating the labyrinth,' according to academics Alice Eagly and Linda Carli.[1]

What is now preventing them from emerging onto a level playing field?

Let us start from the beginning.

Little Girls are Nice

Little girls are still encouraged to be 'nice'. Despite welcome and overdue changes in toys, clothes and activities designed for young children in the past 40 years, there is still an underlying expectation that young girls and women will be compliant. This is not easy for them. 'Tension devours them and the desire for approval agonises them,' writes Elena Belotti.[2] No one would argue that every child needs and seeks attention, but it is the constant need for approval that little girls in particular find hard to shift and too often it follows them into adulthood. The need to be liked hampers their efforts in planning their future. At work they find themselves worrying about antagonising their male colleagues. Those who reject or even rebel against unspoken constraints are still aware of general expectations of their behaviour. They may resist, but resistance takes effort and energy and constant self-examination.

Being raised to seek approval, even strong women find it hard to ignore those who find their assertive demeanour unacceptable, even offensive and confusing. Women who do not conform to the accepted norm are seen as threatening.

Two very different reactions to how they should behave from two women we interviewed.

"I was blonde, wore very short skirts and was lippy. Everyone remembered me." (Baroness Young, CEO, Diabetics UK.)

"When I started work, I was happy to be one of the lads," said one senior manager.

Taking this latter stance a stage further, a successful American businesswoman quoted by consultant Denise Cormier[3] says, 'I speak sport. I do what the boys do. I speak their language,' and yet the same woman admits dejectedly, 'I sometimes feel like I crashed the party.'

So although both the women quoted above and their American counterpart consciously chose how they would behave, opting for short term tactics instead of long term strategies seems not to have worked.

Living with Borrowed Concepts

Sheila Rowbotham[4] describes women as living '… with borrowed concepts that do not fit the shape we feel ourselves to be'. She calls it 'a gentle tyranny'. For some women the tyranny seems anything but gentle.

"I'm failing at something I don't actually want to be," admitted secondary teacher Sarah Beeson.

"There is a mismatch between the little person inside me and the public speaker," said Maggie Baxter – Chair of Trustees of Rosa.

In order to seek approval women apparently smile 17 per cent more often than men and are discomfited when other women do not reciprocate.

Rowbotham's 'borrowed concepts' are clearly not designed to fit and are uncomfortable to live with.

At the other end of the spectrum, terms like queen bees, iron maidens and battle axes are frequently invoked to describe women who successfully stray from the comfortable stereotype of an amenable non-combative workmate.

Cordelia Fine[5] in *Delusions of Gender* warns us that 'self-concept is permeable and people tune their self-evaluations to blend with what others think of them'. For women this probably means acting against their own instincts to fit in with stereotypical expectations.

This constant need to meet others' expectations leaves many women exhausted, disappointed and disillusioned.

The Toll of Seeking Approval

Perhaps the picture being painted here seems out of date. Surely things have moved on? Women are more confident and assertive. Indeed it would be foolish to deny that more women are daring to challenge the apparently immutable status quo we described in Chapter 3. But if women are now more confident why do so many of them "routinely underestimate their talent, skills and experience?" asks Eleanor Mack.

Jean Venables, first woman President of the Institute of Civil Engineers was amazed to find that she had passed the 11 plus "because no one ever told me I might be clever". She received no encouragement from her parents, who dismissed any sign of aptitude or academic success as 'showing off'.

Patricia Hollis, former Leader of Norwich Council and now in The House of Lords told us that in the small South Devon village in which she grew up there was a strong feeling that no one should "get above themselves". She still has the autograph book in which a family friend wrote when she was nine years old: 'Be good, sweet maid, and let who will be clever.'

Ironically Jenny Tongue, who had to attend the sixth form at the local boys' school for her science lessons before going on to study medicine, says she probably benefitted from subconscious prejudice when she was selected to stand for Parliament, not because she had served as a local Councillor for ten years but because "I was a *lady* doctor!": winning approval for being a woman in a man's world.

The Imposter Syndrome

Will they also, as many admitted they do, be constantly looking over their shoulder, afraid of being found wanting, of being found out? The 'imposter syndrome' is very powerful, as even the astronomer Jocelyn Bell Burnell[6] confessed in a radio interview, remembering that after she had been accepted to study for her PhD at Cambridge University. 'I kept thinking they've made a mistake. I should leave before they find me out.' Glenys Kinnock, former MEP and Foreign Office Minister, now in The House of Lords, said, "Oh yes, I feel it every day. It's always there. And in The House of Lords the formality, the vocabulary and the stiffness are daunting."

And the immensely successful academic Dorothy Wedderburn[7] wrote, '... I retained a sneaky feeling that it was all a mistake and at some point I would be found out.' Deborah Bull, former Creative Director of the Royal Opera House understands these feelings but adds that she compensates through hard work.

Most surprising of all perhaps is Ninette de Valois[8] who, in an interview in 1981 when she was 82 years old with a history of success to look back on, still said, 'I kept waiting for them to find me out.'

Brenda Hale, the only female Judge in The Supreme Court, mused, "I wonder whether the imposter syndrome is a woman thing or whether we are simply more ready to own up to it?" Possibly, but this proposition in itself illustrates the vulnerability of women. Controversially, on the other hand, Tanya Slavkin, Senior Analyst at Moody's Investment Services, is of the opinion that this insecurity drives women to excel. "It is replacement for testosterone."

Men Feel Entitled to Their Success

By contrast, what most men appear to feel is a definite sense of entitlement to their successes. Research tells us that men feel that their achievements are based on recognition of their merit; women, on the other hand, believe they are rewarded for hard work, perseverance against the odds and being more fiercely competitive than they feel comfortable with.

Let us explore some other contributory factors to these unequal expectations.

The Importance of Language

In *The Language of Female Leadership*, Judith Baxter[9] attempts to answer the question: 'Is language a reason why female leaders are under-represented at senior level?' Her contention is that there are contradictory 'discourses' in the business world which form the context in which women and men communicate. Put simply, this means that the way we use language reflects our way of looking at ourselves and the world. External forces can have the effect of making us adapt our ways of expressing ourselves.

Constantly being on guard influences our language: the words we use, expressions and the way we use them. Linguist, Deborah Tannen[10] makes a distinction between *report* speech (male) and *rapport* speech (female). Report speech is used by men to state facts confidently regardless of their audience. Women are more likely to adopt rapport speech to connect with those they are communicating with. Women often soften their remarks, inviting comments and using expressions like 'I wonder how you feel about this?'/ 'perhaps we can look at this together'/ or simply using an interrogative inflection in their voices. In a commercial setting this can make them seem inappropriately tentative, even unsure.

National Union of Teachers (NUT) General Secretary, Christine Blower, feels that, "Women speak to engage and build a bridge between themselves and their audience." During a Q&A session at the NUT Annual Conference she noticed that more men spoke than women 'because they put their hands up to speak almost before they have worked out what they are going to say and they keep their hands up even if their point has been made but choosing to repeat it rather than withdrawing it'.

A woman we interviewed who has held senior positions in several companies advises women to "behave as if you expect people to listen to you, make eye contact, keep very still, sit very still … and give your opinion as if you expect your opinions to gain support". She admits that before she learnt these lessons her remarks "disappeared into a cone of silence".

As the sole woman on a European-wide Board, Lesley Wilkin spoke of the 12 other members "who frequently talk over each other and I have to wait for the hubbub to die down before I can get into the discussion".

One woman who did not want to be named told us that the style of discourse in a FTSE 100 company is very masculine. She strongly dislikes the big unstructured meetings where the loudest voices get the most attention and the aggressive approach could even be described as borderline bullying. Being small, in order to make herself heard, she feels she has to stand up.

Feminists rightly insist on careful use of language: the way we express ourselves in speech is indicative of how we think.

Let us consider some examples.

In a recent political debate a man promoted himself as the best candidate to 'take on' a Government minister because he 'would stay in the ring' and later in his speech promised to 'put tanks on the lawn' of his opponent. We are all familiar with sporting metaphors frequently used when men are speaking: 'kicking the ball into the long grass', 'punching above your weight', 'boys playing against men'. And like the man at the political hustings, they also use warlike references: 'being outgunned', 'pincer movement', 'in the firing line' and so on. Being concerned about the use of language may seem either obsessive or trivial but the words we choose are powerful indicators of how we see ourselves and others. Most of the phrases above and other similar ones are commonly used by many of us, and it is easy to forget their provenance. On the whole these expressions evoke images of tough men. We all understand what is being said but using this kind of language can marginalise many women and should be considered inappropriate in work situations.

As evidence that words matter, one has only to look at the fall out for Julia Gillard, Australia's first female Prime Minister, after she accused Tony Abbott, the leader of the opposition, of being a misogynist. His campaign urged voters to 'ditch the witch'. Applauded by women across the globe, Julia Gillard unfortunately suffered a backlash in her own country. However, the Macquarie dictionary – Australia's most authoritative dictionary – did alter its definition of the word misogynist to include 'entrenched prejudice against women' in the wake of this dispute – victory of a sort!

Many men and some women do not have, or feel disinclined to use, the vocabulary to discuss gender and equality issues. They hesitate before key words like 'sexist' or key phrases like 'sexual discrimination' and have not thought out which words to use when they are describing particular occupations or events. Workers employed to put out fires are now called 'firefighters' but the word fireman is still commonly used. 'Police officer' has not yet replaced policeman as the normal usage. The male pronoun is still often used even when men and women are both involved.

Middle-aged men in particular are still inclined to refer to women as girls or ladies. The real giveaway is what people call a woman who chairs a meeting.

The authors have heard her called 'Chairman', 'Chairperson', 'Madame Chairman' and 'Madame Chairperson'. The imaginative have probably come up with other variations. We asked one successful woman why she called herself 'Chairman' rather than just calling herself 'Chair'. The answer was startling: "Because I don't have four legs." We repeated that sentence to another interviewee who grinned and asked, "Does she feel obliged to do a graceful dive every time she goes to sit on a Board?"

We need to learn a modified language which allows us to debate sensitive issues without embarrassment. Maria Adebowale suggested that the problem is not limited to gender. She says that sometimes when race, gender or class issues are raised this can cause tension or discomfort in meetings. "People sometimes feel they do not have the experience or the vocabulary to discuss racial, gender or class issues – so these issues can get side-lined." Discussions about people who are disabled are similarly constrained.

The good news is that men and women in sensitive collaboration begin to modify their speech and take on some verbal characteristics of the opposite sex. Working together as a team allows men to behave differently. "Dialogue is necessary for men to take down their defences," says Civil Service trainer, Hilary Cotton.

The Behaviour Trap

However, the dominant group remain privileged because they write the rules. The academic Davies-Netzzly[11] puts it this way: 'Male ideologies are embedded in structures and practices of organisations and constitute the regime of "truth" in which women managers have to engage.'

Showing anger is frowned upon: "If I lose my temper I am judged as emotional but a man who flies off the handle is applauded for being passionate," says an influential Company Director. In their research on this subject Victoria Bescoll and Eric Uhlman[12] found that, 'Men expressing anger in professional posts gain status, power, independence. Women are expected to be kinder and more modest. If they do not exhibit these characteristics they violate the feminine norm.'

And research by Madeline Heilman[13] has shown that 'violating the feminine norm' can be detrimental for a woman's personality and for her career.

The behaviour trap that threatens to engulf every ambitious woman works in a subtle but relentless way. Women are taught to be nice, to be sympathetic, to be compliant, not to be boastful or aggressive and not to make trouble. These are the qualities that society expects of girls and women. Unfortunately these qualities are almost the exact opposite of those expected of a leader, who is required to be forceful and decisive even if this means upsetting other people. In Chapter 2 we described how this definition of leadership came about. Sadly, we also had to recognise that it is extremely persistent and resistant to modification.

Management Styles

Many women told us how difficult it is to find a management style with which they can feel comfortable. With no prompting, several women we interviewed described successful women as 'Queen Bees'. Liz McMeikan spoke of "the tendency of successful women to adopt a Queen Bee mentality and bask in their position as the only woman in a senior position, resenting the promotion of a second woman who might take attention from them" and Deirdre Hutton regrets the fact that "so many successful women develop a Queen Bee approach and regard other women as competition for the limelight". Jill May feels that "a number of female CEOs and women who have reached the top echelons of management seem quite comfortable with their Queen Bee status and are by no means eager to help other women arrive there". Helen Wells is not so sure. "Many top women are perceived to have Queen Bee syndrome where they are happy to be one woman amongst many men. I wonder if this perception is just another example of women being judged more critically than men?"

Others are forthright in their condemnation of some of the ruthless and divisive styles of management they have witnessed adopted by a few senior women. A senior doctor working for the NHS says of the very few female high-flyers in her field, "they are immaculately turned out, childless and pretty nasty to junior women colleagues ... they often behave like intimidating bullies and are not at all supportive". Professor Susan Greenfield understands the feelings of inadequacy that beset many high-profile women but has also seen "women bosses behaving like bitches – getting at other women because they are easy fodder".

Jo Haigh[14] in *Tales from the Glass Ceiling* sums it up thus: 'Nobody objects to a successful woman if at the same time she manages to be a good mother, good looking, good helpmate, well dressed, well groomed and unassertive.'

Academics often suggest that men and women have different management 'styles'. For autism expert Simon Baron Cohen[15] this is due to innate qualities: 'Men's brains systematise, women's brains empathise'. Unfortunately, whatever reason and experience tell us on this issue, men and women are too often believed to function stereotypically. Baron Cohen's line of argument is unthinkingly accepted. In his opinion male brains produce people who are good at hunting and tracking, achieving social dominance, showing aggression and leadership. Even if he is right (and the evidence tells us that this is extremely unlikely) none of these attributes include communication skills which are vital in today's society. None of them are exclusive to one sex and none are immutable. More importantly, as neuroscientist Cordelia Fine[16] retorts: 'Biology is never irrelevant – nor determinant.'

The fact remains that men and women's behaviour at work is judged by different criteria: *prescriptive* (what society expects) rather than *descriptive* (how they actually behave). In the jargon used by commentators, men are considered *'agentic'* (they act) and women are supposed to be *'communal'* (they respond on an emotional/intuitive level).

Obviously both sexes are capable of both agentic and communal behaviour but because the norm is predicated on a set of stereotypical expectations, colleagues find it hard to accommodate deviations. When a man listens to, sympathises with and responds to the needs of female colleagues he is very likely to be praised for his sensitivity. Women, on the other hand, are looked upon unfavourably when they conduct themselves assertively. What a woman might see as efficient, assertive, business-like behaviour is interpreted as bossy, inflexible and aggressive.

The conclusion reached by Rudman and Fairchild[17] in *Reactions to counterstereotyping* is that an agentic woman applying for a job is regarded as 'competent but not likable and a communal woman is regarded as likable but not competent'.

'Women in authority find themselves in a double bind. If they speak in ways expected of women they are seen as inadequate leaders. If they speak in ways expected of leaders they are seen as inadequate women,' says Deborah Tannen.[18]

Like her male counterparts, a senior woman will have goals and also strategies for attaining them, using her own and her colleagues' skills, talents and expertise. She will manage meetings, briskly and effectively, adhering to the agreed agenda. Her methods are shown to yield positive results. Because she is a woman, however, her style causes problems. What would be acceptable in a man will be viewed as calculating and ruthless: basically unfeminine. She may succeed professionally but at what cost to her personal reputation? Lawyer Pamela Castle admitted that she coped by sometimes behaving "as much like a man as possible" but was aware that this brings its own penalties. "I have often been criticised for forthright behaviour that would have been applauded in a man."

To return to Madeline Heilman:[19] she sums up her research conclusions by saying that ambitious women face formidable obstacles. 'If there is any ambiguity about their competence they are likely to be viewed as incompetent, and if their competence is unquestionable, they are likely to be socially rejected.'

Several women told us about the pressure they were under to behave like a man. Lucy Neville-Rolfe, Executive Director at Tesco mentioned Margaret Thatcher who "behaved very much like a man but mixed that aggression with flirtatious behaviour".

Even more poignantly, a lone woman at the top of an organisation is liable to suffer doubly. 'Solos … are the subject of inordinate gossip and scrutiny,' says Deborah Tannen.[20] Such unwanted attention often leads to negative consequences. In fact Eagly and Carli[21] state 'without a critical mass of women … a woman's style becomes autocratic'.

As Elizabeth Kelan of Cranfield Business School observes, "We need to fix the system not the women." We shall be returning to this theme in Chapter 11.

The Need to be Liked

Most of us want to be liked, but in women this need is much stronger than in men and can affect their outlook and actions.

"Women seem to care more about being liked and notice it more when they are not," says Heather Hancock. Running courses on confidence and assertiveness for women of varying seniority over many years, one of the authors of this book certainly found that the over-riding reason women gave for not challenging other colleagues – male and female – was their fear of not being liked. Losing favour was more important than stating their objections.

Stereotyping also plays its part. In recent research, business school students in the US identified masculine managerial behaviour as delegating, disciplining, strategic decision making, problem solving and pushing. Feminine behaviour is seen as recognising, communicating, informing and supporting (but not leading). It would be easy to dismiss these findings as invalid because the students are using hypothetical examples but they are the potential leaders of the future and such prejudices make depressing reading.

Waiting for Recognition

Women often seem to wait for recognition from others, usually men. Even Helena Kennedy said, "I didn't apply for silk until it was suggested to me by a man." Turning points in former Head Teacher Sally Barnes's career came about through the recognition of others: "And I was always surprised by what they said." As her own close friend Hilary Cotton would ask, "Whose permission are you waiting for?"

Unlike their male colleagues, women usually expect their work to speak for itself. They expect to get noticed without actively promoting themselves. Sally Martin said, "If I was doing good work, that should be enough. Like many women, I don't like promoting myself and I rarely think of doing it."

This reluctance to make themselves too visible can hold back equality in remuneration. More than 40 years after the Equal Pay Act women are still earning less than men performing similar or equivalent work.

Several of our interviewees realised that they were being underpaid. A few confronted their employers and demanded justice but others, through fear – knowing that they may face hostility or refusal – put up with this basic inequality. One or two, particularly women returning after maternity leave, simply feel grateful to be employed and do not want to 'rock the boat'. Susanna Jones, working part time as a solicitor after taking time off to raise her children, knew that she was being paid less pro rata than some of her male colleagues doing equivalent jobs, but said, "I was just grateful to have a job."

As we have discussed in detail in Chapter 5, many women actively dislike discussing pay, although they are aware that most men would negotiate for more.

Men Take Up Space

Men take up more space than women. Taller, bigger men take up even more space. Women visiting the male-dominated House of Commons will confirm that many MPs are well above average height. This confers additional physical power to their already acquired status.

One of the authors, having taught in two boys' schools, remembers her experience in the staffroom room well. As one of the very few women on the staff, teaching in a school in which sport was considered the main defining quality of masculinity, she found herself constantly tripping over the sprawling legs of any male member of staff under the age of 40, most of whom seemed to spend most of their working day in track suits. Although none of the men tried to patronise or intimidate her, being small, she inevitably had to look up every time she had a conversation with the majority of her colleagues.

In offices men move about more. 'There was a herd of roaming men,' says Dawn Steel[22] a film industry Executive. 'Guys wandered in and out of each other's offices … all the important decisions were taken before the monthly production meeting …you have to join the roamers.'

Low-Level Sexism

As we revealed in Chapter 5 many women seem to put up with low-level sexism. 'Putting up with sexist behaviour and jokes is part of most women manager's repertoire,' writes Valerie Hall[23] in her study of women managers in education.

According to Hannah Rosin,[24] in *The End of Men*, 'Women in silicon valley … recognise sexism but see it as an unpleasant and omnipresent fact of life.'

Newcastle MP, Chi Onwura, Shadow Minister for Science and Innovation says, "Life in engineering and science is a male environment and women often have to put up with sexist remarks, all male dinners and dubious jokes."

"You just get used to it," said Deirdre Hutton, Chair of the Civil Aviation Authority, describing examples of casual discourtesy and snubs by men throughout her working life.

Heather Hancock has suffered many instances where she has been taken for a junior employee. "As I get older I learn to develop a lofty stare."

Part of the problem is that the sexism women encounter at work is usually not intended as deliberate or malign. "It tends to be a thousand little things," says Deborah Hargreaves. Openly hostile sexism is comparatively rare and when it is blatant it may be more easily dealt with than 'benevolent' sexism experienced by women as infuriatingly patronising. When she was at Opportunity Now, Helen Wells called it 'subtle discouragement'. Whatever the intentions of male colleagues who genuinely try to help when they feel that women may not be up to handling difficult situations, or explain matters that they feel may be too difficult for women to understand, the effect is to defeat and sometimes silence their female colleagues. We are back to women's desire to be liked which can undermine the need to challenge people one works with on a daily basis. It is hard to object to apparently inoffensive words and deeds but women have to accept that unless they show their displeasure they end up colluding against their own interests.

Collusion Hinders Progress

Essentially the games that are played here are to do with wielding power unfairly and women find themselves putting up with unacceptable behaviour: indeed, according to Veronica Jarvis Tichenor,[25] 'part of being a member of the less powerful group is developing the ability to anticipate the needs and desires of those in power'. Tichenor's research concentrates on the home life of successful women but it is possible to transpose the power play that takes place in personal relationships to the workplace. In practice, for Executive or Personal Assistants, this involves spending emotional energy watching for signs of enthusiasm or impatience in your superiors at work and trying to accommodate them. It could be as simple as sympathising when their children lose a match at school or fail an exam or, more seriously, agreeing to reschedule a meeting which suits your boss even though the change of time table may seriously inconvenience you and others in the team.

"I'm obliging," confesses a successful feminist writer. It is difficult to explain the compulsion that drives women to act in ways that are detrimental to their own self-respect, but the main point is that this accommodation is rarely reciprocated and leaves the less powerful (often a woman) feeling somewhat demeaned. They do not complain because it seems petty to do so. Understandable though this is, sexist attitudes will persist and grow until women have the courage to say stop.

Unless women, particularly those in senior positions, react against insidious, pervasive forms of sexism they are doomed to constant unspoken denial of their justified irritation, even anger and this begins to have a corrosive effect. As Jocelyn Bell Burnell[26] says, 'I played the men at their own game. But I wonder now what this has done to me as a woman.'

Challenging those more powerful than oneself is easier to do if one has allies and one of the more dispiriting things we have found in speaking to younger women is that they appear to believe that the battle against sexism has been largely won by a previous generation of strong women and that if they are experiencing difficulties at work then they have only themselves to blame, which forces them to fight on alone and unsupported.

Because gender equality is not often discussed in the workplace, is taken for granted or is not taken seriously, the position often remains stagnant.

Sometimes we may feel shocked by the few who have made it to the top. Ninette de Valois,[27] herself an accomplished choreographer who virtually single-handedly introduced ballet to the British public, wrote, 'It is essential that you realise the real history of ballet – and by this I mean its creative work, its organisation, its pedagogy – has been the history of great male choreographers, directors and teachers.'

She went on to say with apparent approval, 'We want the public to realise that once again the development of ballet is rapidly passing into the care of the mature male element.'[28]

The 'Glass Cliff'

> *Women are like teabags. You don't know how strong they are until you put them in hot water.*
>
> *Eleanor Roosevelt*

In an effort to gain promotion women can find themselves accepting positions in companies that are failing, or taking jobs which feel precarious. This has been named as the 'Glass Cliff' phenomenon: described by academic Michelle Ryan[29] as 'teetering on the edge … with a constant risk of failure'. The women she interviewed talked about, 'being set up to fail' and not being in control with 'no one to turn to for help'. Some accept these unenviable posts in desperation, having been unsuccessful in applications for senior positions over a long period, others are offered 'Glass Cliff' opportunities by managers who think that women cope better in a crisis than men.

Although a surprising success rate is reported, businesses and other organisations turned round, the toll taken in terms of hours worked and unmanageable stress levels makes this a questionable strategy. Libby Blake, previously Director of Children's Services in Haringey, admitted that she was asked to take on the role of Area Manager in another London Borough, only to discover that she was expected to save £10 million and sack most of the staff. She agreed that this was indeed a 'Glass Cliff' appointment. She saved the money and miraculously managed to redeploy most of the staff but soon moved to another less challenging post.

Sometimes the situations that women find themselves in may not be so risky but nevertheless they are offered work because they are seen as 'a safe pair of hands' (as Deirdre Hutton, Chair of Civil Aviation Authority, described herself). Anglican priest, Ruth Bushayager says, she is "regarded as a safe woman to have on committees". Helena Morrissey, Chief Executive of Newton Investments says of herself, "I'm a coper."

Support Groups

The value of support groups and networking inside and outside work was mentioned by many people we spoke to.

Helena Morrissey began to hold lunch meetings of professional women: lawyers, businesswomen and academics to discuss how they might increase opportunities for women. The ages of the women attending ranged from 25 to 35 and the groups were culturally diverse and international. The influential 30% Club grew out of these lunchtime meetings. Its aim is to ensure that women make up at least 30 per cent of the membership of the Boards of FTSE 100 companies with the hope that this will lead to progress in smaller companies.

Helena Morrissey herself says that it sometimes feels like "two steps forward and one step back". A study conducted by www.ukjobs.net in 2010, highlighted by *Observer* journalist Barbara Ellen,[30] telling us that three-quarters of men preferred to work for male bosses and that (even more depressing) two-thirds of the women interviewed agreed, would seem to justify Helena's caution. The reasons given were that 'men were more straight talking and reasonable, less bitchy, cliquey and prone to mood swings … and there was no "time of the month"' (sic)! When women collude with this sort of prejudice, it is clear that we still have far to go.

Mentors also matter: 'Mentors are more important to career success than hard work, talent, intelligence. Mentors can show you the ropes. And pull strings,' says Sheila Wellington[31] of Catalyst.

However, as discussed in Chapter 4, networks have to be fit for purpose and mentors suitable and sympathetic for such support systems to succeed.

The fact that women are not visible at the top of most company hierarchies deters female employees from applying for promotion. This invisibility affects the whole organisation. 'The presence of women at higher management levels influences the entry, retention and perception of women at lower management levels,' writes academic Gary Powell.

What is needed is an enlightened dialogue rather than battle lines. The difficulty is that we are not considering an emotionally neutral situation.

Writing about their research Ann Halpern and Weedie Sisson,[32] are saddened by the fact that women are unwilling to help change the leadership culture: 'Women with the power rarely use that power to promote the interests of other women.'

Helena Morrissey again: "I am aware that I need to beat the drum for women … but I do despair that women don't support each other. Perhaps the next generation will be braver."

Perhaps women who are reluctant to use their power to encourage other women need to be reminded of former Secretary of State, Madeleine Albright's dictum:[33] 'There is a special place in hell for women who don't help other women.'

On a lighter note Maura McGowan, Chair of the Bar Council, told us that the small group of women Barristers and Judges who meet informally on a regular basis is named 'the thundering bitches' by one of their husbands!

The Second Shift: What Happens on the Domestic Front

Airlie Hoschild's[34] *The Second Shift* was published over 30 years ago. She had spent many years interviewing professional couples in Berkeley and, with their permission and active participation, observing 12 of them in their own homes.

Her aim was to see how successful women functioned in the domestic environment. How did their partners/husbands respond to life with women who outstripped their earning power and influence? How did these confident women behave at home?

'The myth believed in by women as well as men is that men should do 50% of work at home. In fact they don't.' Such is the power of society's expectations of the conventional role of men and women and because work at home is devalued by society, some successful women, whose husbands either earned less or stayed at home to look after the family, started to make up for their status at work by doing even *more* housework. Hoschild says they did this 'to salve the male ego'. When pressed, the women occasionally admitted to feelings of resentment but Hoschild never heard these matters discussed by the couples she interviewed and her conclusion was that 'marital myths are sustained (usually by women) in an attempt to avoid conflict'. She refers to what she calls 'underneath feelings', too dangerous to express. Their partners tended to offer support rather than real involvement. Sometimes the situation was made worse when husbands compensated by spending longer at work in an attempt to earn more, which resulted in their wives having to expend even more energy at home. As Hoschild writes somewhat wryly, '"Gifts" (i.e earning more by working longer) in the eyes of men are not "gifts" in the eyes of women.'

Veronica Jarvis Tichenor,[35] writing in 2005, continues where Airlie Hoschild left off, using almost identical phrases to describe what she found: 'as a woman's income surpasses her husband's she takes on more housework voluntarily to avoid further assaulting her husband's masculinity' (sic). 'Women avoid conflict over domestic labour to preserve marital harmony'. She describes women's work in the home as 'specialised, intimate … and because it has no price … it has little value. Caring work is simultaneously revered and devalued'. Indeed this may lie at the heart of the problem.

An added complication is that the wife's job tends not to decide the family's social status.

The problem appears to have as much to do with society's expectations of gender roles as with individual concerns about personal identity. Understandably, this is an issue that both men and women are reluctant to engage with.

Because the domestic sphere is private, we did not press the women we interviewed about their life at home, although this aspect of their lives has a huge impact on their emotional and physical wellbeing. However some volunteered that it undoubtedly put a strain on their relationships, a few candidly admitting that the partnership did not survive.

It would appear that if a woman is earning more or has a much higher public profile, relationships seem to survive more easily if her partner is older and has already established a successful career, is working in a totally different field (like a musician, artist, entrepreneur and so on) or is genuinely happy to stay at home whether working or not. One influential woman is married to a successful journalist who could often work at home and could therefore deal with domestic emergencies. Susan Street, formerly Permanent Secretary of the Department of Culture, Media and Sport, values her husband's support. He backed her return to work after the birth of their two children even though, at the start, childcare would cost them more than she would earn. She also tells the story that underlines the equality in their relationship. She apologised one day for getting too little milk and he corrected her by saying, 'We all drink the milk and it is just as much my fault if we run out.' An apparently trivial example but it speaks volumes.

Anne Marie Carrie adds, "I think that women have great strengths in the domestic sphere which they don't value enough to bring to work. They juggle all those balls."

In a memorable phrase, Hoschild[36] describes the situation as 'a stalled revolution'.

Some Distance Still to Travel

Women are effectively caught in two behaviour traps. The first is that they have to choose to behave as women are expected to behave and are therefore likely to be overlooked for senior jobs. Otherwise they can behave as men are expected to behave, perhaps gain promotion, and be condemned and disliked for not conforming to the stereotypical womanly ideal.

The second trap concerns the domestic responsibilities that society expects of women. However successful they are in their career, however many hours they work and however high their salary, the expectation is still lodged in their consciousness that they have the primary responsibility for looking after home, husband and children. This means that after doing a demanding job at work they are then required – or require themselves – to do a second job (or second shift) at home.

Developing changed expectations of women, and allowing women to develop changed expectations of themselves, is possible but difficult.

The answer has to consist of seeing more women in top jobs. Visibility is crucial. Otherwise, as TUC General Secretary Frances O'Grady says, "Women have to be taught to behave with a high level of confidence: men have seen other men doing it for years."

A congenial atmosphere based on respect is a good start and can make a huge difference to personal confidence, as Deborah Hargreaves found when she went to work for *The Guardian*: "I felt that the steel stays that had enclosed me were bursting."

Chapter 8

The Maternal Wall

Taking the Decision

Women still have to jump through hoops and over hurdles simply to get some career satisfaction and the possibility of advancement. But for many women the decision about whether and when to have a child is the most difficult one they face. What should be a natural and joyful right can become a minefield.

There is still a mismatch between how powerful people say they feel about the value of mothers and motherhood and how this is experienced by the women themselves. In answer to former President of Harvard and Secretary to the Treasury Laurence Summers's grandiose statement, 'Raising children … is the most important job in the world … The differences between men and women are innate', academic Ann Crittenden[1] retorts: 'Raising children may be the most important job in the world, but you can't put it on your résumé' when you are searching for employment.

Towards the end of our interview with Brenda Hale, we asked her how far she felt we had come in the battle for equality. "The problem is systemic," she replied, "The baby question will always be there. It won't just go away" – words that will ring true for almost every working woman.

Liz McMeikan feels that "childbirth causes a career crisis for women. In her opinion private sector company career structures tend to be "rigid and unforgiving and some women's careers never recover momentum".

Helen Wells, who was Director of Opportunity Now, agrees. "For most women who are on the way up childcare responsibilities represent a huge problem." Emma Howard Boyd goes further, saying, "At present many women feel that they must either not have children or behave as if they have none."

Perhaps the biggest failure in western society is to have developed systems of work and power structures that do not take adequate account of the need for women to have babies and bring up their children.

The decision whether or not to have children is never taken lightly. For working women, with some idea of their future career prospects, it is a choice often made with an incomplete knowledge of potentially major implications.

Most of the women we interviewed do have children. Of those choosing not to, some said quite openly that their achievements would not have been possible if they had been mothers.

Christine Blower, General Secretary of the National Union of Teachers and herself the mother of two daughters cautioned: "For some women being 'childfree' is a genuine decision but for others it is a 'constrained' choice and that is terrible."

Many women in jobs with a clear career trajectory decide to have children in their late thirties or early forties, making sure that they are firmly on the promotion ladder before risking maternity leave. Although this has advantages from a career perspective, delaying having children till later may affect fertility, so even this decision can be fraught with difficulties.

In answers to a questionnaire[2] sent by Opportunity Now to 3,800 senior women managers and followed up by interviews, nearly three-quarters of the respondents agreed that commitment to the family is a barrier to women's achievement and that advancement depends on putting career before family.

It was Joan Williams who coined the phrase 'the maternal wall' in 2001. In a later article published[3] in 2004 and written with co-authors Faye Crosby and Monica Biernat she gives ample evidence that motherhood carries particular penalties. In 2004 mothers in the US earned only 60 per cent of the average pay for fathers. They suggest that this differential in pay is caused by the fact that jobs are still defined in terms of the way men live their lives. Continuous unbroken employment is assumed to be the norm.

Maternity Leave

A number of the women we interviewed expressed the fear of being 'forgotten' by their employers and the consequent pressure to return to work, often too early. We heard numerous instances of women not taking (or not being offered) sufficient maternity leave – one scientist working right through until the day her baby was born and returning within a few weeks.

Jill May, who was Director of Strategy at UBS Bank, never took more than 12 weeks maternity leave because she was worried about the effects of a long absence. She said explicitly that, "I thought I should get back quickly or I might be forgotten." Three months was the norm in the 1980s, she feels. A series of three-month maternity leaves also worked for Lucy Neville-Rolfe, Executive Director of Tesco. "This length of absence did not damage my career as longer breaks would have done." Helena Morrissey told us that "I went back too early because I was afraid of the outcomes if I didn't."

Anna Dugdale, CEO of Norfolk and Norwich University Hospital, even stayed on for an important meeting after her waters had broken. She then returned two days after the birth of her baby, "for an hour or two". She said in explanation, "I was in the right place for treatment if anything went wrong."

Julie Towers, now Managing Director of Recruitment Services at Penna, used to work for a local authority. Feeling under some pressure, she returned to work two and half weeks after the birth of her first child but feels strongly that in this respect she was a bad role model. "Women should take sensible periods of maternity leave and should also insist on returning to work at the same level, not accepting downgrading." Her own experience was discouraging. When she told her boss in the local Council that she was pregnant he said, 'Come back when you are better (sic) and we will try to fit you in …'.

Another senior woman told us that when she returned to work after having children, she noticed a distinct difference in the way she was treated. A senior manager said to her, 'I am surprised that you are here – I thought you were having a baby.' Similarly, when BBC Trustee Suzanna Taverne took maternity leave from her job in newspaper publishing she was told, 'We will try to find something for you if you come back.' In the event she was forced to take legal action against the company and achieved a satisfactory outcome, but, "it was a very uncomfortable 12 months".

In 1995 when Sue Vinnicombe and Nina Colwill[4] wrote the book, *The Essence of Women in Management*, they recorded not only that throughout Europe women managers were much more likely than men to be single or childless but also that the UK had the poorest statutory maternity provision in Europe.

One interviewee took maternity leave from a merchant bank, where she held a senior position, in the early days of the development of maternity leave policies. She was offered three months' maternity leave. She kept in touch with clients and business development but avoided direct contact. Nevertheless, three days after the birth of her second child she was asked to join a telephone conference call when no other senior colleague was available.

We were told of a more recent experience which was particularly unpleasant. When one woman took up the matter of her bonus payment being cut back while she was on maternity leave (an illegal reduction) her employer answered, 'I have a bunch of men who are working their arses off while you are sitting at home.'

Things have improved in the last 15 years but not by as much as we might have expected. The period of maternity leave has increased to a maximum of 52 weeks but this improvement is undermined by the fact that statutory maternity pay is so low. Indeed, according to a study conducted in 2014 by Mercer Human Resource Consulting,[5] maternity pay in the UK is the third lowest in the European Union: only Greece and Luxembourg have lower rates. The best payments are in the Scandinavian countries where women received between two and three times as much in statutory pay compared with women in Britain. Gary Bowker, employment law expert at Mercer, commented on the results of their study. "With the Government's emphasis on family-friendly policies, it's surprising that UK statutory benefits are so much lower than in the rest of the EU."

The attitude of employers remains a problem. A study by Nelarine Cornelius and Denise Skinner[6] in 2008 compared the careers of senior men and women. Two-thirds of the women interviewed reported that their employer's negative attitude to maternity leave was a barrier for them.

At Home with Young Children

Looking after a child from babyhood is physically and emotionally satisfying. The experience of watching developments, however minute, is precious and needs to be cherished. However, being at home as the only adult with young children all day can have its downside. A surprising number of the women we interviewed mentioned the boredom of staying at home to look after very young children. "Looking after young children was boring. I had to work," said Stella Paes, Head of Science at AQA. "I had to work for my sanity," agrees senior former hospital manager, Deirdre Mackinlay and environmental lawyer Pamela Castle told us that she needed to do something worthwhile and "to keep my brain working". One civil servant says that she spent six years at home with her children before "boredom eventually drove me back to work".

Matt Gaw,[7] now a stay-at-home father, wrote recently, 'I was amazed at the brain-mushing drudgery of large parts of the day ... I was always exhausted, often irritable and sick of Fireman Sam.'

Returning to Work

The difficulty of returning after a break was mentioned by several women. There seems to be little help in easing back, and few employers make much effort to keep women on maternity leave informed about what is going on in the workplace or about changes that may be taking place.

For some women, having spent four or five years at home raising their families, the thought of returning to work can be daunting. They have developed confidence in their role as a mother and this has become their identity. They no longer see themselves as the person they were before the birth of their child. Venturing back into the alien world of work can be terrifying. Will they be taken seriously? Have they lost the necessary skills? Many of us are familiar with that feeling that being with a young child or children all day has led to a diminished vocabulary and even concentrating on uninterrupted adult conversations may be hard to sustain at first.

These feelings are not exclusive to women, Hannah Rosin[8] in her book *The End of Men* describes Andy, the stay-at-home carpenter who is wistful about his old job. However, when his wife suggests that he might go back to work, he is terrified. 'It's been a long time and he's lost the stomach for it,' she says.

Having returned to work, what the vast majority of women say they need is flexibility. Lesley Wilkin, Managing Director of Hay Consulting Group (UK and Ireland), has expanded and formalised a scheme for keeping women consultants on contract as associates while they take maternity leave. She insists that this system is of great advantage to Hay: "We don't lose their experience," as well as bringing advantages to the mothers. "Very few mothers want a complete break from work," she says, "They just need greater flexibility."

When she returned to work after the birth of her first child, Liz McMeikan, was advised by a senior manager that she should copy the methods of another woman in the company who behaved as if her children did not exist. She says that the advice was given in all seriousness.

Small things can make a big difference. When asked by her boss what help she would need now she had a child, Helena Morrissey made a wonderfully simple request. She asked for and was given one of three allocated car parking spaces in the company car park so she could drive to the office after dropping her child off at nursery.

Kate Grussing is the founder of Sapphire Partners, the executive search consultancy with strong expertise in helping companies recruit senior women. She told us that, in her opinion, "Women who take a year off for maternity leave risk stalling their careers and losing momentum, although it feels politically incorrect to advocate maternity leave of three to six months in length." She went on to say that women should not have unrealistic expectations about finding a new job after a career break. "Unfortunately, most head hunters won't touch mothers with young children."

This somewhat brutal-sounding judgement was softened when she shared with us the advice she gives to women who want to return to work. The main message is that women need to be proactive in keeping abreast of developments. They also need to keep in touch with former colleagues, keep their CV up to date, regularly remind their company of their existence and know what the going market rate is for their work. Clearly, this is sensible advice, but it accepts that most companies are under little pressure to adapt or change their practices. It is still the women who have to fit in.

In 2013, Research company One–Poll[9] questioned 1,000 women about what happened when they returned to work. Almost a third of the new mothers felt they did not fit in anymore and two in five felt they lacked support. Almost 20 per cent felt that no one understood what it was like to be juggling work with new motherhood.

As Ivana Bartoletti, Chair of Fabian Women's network, says, "There still has to be a shift in culture at the workplace."

The Visceral Pull of Children

Parents in the twenty-first century appear to share childcare much more equitably but the main burden still seems to rest with the mother. Let us not misunderstand: most women, and indeed many of the women we spoke to, are not altogether unhappy about this situation. As Jan Royall, Labour Leader in the House of Lords says, "Women like being mothers." Fiona Millar[10] in *The Secret World of the Working Mother* vividly describes what she calls 'the pull' to be with your child. For many women this strong attachment is visceral. MP Julie Elliott agrees. "I really enjoyed being at home with my four children."

Liz McMeikan took six weeks maternity leave and assumed that when she returned to work she would simply take over where she had left off. In fact the physical and psychological need to look after her baby took her completely by surprise. On her first day back she had to attend a conference and could not concentrate. Her brain was somewhere else. "I was gibbering," she says.

In her book, *Madonna and Child: Towards a New Politics of Motherhood*, Melissa Benn[11] describes her own conflicts:

> As the new mother of a young child and as a self-employed writer, I had been back at work, if fitfully, within weeks of the birth, resentfully taking transatlantic calls at some unearthly hour of the night on an article that needed more work on it. This was at a time when all I wanted to do was gaze at my new baby girl and not worry about money or the outside world, or whether I was still considered a serious person.

The Need to Be in Charge

Some mothers, whilst railing against their partner's apparent blindness to the daily routines and chores that need to be done if the household is to run smoothly, nevertheless admit the need "to control their families and find it hard to relinquish that power," says Deirdre Mackinlay. Publisher, Ulli

Drewett, feels that some women have a constant struggle not to be in charge at home. Watching her husband with their three children, she has to bite her tongue not to say, "I want it done my way." When Jan Royall went to work for the EU in Brussels, her husband took on the caring role for their three children which he enjoyed and managed very well. "But," she admits, "I still wanted to be the mother – with all the responsibilities. I found it difficult to take a back seat."

Sheryl Sandberg,[12] Facebook's COO, in her book: *Lean in: Women, Work and the Will to Lead,* describes this as 'maternal gatekeeping'. 'I have seen so many women inadvertently discourage their husbands from doing their share by being too controlling or critical,' she writes. Hannah Rosin[13] says that, in the course of many interviews, 'I did not talk to a single breadwinner wife who has entirely ceded the domestic space.' Suzanne Warner concurs, "I have never met a woman who was not the default carer for her children."

Even where the husband or male partner stays at home to look after the children, the working mother still often finds herself doing the routine household chores at home. Ruth Bushyager is "very grateful" to her husband for looking after their children while working part time himself but says she does "the cooking, cleaning and laundry".

Perhaps what Veronica Jarvis Tichenor[14] calls the 'selfless devotion of motherhood ... tied up with issues of love and identity' needs to be analysed and confronted by all of us. Changes in culture are difficult to achieve. Every day women receive messages from family, the media and adverts that they are primarily responsible for looking after the home. Gloria Steinem[15] says that men should take equal responsibility. 'The idea of having it all never meant doing it all. Men are parents too and actually women will never be equal outside the home until men are equal inside the home.' But these matters are complicated. When women complain that their partners do not take equal responsibility in the home it may be that in some cases their own attitudes, ingrained since birth, are not encouraging their partners to do so. The best compromise seems to be for men to accept that women want to retain responsibility but also need more help and support than they get at present. This conclusion has important implications for future policy and we explore them in Chapter 11.

Childcare

Childcare remains a difficult issue in Britain. The choices are few and not always satisfactory. Reliability, distance from home and the cost are all factors that have to be taken into consideration. For women working long hours and perhaps travelling too, having a partner at home seems to be the most popular option. Childminders, nannies, au pairs and nurseries and, more common these days, grandparents, all take on childcare. For most families one, or a combination, of these arrangements generally works well, although the cry of a woman quoted in Breaking the Barriers,[16] 'I only see my little boy for half an hour a day during the week,' pulls at the heartstrings.

Understanding women's need to work, Patricia Hollis, now in the House of Lords and formerly Leader of Norwich City Council, advises young women to "spend your entire earnings on childcare if necessary …"

In a speech to the 2013 Labour Party conference, Ed Miliband promised to keep schools open from eight in the morning until six in the evening to help parents with childcare. On the surface this sounds like a good scheme but, as experienced childminder Beatriz Lees points out, this may help businesses and parents but it does not answer the needs of the child. "Remaining at school for ten hours is a very long day for a child in an environment designed for formal learning, not as a place able to cater for a child's individual needs."

For some women employing nannies is the best solution because this allows greater flexibility and the child feels secure with one known adult. But this can be an expensive option. One interviewee says she is now a senior manager and earning enough to employ a full-time nanny and is even able to build her children's events into her 24-hour diary. However, she acknowledges that for most women this luxury is very unusual and that even women who eventually get to the top normally have their children when they have much less money and even less control.

"The choice for most working women with children is between using a succession of nannies which leads to misery and guilt or to make it explicit that you want to reduce your workload and accept the consequences of that at work," said one woman rather despondently.

A rarely mentioned drawback to employing nannies and au pairs is that the children can become extremely attached to them. Compounding the guilt felt by many women at leaving their child to go to work is the scenario they paint of finding that their child, when upset, runs to the other woman. A working mother might feel relief that the child is obviously secure in the care of the other woman but there must also be a natural resentment that the affection, that she thought was reserved for her, has somehow been forfeited. Journalist Gaby Hinsliffe describes[17] 'the fierce feeling of possessiveness, a rather shameful sense that someone else had something that was mine. Even now, at the end of a working day, there is a small primal shock when my son hurls himself at me smelling faintly of his childminder's perfume'. Irrational and momentary, perhaps, but painful nevertheless.

Anna Dugdale wanted stability for her children and that meant hiring nannies who would stay for long periods. On the other hand she realised that long-serving nannies meant that the nanny would be special to the children and this might diminish her own importance in their eyes. So she thought out what was important to her and managed her working day to make sure that she could be home every evening to spend time with her children and put them to bed.

These are very complex issues. Deirdre Anderson et al.[18] in their research paper *Women partners leaving the firm: Choice, what choice?* quotes one woman who had examined the options for childcare and decided, 'I didn't want … to *outsource* (sic) my family and get a live-in nanny.'

Leaving Work on Time at the End of the Day

Tensions arise when women need to leave work in time to see their children. Even when their working hours have been agreed, it can be hard for women to leave in the middle of a meeting, sometimes leaving unfinished business. Jan Royall described how she used to feel guilty leaving her office in the House of Commons to be with her children, even when she had already worked after her agreed finishing time. Often an urgent matter had arisen and that is a common event in politics. "But people seemed to be in the habit of working late and there was a definite 'jackets on chairs' syndrome." Pamela Castle admits to "mixed feelings" when a young woman made it clear that she had to leave a vital meeting at six o'clock in order to get home before her nanny left at seven. Reflecting on the incident, she accepted that the woman had every right to leave when she did and wondered whether the work needed to be organised so that it went on into the night. However, whatever the rights and wrongs, it meant that Pamela Castle was left without crucial support.

Coping with Guilt

The good news is that research tells us that children and families benefit from working mothers. Contrary to generally accepted beliefs, mothers who work are said to spend more time reading and talking to their children than their own non-working mothers used to do.

In *Through the Labyrinth: The Truth about How Women become Leaders*, which many consider a seminal book on women and leadership, Alice Eagly and Linda Carli[19] found that 'employed mothers in the USA in 2000 spent as much time interacting with their children as nonworking mothers did in 1975, even though phone calls and emails now intrude upon personal lives'. Intriguingly the authors go on to say, 'Mothers these days are often critical of their parenting skills – especially educated mothers.' Perhaps childminder Beatriz Lees understands why. She meets some mothers who are very confident in their work outside the home and are used to running tight and demanding schedules, "but babies and little children have their own agenda," she says.

Some working mothers, like Liz Nelson, want to make the time spent with their children very special. When her three children were young she had a full-time nanny. "I was not there 24 hours a day but I genuinely believe in quality time." These children benefit from concentrated periods of time with their mothers talking and playing with them, ignoring any potential interruptions.

The enhanced wellbeing of working mothers and of their families is now also well documented. Unfortunately these facts will not prevent many mothers who work being engulfed by feelings of guilt. Indeed very often children suffer less from the anxiety of separation than do their mothers.

On the other hand, working at home may not always be the solution. Patricia Hollis told us that when she was a university lecturer,

> *I used to do all my university research, writing and marking at home, with a nanny/childminder looking after my children so that I could work while still being at home. Until my three-year-old son came into the study demanding my typewriter. Assuming he wanted to thump on it, I suggested we find a xylophone. Oh no, it was the typewriter he wanted. Why? Well, he wanted to take it into the garden and bury it. Then I would play with him. Ouch! Whatever you do, you can't get it right all or even most of the time. You just have to be good enough, not perfect.*

Mercer's survey of maternity pay throughout Europe showed that situation for new parents in Finland and Sweden is to be envied. Parental leave in Finland is 281 days on full salary. In Sweden parents are allowed 15 months leave on 90 per cent of their average earnings and fathers are obliged to take three months paternal leave. An important point is the inclusion of men in the equation.

Men at Home

As we were ending our conversation Patricia Hollis said,

> We have one battle left: part-time work for men who choose it. We need to change the culture of middle management for men, so that they are not considered wimps if they choose to work part time. This is about how couples manage children and are guilt free.

In *Men Can Do It*, Gideon Burrows[20] is adamant that more men could share care equally with their partners if they were more determined to do so. He admits that traditional views about men and women's roles can act as a deterrent and, as a full-time non-working parent of young children, he recounts how women at the playgroup sit at the opposite side of the room to avoid him and ignore him at the school gate, making him feel isolated. However he firmly believes that men should quash feelings of discomfort and be braver about approaching these groups of unwelcoming women. Gradually they will come to accept the fact that men also need to join in the conversations and break down barriers. He is impatient with the excuse of alienation. 'Since when has a little social embarrassment stopped men from doing exactly what we want?'

At parties in Brussels, where Jan Royall was working for the European Commission, her husband Stewart found that people would ask him what he did for a living and when he said he looked after the children "they would look down and walk on". She found that very hurtful to witness. He felt he had no real identity and this situation occasionally caused tensions between them.

Rebecca Gill is the Policy officer of The Young Women's Trust. When her husband asked his employer, which happened to be a trade union, if he could work part time in order to help with childcare, he was met with resistance and finally with a refusal. An experience he found deeply upsetting, although he admitted that this was a situation women frequently encounter.

More sharing of childcare does seem to be the best answer. Research carried out by Rosalind Barnett and Karen Gareis[21] appears to demonstrate that the quality of life for mothers who work improved. 'They suffer less depression and have a greater sense of wellbeing if they work ...' The researchers also conclude that, 'Men's lives are improved by taking on more of the family responsibilities.'

Pressure Points

The arrival of a second child in the family seems to alter matters considerably. Most people concur that arrangements for two children are far more complicated than managing satisfactory childcare for just one. Apart from the time factor, children have individual and differing needs and some women who coped at work with the first child admitted to having difficulties with two, occasionally even taking the decision, sometimes with great reluctance, to stop working for a while.

Lesley Wilkin's associate contract scheme for women on maternity leave has already been mentioned and she says that she has seen the enormous pressure on women who try to handle a demanding job after the second child.

Because Helena Kennedy QC was working in a freelance capacity when her children were young and, being under pressure, she took only four months leave with her first child, gradually taking more time off as she became more confident after the births of her subsequent two children. She made the vital point, too often underestimated, that it is not just young children who need their mothers. Many children also need their mother very badly when they get to their teens, facing the problems of puberty and taking exams. During her second daughter's A Level years, Deborah Hargreaves managed to arrange her work to spend time with her. She spoke of her relief at having time to chat to her. "Up until now there had only been time to talk schedules and issue instructions."

Research has come to the same conclusions. Deirdre Anderson[22] and her colleagues quote a woman whom they interviewed as part of their research. She said, 'I wanted to be more involved in their teenage years than their toddler years.' This need should be more widely recognised. Fiona Miller[23] quotes writer Kate Figes who 'believes society hasn't yet worked out that it needs to allow parents extra leeway to cope with adolescents in the way we forgive the need to deal with smaller children'.

Career Penalties of Having Children

In *The Price of Motherhood: Why the Most Important Job in the World is Still the Least Valued*, academic Ann Crittenden[24] reflects that, 'Economically, motherhood is the worst decision a woman can make.' A devastating comment, corroborated more recently by Sheryl Sandberg[25] who quotes some alarming statistics from the USA: only 74 per cent of women rejoin the workforce and only 40 per cent return full time. Their household income drops accordingly. In the UK, mothers' earnings decrease by roughly 13 per cent per child.[26]

An unbroken career is still the expected norm. Even in a working life currently likely to last over 40 years in total, the notion of a woman taking four or five years away from paid employment is not something that most companies will contemplate. It is as if employers expect a mother's brain to atrophy in that short time and that women will not be able to retain any skill or competences from their previous years in employment.

It has to be acknowledged that for a small company, paying for maternity leave can be a serious financial burden. Despite strong feelings of solidarity with female colleagues, Pamela Castle reluctantly recognised that just putting up the costs of employing women of childbearing age without making other changes might simply mean that employers are even more reluctant to take them on.

Liz Nelson, a champion of women at work who opened our conversation by stating unequivocally, "I'm in favour of quotas," said equally firmly, "If I were an employer now and a woman took 12 months off after having a baby expecting to come back on the same salary, I would refuse." And making such actions illegal has not solved the problem. We search for a better solution in Chapter 11.

Part-Time Work

Part-time work is still stigmatised. In *No Seat at the Table*, Douglas Branson[27] reports on the 'isolation, loss of status … loss of desirable assignments, elimination of advancement opportunities … and relegation to (what he calls) sub-par office space'.

Edward Craft is a solicitor and a corporate governance specialist. He has two young daughters and spoke passionately about the need for it to be made much easier for women to return to work. He cannot understand why companies refuse to introduce flexible working. "The morale of employees improves, turnover is reduced and people working part time usually work longer than their contracted hours." He has managed to persuade his (female) boss of the value of flexibility in the workplace. "The whole organisation benefits from work of better quality from more satisfied people."

At present his enlightened views are unusual. Part-time work is still undervalued, even though study after study has proved that contented part-timers work much harder than tired and worried full-timers. When children are ill, parents (usually mothers) are sometimes too worried to admit that they are taking days off to look after them, pretending that they are sick themselves or they even risk sending their sick children to school. In these circumstances, as Margaret Littlewood, former lecturer in Gender Studies at the Open University put it, "Children can become invisible for working women."

Despite often being accused of lacking serious commitment, most women who work part time do far more than the 'official' hours they are paid for. It is more acceptable now to work three or four days a week, particularly since the use of computers has facilitated working at home for part of the time.

For many women working part time brings great advantages: they are part of the working world, making contact with people on a professional level whilst still enjoying time with their children at home.

But there are dangers. Teresa Graham told us that employers expect a full-time commitment from senior managers so "senior women on part-time contracts often find themselves covering full-time hours but only being paid two-thirds of a full-time salary".

Publisher Ulli Drewett describes what can happen if the hours worked are not strictly adhered to: "I felt I wasn't doing anything properly. I was making sacrifices but there was no quality family life. Even though it was officially four days a week I was virtually full time."

The fierce outburst by renowned astronomer Jocelyn Bell Burnell[28] during a radio interview with Jim Al Kalili reminds us that fortunately things have moved on somewhat: 'They just don't understand about the grit needed just to be there. To hold my own. When I returned to work with a young family, colleagues thought I was not serious because I worked part time. People don't realise how difficult it was to work in Britain at all when you were a mother in the 60s.'

Long Hours Culture

Discussing the long hours culture demanded by many organisations, which can deter women from having children, Kay Carberry, Assistant General Secretary of the TUC, told us, "… many choices are made under constraint. They are not choices at all."

University lecturer in psychology, Ellie Dommett, is unequivocal: because of the long hours that have to be put in in the lab and also the important discussions that take place during early mornings or late evenings. "In science as a woman you either have a career or you have children." A powerful statement, challenged by some women scientists, but the long hours that have to be spent in the lab and where some of the experiments may be harmful for pregnant women are undoubted deterrents.

Surgeon Jane Butters told us about "the horrendous hours that new surgeons have to work. They also have to contend with irregularity. The early starts can be managed but there is no guarantee of finishing times in surgery. You are dealing with live patients and you can't just leave them because your shift has officially ended. This makes childcare a nightmare and definitely contributes to the lack of women in this field".

Sympathising with the plight of women with children who nevertheless feel entitled to a decent career, she added, "Why have children you never see?" Certainly a few of the women we interviewed spoke with some sadness of the missed opportunities of actively participating in their children's lives while they themselves were pursuing high-level careers.

Even barrister Cherie Booth[29] in a recent passionately argued article writes, '… I didn't take any real maternity leave with my three younger children, It is only looking back that I realise I wasn't beating the system but reinforcing it.'

We need more employers to adopt General Colin Powell's rejection of what he calls 'busy bastards' who put in long hours at the office without realising the impact they have on their staff.

Making Things Better

Job sharing can be an ideal solution for those who are able to organise it. Former *Financial Times* journalist, now Director of the High Pay Centre, Deborah Hargreaves, eventually managed to persuade her reluctant Editor that sharing an overlapping three-day week with another colleague would work. They were asked to specialise in agriculture where it might be thought they would be less visible, but in fact they secured their job-share just as the BSE crisis story broke and farming was on the front page most days! Their system worked successfully for over two years until they both decided to move to other positions.

Efficient job sharing in any industry requires a close relationship between the job-sharers, very careful briefing of each other on hand over and regular briefing of one's boss.

With determination and a genuine recognition on the part of employers of the value of making conditions flexible, it is also possible to create a working environment which is both efficient and comfortable for all concerned.

Kay Carberry the first woman to serve on the TUC's senior management team, spoke with gratitude of the efforts of the then General Secretary, Norman Willis, to make it possible for her to attend meetings by rearranging the weekly timetable so that she was able to take her son to nursery first. As Kay Carberry says, "It was difficult to charge to the nursery to drop and pick up my son. There are certain things which are totally non-negotiable when you have children." Part-time work and flexible hours are on offer to all staff working for the TUC, whether or not they have children. In addition, half of childcare costs are paid by the TUC, rising to three-quarters for single parents. The TUC finds that such working conditions benefit the organisation as well as the workforce.

Maura McGowan, Chair of the Bar Council, is proud that there is now a central nursery for the children of all staff – barristers and administrators, male and female. Furthermore, she says, "This was definitely pushed through by both sexes."

For civil servant Melanie Dawes, the enlightened support from her male boss was "very encouraging and came at just the right time". When she was six months pregnant he told her that he wanted her to continue in her job after the birth and that she could return on any hours and pattern of days. He also gave her the very good advice to make no decision until well after the baby was born.

Andrew Mackenzie, Chief Executive of BHP Billiton, told us of his company's approach to supporting women at work: "Women who leave to have children are encouraged to return to work by providing flexible work arrangements on return. In addition our Accelerated Leadership Development programme is weighted towards high potential women to support our efforts to improve gender balance among our leadership population."

District Judge Susanna Jones wonders how many professions genuinely need completely unbroken service nowadays. How long does it really take for anyone to catch up on recent developments and the latest technology?

In a digital age when so much can be achieved with no face to face contact, women are frequently offered the opportunity to work from home. This sounds straightforward, but using technology in this way is only a temporary or partial solution to helping women back to work. In the end they complain about isolation. Part of every person's satisfaction at work is the opportunity to meet and interact with colleagues. In her research, Rosalind Gill[30] of the LSE found that, 'In spite of the image of workers enjoying the freedom to work at home, very few wanted to do so because they all valued the opportunity to work close to others doing similar work.' She concludes that working from home is often by necessity not by choice. And of course there is also the added concern that, with no one responsible for overseeing the number of hours worked at home, there is the obvious danger of workers being exploited.

Several dilemmas have been discussed in this chapter to which there are no easy solutions. Women want to spend time at home after the birth of their child. Generally this is an intensely enjoyable and fulfilling period in their lives but most women want more than a long period at home. There must be the opportunity to return to work and continue a career. When their male partners are happy to play a bigger role in the upbringing many women find it hard to 'let go' and allow the men to take over. For most families with one or two children, the early stage of parenthood only lasts a short time, although when things are not running smoothly it can seem endless. The system in Sweden, with both parents obliged to take paid leave on virtually full pay for several months, would appear to be a positive step, with beneficial results for parents and children.

Another set of problems arise when women return to work. In Britain they often find that employers think they are less committed to their job, especially if they ask to work flexibly. And as further pressures develop in the teenage years or at other pressure points, the penalty that women pay for being mothers appears to increase.

Some younger couples in Britain seem to have settled on a more equal system of sharing childcare and this leads us to hope that a new generation of men and women will find more satisfactory answers to the contradictory tensions. But simply hoping for things to change cannot be an adequate response to problems that are blighting the lives of so many women. We need to look at how other countries have made better progress than Britain. New and properly enforced laws must play a part but it is difficult to see how these complex dilemmas can be resolved just through legislation. Other initiatives are required to prompt the cultural changes that are needed.

'You can't do it all,' says Gloria Steinem.[31] 'No one can have two full-time jobs, have perfect children and cook three meals a day and be multi-orgasmic … superwoman is the adversary of the women's movement.' In short, the pressures on women in the modern world are too great.

That is the ultimate condemnation of our system.

It is two centuries since the industrial revolution but the world of work has still not found a way to reconcile the demands of employment with the fact that women have babies. At the moment mothers are, in effect, excluded from much employment and from many positions of power. So women are still forced to choose between a high-flying career and children. That is appalling.

Jane Fuller, owner and Director of Fuller Analysis Consultancy, said, "It helped me not to have children in my career. I could be more flexible and work longer hours if necessary *but you shouldn't have jobs that mothers can't do."*

That is one of the challenges that we address in Chapters 11 and 12.

Chapter 9

Secrets of Success

One word, almost more than any other, was used by high-achieving women as they described their careers to us and sought to explain the reasons for their success. That word is 'luck'. Time after time we were told about lucky breaks, about being in the right place at the right time, about openings that occurred at an opportune moment and about their good luck in having supportive husbands or partners.

Is it Good Luck?

Sometimes it is easy to understand why the word luck is used. Emma Howard Boyd was working for a different organisation in the same building when the whole of Jupiter's green and ethical investment team resigned. The team had to be reconstructed in a hurry, Emma Howard Boyd was close by and, according to her own account, dropped into a senior job. This was certainly a lucky break. But of course, however fortunate the circumstances, she would not have been appointed if Jupiter had not seen great potential in her and she could not have held onto the job if her performance had been below what was required. No doubt some luck was involved but perhaps rather less than Emma Howard Boyd would suggest.

On the other hand it is difficult to find much good luck in many of the other examples that were quoted to us. Anna Dugdale became Deputy Finance Director at the Norfolk and Norwich University Hospital Trust after six successful years with a top accountancy firm in London. She told us that she was lucky because her boss, although well regarded and politically shrewd, was less energetic than he might have been. As a result he was content to let her take on more and more responsibility and do more and more of his job. This provided an opportunity to learn quickly about the Trust's finances but it also meant that she had to work at a higher level than a Deputy would normally expect. And there is no doubt that her 'politically shrewd' boss would not have put his reputation at stake unless he was satisfied that she was highly competent and could be trusted to handle his work effectively. It sounded to us as if the boss was a good deal more fortunate than Anna Dugdale. We put this view to her but she insisted that "the chance to do the job before you have the title is a great opportunity for anyone early in their career".

Adrienne Morgan told us that she was very lucky to be taken on as an articled clerk by a good firm of solicitors. But before she got that 'lucky' break she had the stamina to write unsuccessfully to over 50 firms. Sue Street thought that she was lucky to get back into the Civil Service after a gap of six years at a time when normal recruitment was suspended. Most observers might think that as a starred graduate trainee, with her previous record of considerable success in the Civil Service and her determination to apply after being told that an application would not be considered, was enough to earn what she labelled as good luck. Liz Nelson made perhaps the most startling comment of all. She said that she always felt lucky "because the men who worked for me didn't seem to mind working for a woman".

Some careers involve a succession of setbacks. Nevertheless, we found that a single moment of good fortune is likely to be remembered while the rest is forgotten. One poor woman who is now running a forward-looking charity described her "good luck" in landing a job with a major environmental company. In the days before that successful application, which was entirely merited by her qualifications and experience, hotel bookings had gone wrong, she had been involved in a nasty car accident and a senior colleague whom she worked with had suffered a heart attack. Another Senior Executive extolled her good luck in being offered a temporary contract in another part of the company after her boss, who had evidently taken a dislike to her, gave her a "terrible assessment" and almost ended her career. The appalling bad fortune of having such an unreasonable boss seemed to be forgotten as she described her good luck in getting a "second chance".

Of course not every successful woman takes this view of her career. A minority told us that they did not regard themselves as particularly lucky and Lynne Berry declared unambiguously that most of her success was the result of "bloody hard work". Clarissa Williams took the very clear-eyed view that luck might sometimes create opportunities but those opportunities have to be taken with confidence and competence if success is to be achieved. Nevertheless we found a much larger number of women who denied that their career had been in any way planned and that happenstance had played a big part in helping them get to the top. Frances O'Grady used the phrase, "I ended up as Deputy General Secretary of the TUC," to describe a particularly important promotion in her career. This might have been just a figure of speech but it sounded almost as if fate had intervened. In fact she was appointed to that position and then into the top job at the TUC as the outstanding candidate and with the overwhelming support of the trade union movement.

It is obviously difficult to be objective about what constitutes good luck but, looking at the evidence, we find it very difficult to believe that the women we interviewed had more than their share of lucky breaks. In earlier chapters we have described the obstacles that ambitious women face and those obstacles are formidable. Women who get to the top in Britain achieve that success against substantial odds. And, as we began to explain in Chapter 7, ambitious women also face a unique hazard that can blight their careers.

The 'Glass Cliff'

In 2002 *The Times* newspaper carried an article claiming that companies led by women performed significantly worse than companies led by men. This was a very controversial finding and a team of academics at Exeter University, led by Michelle Ryan and Alex Haslam, put the evidence to the test.[1] What they found entirely overturned the conclusion reached by *The Times*. It transpired that women were not taking top jobs in successful companies and turning those companies into failures. What was happening was that women were being appointed to top jobs in companies that were already in difficulties and were being given the formidable task of saving them. Ryan and Haslem called this phenomenon the 'Glass Cliff'.

As they analysed the evidence the researchers found that 'Glass Cliff' appointments are quite common. Indeed it seems that organisations that are in difficulties are more likely to appoint a woman to a senior position than organisations that are performing well. Why this happens is not entirely clear. Some have suggested that companies in desperate straits might simply be more willing to try something new. Others have made the more cynical suggestion that the men making such an appointment might choose a woman because they want to avoid blighting the career of an up and coming male colleague by offering him a near impossible task. More recent research[2] by Ryan and Haslam suggests that the stereotypical qualities that women are widely believed to possess – like resilience and the ability to support people in trouble – makes them particularly attractive to organisations facing serious problems. But, whatever the reasons, the evidence certainly suggests that a disproportionate number of women are offered leadership jobs in circumstances of exceptional difficulty.

During our interviews we found many examples of what seem like 'Glass Cliff' appointments. Mary Chadwick was appointed as the boss of a loss-making bank with a tight timetable to turn it round. Another private sector Executive was given the job of sorting out a high-profile and politically sensitive company that was universally described as 'a pile of shit'. Deborah Hargreaves was given two jobs in succession that involved major and very unpopular reorganisations at the *Financial Times*. A public sector manager was surprised to be offered a big promotion but then found that the new job involved managing massive cutbacks in staff and a big reduction in service. Suzanna Taverne was appointed Managing Director of the British Museum when the £100million Millennium Project to build the Great Court was proving hard to deliver. The Government ordered an inquiry which found many faults in the management of the Museum. The Trustees did not want to appoint a Managing Director but the Government insisted. It was a classic 'Glass Cliff' scenario: the Trustees had to appoint a competent manager to take on a tough, high-risk job but wanted someone whom they thought would be easy to get rid of at the end of the project.

As far as we have been able to check, these examples have one thing in common. In each case the women who were appointed to take on these difficult and demanding jobs were replacing men. A significant feature of the 'Glass Cliff' phenomenon is that a man leaves behind a mess and a woman is then given the high-risk task of clearing it up.

The most spectacular example we found of a 'Glass Cliff' appointment involved the Ratner jewellery business. Its eponymous boss Gerald Ratner made a well-publicised speech which included the famous confession that 'we sell crap'. In case his message was not fully understood he went on to explain that some of the earrings in his shops were 'the same price as an M&S prawn sandwich but probably wouldn't last as long'. The public reaction was devastating. The company went into free fall. £500 million was wiped off the share value. Sales plummeted. Jewellery worth £25 million was returned by angry customers. Graffiti was painted on shop windows. Shop staff were abused and many of the senior managers were sacked. That was the point at which Dianne Thompson was offered the job of becoming the new Marketing Director.

The company's motive was obvious. It wanted to recruit someone completely different from Gerald Ratner and a successful woman fitted the bill exactly. What is less obvious is why Dianne Thompson accepted the job. She says that she relished the challenge and she wanted to test herself as a manager in difficult circumstances. But the job took its toll. When she eventually left the company to move to Camelot, she realised that she, "had not laughed once" during the time she had spent dealing with the mess at Ratner's.

Dianne Thompson took the job at Ratner's with her eyes wide open and in preference to another attractive job offer in the hotel industry which many managers would have preferred. We found other women who were also prepared to take on high-risk appointments for similar reasons. In our society ambitious women are under great pressure to prove themselves. But for most women other considerations also apply. Dianne Thompson had a choice of important jobs but for most women the offer of a top job does not come along very often. A man can turn down a high-risk appointment and know that he has a reasonable chance of getting a better offer in the future. A woman cannot be so confident, particularly in the private sector. As we explained in Chapter 4, only 5 per cent of the most powerful jobs in FTSE 350 companies are held by women. In these circumstances a woman has to think long and hard before she turns down any high-profile job, even if it looks risky and difficult.

All the women we have named made a success of their 'Glass Cliff' jobs. But we also found occasions where the task was just too difficult, the woman manager had to accept defeat and her career suffered a setback. Very few of these women blamed bad luck. Almost without exception they took full responsibility for the failure. They did not regret taking such a difficult job. They just regretted not doing it better.

We explored the many references to luck with Helena Kennedy. She stated firmly that luck had not been particularly important in her career but she understood why women might be inclined to suggest that they had been lucky. Women, she explains, are so often cast in support roles and are so frequently taught to regard their careers as secondary to men that they are bound to think in terms of luck if they go against the trend and achieve a premier position. Men, on the other hand, do not need to explain their success because, as Helena Kennedy put it, many of them are taught from a young age that they are "the centre of the universe" and feel a sense of entitlement that women do not have. Yet, in spite of her confident assertion that luck was much less important than women think, Helena Kennedy surprised and amused herself at the end of the interview by telling us "how lucky" she had been to have a husband who had been given the right upbringing by his mother. "Oh there," she said with a broad grin, "Now even I have said it."

Is it Background and Education?

Having discounted luck, we looked for more conventional reasons for success. Much sociological research demonstrates that success in life comes most easily to people who are born into an affluent family and who have the advantage of a privileged education. So we expected to find that most of the successful women we interviewed would have come from wealthy families and that a high proportion would have been educated privately. We were surprised that this was not the case. Seventy-eight of the women we interviewed mentioned the class of their family. Of these 48 said that their background was middle class and 30 said that their background was working class – a clear middle class majority but not overwhelming. And it was noticeable that many of the women who talked about a middle class upbringing had parents who were teachers or doctors. Only three seemed to come from a family that could reasonably be described as rich.

The absence of notable privilege extended to their schooling. Fifty-three mentioned their secondary education. Of these 44 said that they went to state schools and only nine said that they went to private schools. It is of course possible that a high proportion of those who did not describe their secondary education went to fee-paying schools but we were given no hint of that in other parts of their interviews. Most of the women who talked about their teenage years went to Secondary school in the 1960s and 1970s when the 11 plus was still being used extensively. Twenty-three mentioned that they went to grammar schools and three said that they had failed the 11 plus. Almost all those who talked about their schooling said that they had been to all-girls schools.

So far, so normal. But after Secondary school we come to the feature of their educational profile that is entirely exceptional. An amazingly high proportion of the women we interviewed went to university or its equivalent. Of the 100 women for which we have the relevant information, 92 have a first degree and, of those, 35 told us that they had a second degree. Only eight said that they do not have a degree and even this small group includes two women who won a university place but did not take it up. Seen in the context of the times, these figures are very surprising. When the women we interviewed were growing up, the proportion of women who went to university was tiny compared with what it is today. Most of the women we interviewed would have been aged 18 between 1960 and 1990. In 1960 only some 10 per cent of women went to university and that proportion did not reach 15 per cent until late in the 1980s. By contrast over 90 per cent of the successful women whom we interviewed went to university. This means that they were six or seven times more likely to go to university than an average young woman living in those times.

There can be little doubt that a high level of intelligence is a very important factor in explaining the success of this group of women. In a world where the top jobs are normally held by men and where the safe and comfortable option is to appoint another man, women need to show that they are special. Sue Street identifies intelligence as one of the crucial elements in the make-up of an ambitious woman who wants to succeed. "You have to be bright enough to impress people and ensure that they remember you – not an Einstein but bright enough to stand out." Liz McMeikan says that having a degree from Cambridge was very unusual when she worked in Tesco and she was regarded as a bit of an intellectual. She insists that this description was wide of the mark but she allowed the "illusion" to flourish as it gave her a distinct identity.

Having high intelligence, and the wisdom to make the most of it, are great advantages but moving from an all-girls school to a university where men heavily outnumber women and then into a job where almost all the top people are male involves a period of uncomfortable transition. The support of parents and close relatives is a great help. But while we found that high intelligence is a defining characteristic of all the women, we found that the attitude of families to their able and ambitious daughters varied considerably.

Is it the Attitude of Parents?

Just over half of the women talked about the support, or lack of it, that came from their parents. Fourteen said that both parents were supportive while 13 picked out their mother and a slightly larger number – 15 – mentioned support from their father. However, although the number who specifically mentioned one or other parent is quite similar, it was noticeable that the nature of the support from fathers and mothers was distinct and that the women seemed to value the support given by each of their parents quite differently.

We heard that the support given by some mothers was strong and unwavering. Leslie Wilkin said that her mother was "very aspirational" for both her and for her older brother. Melanie Dawes told us that her mother gave her constant encouragement and was enormously proud of her academic success. In a few cases we were told that maternal support probably arose from the mother's frustration at the limitations imposed on her own career. Liz Nelson told us that her mother was "a wonderful kindergarten teacher in the slums of New York but forever frustrated. She was a driven woman and she lived through me." We were also told how this kind of maternal support also produced pressure to succeed. Dianne Thompson was an only child and when she asked why she had no brothers or sisters, her mother said, 'We wanted to give you the opportunities that we never had.' Dianne Thompson says that she has carried the burden of expectation throughout her life.

But these examples of up-front and positive encouragement from mothers are not typical. More often maternal support was in the background, providing security and comfort while support from fathers was more assertive and vocal. Anne Marie Carrie made the distinction like this: "My father had a very strong belief in his daughters' abilities and encouraged us. All three of us are successful. My mother also wanted us to do well but she would say 'Don't get too big for your boots. Remember to be nice!'"

The women who talked about encouragement from their fathers seemed, without exception, to find that support to be liberating and enabling. Jenny Tonge recalled her father urging her to "do something now with your education while you are still young and before you marry and have children". Mary Marsh said that she was close to her doctor father, drove with him on calls, and answered the telephone from patients. She discussed many things with her father and only later realised how much attention he had given her and how much she owed him. Patricia Hollis said that she adored her father and he "gave her licence" to succeed. She added that Barbara Castle, Margaret Thatcher and Jennie Lee are amongst the many successful women who had an adored and supportive father. Brenda Hale said that her parents, particularly her father, were her greatest influences. They expected their three daughters to go to university. Her father's death when she was only 13 affected her deeply. "It pulled the rug of security from under me."

The different manner in which most women spoke about the influence of their fathers and their mothers was very striking and, in most cases, the support of the father seemed to count for more. We discussed this conclusion with Carole Elliott, who – with Valerie Stead[3] – has made a study of women leaders. She thought that there might be a straightforward explanation. When the women we were interviewing were growing up, men were even more powerful in society and their authority was even greater in the family than it is now. So perhaps the women were simply reflecting the fact that their fathers seemed to be more important than their mothers. There is some support for this interpretation in the interviews. Several women told us that their mothers expected them to marry and accept the restricted job opportunities normal a generation ago. Their fathers often expressed a wider view of the world and talked differently about ambition. Others noted, with approval, that their fathers treated them the same as their brothers, acknowledging that this was unusual. One added that, as the oldest child, she was given encouragement by her father "even though I was a girl". In a male-dominated society, everything men do is liable to be given an elevated importance.

However, whatever the relative value of encouragement from mother and father, the bigger contrast is between those with parental support and those who had none. At one extreme is Joan Ruddock whose parents were "hugely ambitious", encouraging her and her sister to travel and seek opportunities outside the South Wales valleys where she was born. At the other extreme is Stella Paes who says that her parents showed little interest in her schooling and she only remembers them going to the school once for a parents' event. "They could never understand why I wanted to go to university." One manager in the private sector told us that both her parents thought that going to university was pointless and wanted her to go straight out to work. Very recently she was outraged to find that her own daughter had been given the same advice. "Granny has just told me that going to uni is a waste of time."

Sometimes a big part was played by other family members. Pamela Castle recalls that she was supported by her maternal grandmother who was determined that she would do well at school and should talk properly. Another woman remembers how her grandfather gave her particular support when she wanted to go to university. Jean Venables pays particular tribute to the support she had received from her husband's parents. However she explained, with some sadness, that this was "the first time any family members gave me any real encouragement".

Modesty

All in all, the variety of family experience is so great that we found it impossible to regard any advantage of background or upbringing as an adequate explanation of success. Sarah Anderson's family owned a chocolate company and she says, with admirable honesty, that she was born with a silver spoon in her mouth. Ann Robinson failed the 11 plus and was relieved because, "I knew that my parents could not afford to buy the uniform for the grammar school." But what unites Sarah Anderson and Ann Robinson is an extraordinary modesty that seems to be a defining characteristic of almost all the women that we interviewed.

Sarah Anderson has achieved success in the public and private sector, founding her own companies and helping others to succeed, representing small businesses at the top of the CBI, chairing public bodies and leading important public enquiries. Yet she recounts it all in a matter of fact style, dwelling mostly on her surprise that others should believe that she is capable of such important work.

After failing to get into the grammar school, Ann Robinson managed to win a scholarship to Harris Technical College in Preston to do a two-year commercial course. Like the grammar school, the Technical College also had a uniform and she says that she "had to save up for ages to buy that". After completing the course she took a typist's job. Less than ten years later she was a high-flyer in the Civil Service and had caught up with people who had entered the Civil Service as graduate trainees with a good degree from Oxford or Cambridge. But she made no mention of just how exceptional her success had been.

The modesty of most of the successful women we interviewed is palpable. Although Sally Martin omitted to say so, she transformed the Shell UK and Ireland distribution organisation from a "tremendously challenged" part of Shell's business into an effective operation. A failing distribution contract was reassigned to two new companies, a deal was struck with the Union to improve reliability and the service to petrol stations was greatly improved. This was achieved with the Government looking over her shoulder and seeking constant reassurance that there would be no disruption in the supply of fuel. Sally Martin explained all this by saying that she enjoyed working with such an effective team.

Alongside this modesty goes a ready willingness to remember the help and kindness received from others. Two civil servants spoke very highly of their bosses who had given them great encouragement. A *Financial Times* journalist told of the strong support she received from the Editor, Richard Lambert. Helena Morrissey remembers how helpful and brave Schroder's had been in giving her a chance in the New York office when she thought that she was not the obvious candidate. Dianne Thompson recalls the kindness of managers in Woolworths when she came south, knowing next to no one, with a young daughter and needing to find a house very quickly. Our interviews were full of expressions of appreciation and gratitude to former bosses and colleagues, nearly all of them men.

Using Advantages

Most of the women we interviewed were adamant that their career was unplanned and that they just made the best of the advantages they had and the opportunities that were presented. As with so much else that was said, we had to cut through the modesty to get closer to a more objective judgment. Being a woman amongst many senior men is the source of many difficulties but it also means, as Emma Howard Boyd recognised, that it is easy to be visible and to be remembered. But, as she went on to explain, this apparent advantage has to be exploited with care. Women have to behave cautiously when they enter new situations because negative impressions are formed so quickly. Men can 'plunge in without paying much of a penalty' but, if they are wise, women will move slowly and avoid dramatic public statements at least until they are known and trusted.

Helen Phillips used this extra visibility to gain a strategic advantage for her organisation. She was still in her twenties when she became an Area Manager in the Environment Agency. In its flood management work the Agency has to persuade many public authorities to work together. So Helen Phillips took the unusual step of inviting the top people to an informal meeting to discuss common concerns. With a nice touch of humour, she called the meeting, 'a tea party'. Most of the public authority leaders accepted, no doubt curious to meet this young woman manager who had been appointed to a senior management position usually held by an older man. The tea party was a success and became a regular quarterly event.

Pamela Castle's advantage was that, before she qualified as a solicitor, she had trained as a scientist. This made her a great rarity in the profession and an attractive employee to some legal practices. However the firm who recruited her wanted her to concentrate on patent law which was very remunerative for the practice but as she said, 'rather limited'. She aimed to make the most of her unusual background by applying the methods she had learnt as a chemist, following the main thread of argument to a rapid conclusion rather than taking the normal legal route of considering an issue from a variety of different angles. Her direct approach proved to be very popular with clients and earned her rapid promotion.

Creating Opportunities

Most impressive, and one of the defining characteristics of successful women, is the determined way in which they manage to create opportunities for themselves. When Suzanna Taverne realised that the five years she had intended to spend working for an investment bank had stretched into eight, instead of looking for a suitable vacancy she decided to create one. At the bank she had advised *The Independent* Newspaper on its financial structure. Judging that the company needed to plan its future more carefully, she wrote to Andreas Whittam-Smith suggesting that she work for him as Head of Strategy. She made a convincing case and he appointed her soon after.

Peninah Thomson was considering consulting as a career when the Director of the Department for External Studies at Oxford passed her a report, *A Challenge to Complacency*, which reviewed the UK's training policy in relation to those of several other countries and was produced by the consultants Coopers & Lybrand (now PwC). The report included a critical analysis of the UK training. Having decided that she wanted to work on projects of this type, she telephoned the Coopers & Lybrand switchboard in search of the author of the report. After many failed attempts to find the author, the telephonist eventually put her through to the Managing Partner who – perhaps surprisingly – took the call. He was not familiar with the particular report. 'We produce several hundred reports each month,' he explained. But he was sufficiently impressed to ask her to come and see him and, after a series of interviews, he offered her a probationary job. She stayed with the consultancy for 14 years and eventually became a Director.

Every successful woman knows that, in a world of work dominated by men, hard work and persistence are obligatory. As we explained in Chapter 4, many women were told explicitly that they would only be treated equally if they outperformed men. Other women quickly learned the same lesson from experience. One journalist told us that, before she was really established, she telephoned the Reuters Area Manager every week for more than six months to get the offer of a fairly junior job. The pressure lasts right through each career. Lucy Neville-Rolfe was appointed the Company Secretary at Tesco after a successful time as Director of Corporate Affairs. There was no obligation on her to take any further training but she decided to study for the relevant qualifications and passed the examination with some of the highest marks in the country. It is difficult to believe that many men would have set about a programme of such arduous study to gain qualifications for a job they already held.

Even the most successful career stalls from time to time and the test is whether a way can be found to navigate out of the difficulty. Early in her career Dianne Thompson was unhappy working for Ronseal but had no early prospect of being offered a better job. So she adopted the, at that time, very unusual tactic of making a presentation to a head-hunter on her strengths and weaknesses. The head-hunter told her that no one had ever asked to present to him before. Barbara Young wanted to change jobs but she was unsure whether her own view of what she was best at was really valid. So she took psychometric advice to give her a more objective view of her attributes and the sort of job that she should seek.

Marriage and Children

There is little doubt that the greatest difficulties most women face during their career come when they have children. A generation ago the popular expectation was that a woman had to choose between being a wife and mother and being a 'career woman'. Fortunately that time is now well past. Eighty-nine of the women we interviewed told us that they were either married or had a partner. Of these 28 or 31 per cent said that they had been divorced. It is notable that this figure is very close to the UK average of 34 per cent of marriages that end in divorce during the first 20 years of marriage – a reasonable comparison given the ages of the interviewees. Our sample is clearly not large enough to draw robust conclusions but these figures begin to contradict the suggestion made in some quarters that women who have high-profile and demanding jobs find it more difficult than others to form lasting relationships.

Nearly three-quarters of the 'career women' we interviewed had children. While our figures seem to show that marriage and career success can co-exist, our society has still not found a way to ensure that work and motherhood sit comfortably together. Indeed one woman told us ruefully that the birth of every child causes a 'career crisis' for the mother. It is sad, extraordinary and true that the extent to which ambitious women succeed in their careers still depends very heavily on how well they navigate their way through the 'crisis' of having children.

As we explained in Chapter 8, most women find that coping with one child is difficult but manageable. Much greater problems arise when a second child is born and a new set of needs are added to the first. This is the point at which most women review their career and try to make changes. It is also the point at which many careers stall and some go into decline.

Many women try to scale back their hours and work part time. However, although many employers are prepared to allow junior staff to work shorter hours, most employers are much more reluctant to agree to a senior manager moving onto a part-time contract. Several women we interviewed had suggested to their employer that a job-share agreement could work effectively. Some companies are hard to convince. When one interviewee returned from maternity leave to a FTSE 100 company in the retail sector, she asked if she might undertake her current role, one below Board level, on a part-time basis. The response was that she would have to demonstrate that she could run an international subsidiary of the company working three days a week, despite the fact that she was currently the Change Management and HR Director based in the UK. Apparently the thinking behind this response was that, since both roles were at the same level in the company, she would have to show that she could undertake not only her own job, but other jobs at the same level as a part-timer. To make progress, she suggested a job-share as an alternative. The response was somewhat surprising. She was told that job-sharing was a passing fad and, in that respect, was 'a bit like organic food'.

Even if a job-share is agreed, problems can easily arise. The other party to a job-share might want to vary the arrangements. More seriously, if there is a change at the top, the new boss might want to cancel the 'concession'. This was the experience of Deborah Hargreaves who was sharing the job of News Editor on the *Financial Times* with a colleague. Lionel Barber, the incoming Editor, made it very clear that he wanted the job done by one person and he eventually got his way.

A more radical solution is to change direction entirely and to try to make a new career which gives more flexibility and more control. Sarah Anderson cannot understand why more women do not opt for self-employment or running your own business. "As the owner of your own business you are free to arrange your work and family life so that they fit neatly together." But this is not a unanimous view. Maria Adebowale insists that the increased flexibility is balanced by the fact that the owner carries the responsibility for the future of the business. "It can be difficult for you and your family. It's important to get the balance right between looking after yourself, your family, the company and the people you work with."

At first sight an attractive option is to 'go plural' – leave an Executive position and build up a portfolio of Non-Executive positions. This is more easily said than done. The number of Non-Executive appointments in the private sector is limited, vacancies are very rarely advertised and the favoured candidates are usually people who hold Executive responsibilities in other companies. Opportunities in the public sector are similarly limited and the most powerful appointments go to people with a strong record of past achievement. Deirdre Hutton has had great success in chairing difficult organisations, undertaking government enquiries and leading Committees in the public sector. However she is very much the exception and has built up her considerable reputation over many years. Any woman trying to emulate her success would need great skill, stamina and considerable resilience.

Childcare Pressures

After looking at the alternatives, it is not surprising that most ambitious women decide to hold onto their full-time Executive positions and to try to cope with the inevitable problems as well as they can. One woman says she warns her colleagues that this often proves more difficult than they expect. She told us that most women have what she calls a "surplus of optimism"; they pretend to themselves that it will be easy to sort out any clashes between family and work commitments as they arise. In practice this leads to last minute cancellations and gets the woman concerned a damaging reputation for unreliability. The only chance of success is if the childcare is planned for resilience with several layers of support.

Sue Street says that a woman in a relatively junior or middle management position with ambitions of promotion must expect to spend, or rather 'invest', all her net salary on childcare. Trying to save money by limiting the quality or quantity of childcare cover can lead to a breakdown in the arrangements which, in turn, leads to guilt and stress. This advice was echoed by many others. Anna Dugdale was able to share childcare arrangements with another couple and this provided reassuring support, particularly as the other couple were family members. Many women said that back up support from relatives was vital in giving them peace of mind. Suzanne Warner found that her stress went away when her children were being looked after by their grandmother. She knew that the children were being loved and,

> I also knew that they were being properly looked after. Good food was being prepared and shared with them, games were being played and, if necessary, homework was being done. I did not have to worry that they were in front of the TV or the Playstation with a microwaved dinner while the nanny was on the 'phone. Not having to worry whether the children were OK was true liberation.

Attitude of Partners

However, for almost all the women we interviewed, the most important factor in ensuring that they could cope with the often contrary demands of work and children is a supportive husband or partner. Fifty-seven women talked to us about the role of their husband or partner and 46 of those made special mention of the support they had received. But the extent of the help varied significantly. Susanna Jones said that her husband "provided enormous support and encouragement but the final responsibility for the babies was mine". Hilary Cotton said that her friends were impressed because her husband cooked and ironed his own shirts. Other partners were more directly involved in looking after the children. Christine Blower said that her partner did more than his "fair share" of childcare and a senior civil servant told us that her husband provided a good deal of support for their daughter as she was growing up. Her husband worked at home and his availability was not only of great practical help but also went some way to assuage any guilt that she might feel at leaving her daughter.

We were given several examples of partners who adjusted their career to provide childcare support. One husband who works in the finance sector was said to have decided against working for one of the big Finance Houses so that he could spend more time working at home. Helen Phillips's husband agreed to scale down his work commitments for a couple of years when their children were small and when Helen Phillips herself had to devote a lot of time to her job. Another very successful woman said that her husband had stepped aside from an expected promotion to allow more space for her to go after the very demanding job that she eventually secured.

A few of the women said that their partners had gone further and had taken over most of the childcare for an extended period. Jan Royall's husband took on the caring role and did everything for the children. He enjoyed the role and managed very well. Anne Marie Carrie's career involved a number of moves and she explained that her husband did most of the childcare during this hectic period. "He is a very caring father. When I moved to work in London, our daughter Helena didn't want to leave all her friends just as she was starting Secondary school, so my husband looked after her and I commuted."

Unfortunately social attitudes in Britain have not changed sufficiently for it to be regarded as reasonable for men to take a heavy share of the childcare. In Chapter 8 we noted that Jan Royall's husband was sometimes patronised or ignored once he told people that he looked after the children. That caused Jan Royall considerable sadness. Ruth Bushyager's husband also did a good deal of the childcare. When the family left the Midlands and moved south, they expected to find many other couples in 'trendy' west London with similar arrangements. In fact they found that they were very much the exception and her husband's role was regarded as rather strange. Ruth Bushyager now realises how just rare their arrangement was. Her friends from university have married and in every case the woman has given up or limited her career in favour of her husband. It is not surprising that men dislike being described as a househusband when people still seem to think that a man who takes on a good deal of the childcare is a bit of an oddity.

It was during discussions about childcare and the role of partners that the issue of 'luck' reappeared. Most women who received what they regarded as an unusual level of encouragement and support from their husbands and partners said that they have been lucky. And in this case they are probably right. Pressure on men to conform to the stereotype and to put their own career first is considerable. Men who take the risk of being outshone in their career by their wife or who risk incomprehension and ridicule from family, friends and colleagues as they explain that they take on duties normally assigned to women, are still very unusual. They deserve to be applauded and the women who have the comfort of their support should certainly be regarded as fortunate.

Just how fortunate becomes clear from the examples we found where the woman received little support from their husband or partner. We were told of several instances where marriages were put under stress because the man insisted that his career should come first. Two women told us of ultimatums delivered by their husbands. One was brutal and one was gentle but they both meant that unless she agreed to move home to help his career, the marriage would be over. Another woman with a high-profile career told us bluntly, "My husband could not cope with my success, so in the end I dumped him." Another told us that, during the time when she and her husband worked far apart, there were few problems. But when he came to work in the same town and he had to admit that she was more successful than he was, his pride could not take it and the marriage ended.

Liz McMeikan says that, when she was married, she was always the back-stop when it came to childcare and domestic responsibilities. After their divorce, although she and her ex-husband agreed to share access and childcare duties, he never picked up their children from school and it has always been her ex-husband who "needed to change the days and times of having the children because of the pressure of his job". All this was in spite of the fact that her job – objectively judged – was at least as important as his.

Giving Advice

Recognising the difficulties that women face in navigating their way to a successful career, several of our interviewees suggested words of advice that might be given to young ambitious women as they start out. Elizabeth Buchanan is anxious that young women leaving school or university are given little idea of what they will face in the adult world. "No one tells you what it is going to be like. Young women need to be much better prepared. It will be much more difficult than they imagine." Patricia Hollis gives three pieces of advice to women students. In the first place she suggests that they become extremely well-qualified. This makes up for the extra experience of men who rarely have breaks in their careers and helps women fill up gaps in the CV. Then she tells them to be prepared to spend all their earnings on childcare if necessary. Finally she says, "Agree with your partner about minimum standards of food and cleanliness and then stop worrying!"

Sue Street thinks that there are four significant elements that help to determine the success of women at work: intelligence so that you "stand out", enough confidence so that "you do not take every setback to heart" and a sense of perspective so that you "concentrate on the job and not on personal issues". Sue Street's fourth element is, perhaps inevitably, a large helping of "good luck". And she maintained the importance of luck even after we argued that her own success seemed to have been due much less to good luck than to a great deal of hard work.

Kate Grussing runs Sapphire Partners, which she set up to help better promote senior female talent into the UK's top businesses. She reminded us that conventional head-hunters give little help to women who have children. "By and large mainstream head-hunters avoid them like the plague!" So her main message is that women should help themselves by keeping abreast of developments in their own sector, by trying to get part-time work, by taking professional advice, by seeking out a coach and by making sure that all their recent activities are recorded on their CV so that it is right up to date. If a woman is on an extended maternity leave or on a career break she should take the initiative herself in maintaining contact with her previous organisation because, as Kate Grussing puts it, "You need to keep reminding them of your existence." And she adds, "Make sure that you know the current market rate for your work and do not shy away from asking for any necessary pay rises when you get back to work."

A Convoluted Path

These recommendations are valuable in themselves and the nature of the advice is significant for other reasons. In the first place the advice reminds women that their career path will not be straight-forward.[4] Very few of the women we interviewed had the sort of linear progression that characterises the careers of many men. Helena Kennedy expressed the difference in a graphic image. "There is a real problem in the convoluted path women have to take to reach the top. It's not in the front door and up the stairs as it is for many men. For women it is more likely to be in the door, out of the window and up the drainpipe." Success tends to come to those women who recognise that there will be major obstacles and find a way to navigate round them.

The advice given by the women we have quoted, and by most of the other women we interviewed, is also significant for what it does not include. Throughout this book we have described the unfairness faced by ambitious women who try to get to the top. Those few who have managed to travel the convoluted labyrinthine path to success are certainly outstanding people. By and large they have not reached the top because of great good luck or through some advantage of birth or background. Their defining characteristics are considerable intelligence, the imagination to make the most of their advantages and the great determination to get around the obstacles that an unfair and insensitive society has placed in their way. Some have been encouraged by supportive parents and many more have had the advantage of a supportive partner, but a few have achieved great success without the benefit of either. The main conclusion that must be reached, which is highly complimentary to the successful women we interviewed but rather depressing in its judgment of our society, is that to get to the top in twenty-first century Britain a woman has to be an extraordinarily able individual. As Jane Fuller remarked, "We will know when we have achieved equality because as many mediocre women will get to the top as mediocre men!"

Fixing the System

Almost all of the women we met recognised that it is much more difficult for a woman to get to a senior position than a man. One woman even told us that she would like to be reincarnated as a man, because men's lives are "much easier and more straightforward". But few of the women we interviewed and none of the advice that was offered to other ambitious women stated that the most urgent need in Britain is to change the system in Britain and to eliminate the unfairness. Their focus was almost exclusively on how to work within the system that we have. Helena Morrissey, the most prominent private sector campaigner we interviewed, described herself as a "coper" and that is the position adopted by almost all the women we interviewed. They recognise the injustices in the present system and they seek the best way to cope. But very few of them say that the main priority must be to fix the system so that women and men have an equal chance of success.

Such pragmatism has certainly worked for the successful women we interviewed. Of course it is an open question whether any of them could have achieved more or reached the top more quickly if they not had to deal with the problems of being a woman in a system that favours men. Michaela Bergman, for one, thinks that she would have done better. "My early career would have been more enjoyable and I would have been recognised earlier had I been a man." But that is only part of the problem. We have talked to a large number of very able women who succeeded against substantial odds. There is no way of knowing how many other women might have joined them at the top if the obstacles had been fewer and if the system had been fairer. Our best guess on the basis of the figures given at the beginning of this book is that, with a fair system, the number of women reaching the top would double and treble. So the rest of this book is dedicated to those women and to the changes that must be made to give them the same life chances as the men they work alongside. Having more women in positions of power would change the way women are seen and the way women see themselves. That vital change would help to bring about a society with a wider range of opportunities for all women, whatever their ambition, aspiration and chosen lifestyle.

Chapter 10

Slow and Unsteady Progress

Ten years ago, while she was a Minister in the Labour Government, Harriet Harman explained why she believed that Britain needed more women in positions of power.[1] She argued that having more women in top jobs benefits all women because of their better understanding of women's lives. Women bring new insights to management and break up what she called 'male group-think'. She ended her article on an optimistic note:

> It is inconceivable that there should ever again be an all-male Cabinet. Public opinion would find it unconvincing to be told that the country could be governed by men alone. So too the days of the all-male Board are numbered.

Consensus

Harman's argument came to form the basis of a remarkable consensus that stretches across the political spectrum. David Cameron tells us that the Conservatives want to see more women in the House of Commons. The Liberal Democrats are committed to increasing the number of women on company Boards. The Scottish National Party and Plaid Cymru are pledged to increase the number of women in the Scottish and Welsh Parliaments. Even Diane James of UKIP is gallantly working to convince the electorate that her Party is not anti-women and wants to see more women at the top.

The consensus extends beyond politics. The CBI, the Institute of Directors and the Chambers of Commerce have each declared that Britain needs more women on the Boards of major companies, although their ideas on how this should be achieved are rather different. Every profession and institution seems to have a policy document on the issue and some even have action plans. The extent of agreement pleases and surprises Frances O'Grady, the General Secretary of the TUC, who remarks – with only a hint of scepticism – that nowadays everybody seems to want more women in important positions.

Yet, as our earlier chapters have shown, the number of women in senior positions remains depressingly low. The rhetoric has been strong but the delivery has been pathetically weak. Indeed it is difficult to find another area of public life where there is such a cavernous gap between the expressed aspirations of the powers-that-be and what has actually been achieved.

Some cynics suggest that the failure of the political and business establishments to deliver what they claim to want is evidence of deceit. Do those men in power really want a change or do they just find it politically convenient to say so? A kinder explanation is that these men genuinely wish for reform but, faced with the extent and depth of the problem, their energy has failed and other issues, which they consider to be more pressing, have been given priority. Or perhaps, and this is the kindest explanation of all, the conviction is strong but the men who hold power in Government, business and the institutions have just not found the right mix of policies to produce success.

This chapter attempts to solve the riddle: why has a policy that seems to have such powerful support achieved so little and what are the prospects for early improvement? We concentrate on what is happening in business because that is where Government and business leaders have focused their efforts and expect to see the greatest progress.

We start by considering the arguments that politicians and business leaders use when they make the case for more women in senior positions. It is notable that when the men who hold the top jobs in our society address gender issues, they rarely talk about fairness and almost never talk about equality. This is curious and requires explanation.

Women hold only a small proportion of the most powerful – and best paid – jobs in Britain. The odds against this situation occurring by accident are astronomical. For this gender imbalance to be fair, it would need to be demonstrated either that women have less ability than men and are being rejected on merit, or that women do not want power and its associated rewards. Neither explanation has much credibility. Judged by their success in the education system it is preposterous to suggest that women are less able than men. Girls routinely outperform boys at Primary and Secondary school and each year more university degrees are awarded to women than to men. When they enter the workforce, women seem to display a desire to succeed at least as strong as the ambition shown by men. Catherine Hakim[2] and a few others argue that women's subsequent lack of success is because women do not want power and its associated benefits. However, Hakim and those who agree with her rely on an argument that is both circular and perverse. In the face of a mountain of evidence, they declare that women have the same opportunities as men. From that unsound premise they conclude that the low numbers of women at the top must, ipso facto, prove that women do not want to be there. The evidence presented in this book suggests a more obvious conclusion: that the obstacles and difficulties faced by women in our society explain the imbalance of power. In truth, our current system of appointing the leaders of our society is unfair to women; the men who hold most positions of power should be honest enough to say so. But, as a matter of fact, very few men do.

The 'Business Case'

Instead of talking about fairness or equality, the men who are part of the present day consensus advance a set of arguments that are known as 'the business case'. As the words imply, the 'business case' sets out the apparent benefits to individual companies and to the economy in general of appointing more women to senior positions. This approach can cause some impatience because it gives such small importance to women and fails to recognise the disadvantage they suffer. Moreover, by neglecting issues of fairness and equality, a reliance on the 'business case' understates the importance of changing the status quo. And ironically the 'business case' also tends to exaggerate the benefits to business of promoting women. That misjudgement leads to a number of policy difficulties that are examined in this chapter.

Nevertheless some parts of the 'business case' are undoubtedly valid. Many supporters argue that women constitute an under-utilised resource and that enlarging the 'talent pool' of people available to take senior positions to include more women would bring significant commercial benefits. Like several parts of the 'business case', the tone is rather off-putting but the argument is impeccable. Warren Buffett, that successful and celebrated investor, famously said that he has done so well because, in a male-dominated world, he only has to compete against half of the population. Huge sums are invested in educating girls and women. Using their talents and their education to the full is economically sensible and will increase the wealth of individual companies and of the nation.

The second element of the 'business case' is that having more women in senior positions will improve the quality of decision making. This argument also seems to be valid. Women bring a different range of experience and opinion to discussions at top level and stop decisions being made by the process that Harriet Harman called 'male group-think'. A group of men, from similar backgrounds with similar education and similar career experiences, are likely to look at issues from a similar point of view. As a result they are liable to miss important matters that a person with a different experience of life might well spot. Having women at the top helps to ensure that issues are examined from several angles and not looked at solely from the viewpoint adopted by a group of like-minded men.

Businesswoman Sarah Anderson told us that she had seen the unfortunate results of 'male group-think' at close quarters. She sat as the only woman on the Board of a company led by a charismatic CEO who was a darling of the City. He was rarely challenged by the men on the Board and the questions which Sarah Anderson asked, as the only woman, were sometimes dismissed as irrelevant. However, when the charismatic CEO was killed in a helicopter accident and the Board saw beyond his optimistic presentations to the true position, the company was found to have serious weaknesses that nearly brought about its collapse.

A close observer[3] of RBS told us that, in his opinion, 'group-think' explained many of the systemic problems that led to the collapse of that bank. On the face of it, the Board contained enough people with the intelligence and the experience to ensure that the company was well managed. However, according to the insider who briefed us, 'The Board members knew Fred Goodwin well and assumed that he could be trusted. The Board failed to ask the right questions and too often gave Goodwin the benefit of the doubt.'

A similar problem occurs outside the business community in politics and in the professions. Allowing men alone to decide which issues should be given priority and how those issues should be handled often results in lop-sided decision making. Research carried out by the Hansard Society[4] found that women raise matters in Parliament which may not otherwise have been debated, or which might have been given much less time and prominence. Brenda Hale, the Deputy President of the Supreme Court, believes that, "Our experience of life as women is an important reason why women should go into judging. Our common sense is different because of this."

There also seems to be an increased attention to detail when women are involved. Terjesen, Sealy and Singh[5] from Cranfield University found that Boards of FTSE 100 companies containing women adopted the good governance proposals recommended by the Higgs Review more quickly than all-male Boards. From her experience with the Cross-Company Mentoring Programme,

Peninah Thomson has noticed that when women join Boards they are frequently "rather more curious about the organisation" than male Directors. Women also seem more likely to study the papers for meetings thoroughly, a point noted by one successful woman who told us, "I was shocked. Some of the men on public Boards seem to do no preparation at all and hope that they can pick up the details at the meeting."

Better Behaviour

A recurring observation is that the presence of women improves the atmosphere at Board meetings. In 2008, Alison Konrad, Vicki Kramer and Sumru Erkut[6] published a study of how the presence of a significant number of women changed Boardroom behaviour in the US. One woman said that, "You can see the guys decompress from their normal very aggressive style. The style of debate changed." A Company Secretary noted that Board meetings became "much more conversational and less hierarchical" and "the women are universally more polite" to each other and to staff.

Une Amundsen, one of the most strident opponents of the quota law in Norway, was pleasantly surprised to find that, once women joined the Board of his company, the men were less likely to tell dirty jokes. He even appeared on the front page of a popular Norwegian newspaper saying, 'Mye mindre griseprat!' ('No more dirty talk').[7]

It is also true that senior women often seem to behave with more integrity than men. One of the journalists we interviewed told us that some men working in newspapers seemed to think that the perks of the job included taking gifts from marketing organisations who were clearly intending to buy a "favourable reference" in the paper. She insisted that women journalists were much more fastidious. It is also notable that it was three determined women who exposed the corruption in Statoil, the Norwegian state oil and gas company, after the men on the Board had decided that nothing untoward had taken place.

Such examples, and we heard several more, are thought-provoking but of course they do not prove, as some have claimed, that women, as a gender, are more moral in their business dealings than men. During the interviews we heard many examples of men behaving with admirable rectitude. One woman told us of a rather distasteful training session run by a large consultancy company. The aim seemed to be to show people what tricks they could use to avoid paying tax on very high salaries. The audience grew more and more uncomfortable with this cynical approach. However while many of the women clearly disliked what was being said, it was a man who intervened to criticise the tone of the session and force the consultants to change direction. Fortunately there are many men who are as keen as any woman to act with integrity and uphold moral standards.

Performance and Profit

So, in two of its elements – enlarging the talent pool and improving the quality of decision making – the 'business case' seems to deliver what it promises. However a third element is much more controversial. Most advocates of the 'business case' claim that having more women at the top of a company will lead to an improvement in performance and an increase in profits. For obvious reasons, this third element is regarded by some people in the commercial world as the most important part of the 'business case' and great efforts have been made to demonstrate that it is true.

A number of studies are cited to demonstrate that more women at the top mean an increase in profits. In 2004 Catalyst[8] found that companies with the highest proportion of women in top leadership positions had a return on equity that was over a third higher than companies with the lowest proportion of senior women. In 2011, the accounting firm Deloitte reached a similar conclusion but found a smaller differential:

> In Europe, of 89 publicly traded companies with a market capitalisation of over 150 million pounds, those with more women in senior management and on the Board had, on average, more than 10% higher return on equity than those companies with the least percentage of women in leadership.[9]

Unfortunately for people who rely on the profit argument, the evidence is actually rather ambiguous. A number of studies have looked at what happened to the performance of Norwegian companies after 2008 when, as a result of the introduction of quotas, the number of women on the Boards of large listed companies was greatly increased. Some of the studies have found a small deterioration in performance and others have found no discernible difference at all. And of course the studies only look at whether there is an *association* between having a relatively high proportion of senior women and high performance. Research by Morten Huse and Anita Solberg[10] showed not only how difficult it is to find a causal link but also how hard it is to identify the specific contribution of women on a Board. Huse and Solberg note that so much of the work of company Boards is informal or is not recorded. They talk about the need to unlock the secrets of what they call the 'black box' to discover what really goes on in the Boardroom.

Work by Siri Terjesen, Ruth Sealy and Val Singh[11] in 2009 tried to take the story a little further. The researchers reviewed 180 books and articles about women on Boards but found that only 20 of them actually dealt with the contribution of the women concerned and unfortunately these were mostly old and thin in their conclusions. After a detailed study of the available material, the three researchers found little evidence of any significant impact on shareholder value.

At last, in 2012, an important study by Credit Suisse[12] gave a deeper insight into what seemed to be happening. Credit Suisse looked across the world and compared the performance of companies that had women on their Boards with companies that had none. The initial results seemed to support the 'more women mean more profit' school of thought. Over a six-year period, companies with at least one woman on the Board outperformed those with no women. However a closer look at the results leads to a different conclusion. Between 2005 and 2007, when the world economy was doing well, there was little difference in performance between companies with or without women on the Board. But, after the financial disaster that occurred in 2008, those companies with women Directors on the Board did noticeably better than those without. In other words, when times were good, having women on the Board made little difference but once the world's financial system started to collapse and companies faced the worst recession in living memory, having women in the Boardroom proved to be a significant advantage. In Credit Suisse's rather uninspiring prose, 'More (gender) balance on the Board brings less volatility and more balance (to company performance) through the cycle.' In plain English, Credit Suisse found that those companies with women on the Board rode out the financial storm better than those with all-male Boards.

This is a very important conclusion, and it tends to confirm what several researchers and a number of our interviewees women have suggested. A Board that includes women tends to be more cautious than a Board made up entirely of men. Human relations specialist Julie Towers told us that in her experience men and women approach difficult issues quite differently. Men focus on the outcome and tend to say, "We need to do it so we had better get on with it". Women often bring stronger people skills and are likely to think about the process, how people will react and what could go wrong.

"Women are prepared to give more time to talk through the consequences while men can come to a conclusion quickly and cannot see the point of long discussions. Both approaches are needed in business."

At a conference that we organised at the House of Commons in 2013, Arne Selvik,[13] who has sat on the Boards of over 50 companies across Europe and Asia, said that he had seen groups of men being carried along by their own enthusiasm and taking unwarranted risks as a result. Selvik thought that the presence of women 'slows the men down'. He quoted research from John Coates,[14] the Cambridge University neuroscientist and former Wall Street trader. Coates studied the biology of financial risk taking and summed up his findings by concluding that, 'When it comes to making and losing money women may be less hormonally reactive than men … Greater numbers (of women) among risk takers in the financial world could therefore help dampen the volatility.' In other words, high levels of testosterone can lead to high levels of risk.

Unravelling

At this point the 'business case' begins to unravel. Having more women in senior positions seems to lead not to an increase in profits but to more careful discussion of the issues and a more cautious approach to risk taking. Companies might well be more resilient in the bad times but they are unlikely to be much more profitable through the economic cycle. It is worth considering why women are inclined to follow this more cautious approach. Sarah Anderson has a convincing interpretation of the evidence. She suggests that women usually come into senior positions feeling and behaving as if they are outsiders, a phenomenon described in Chapter 4. So women tend to question decisions and practices and ask for explanations because, as outsiders, they do not feel responsible for the traditions of the Board and feel no close bond with the men around them. Conversely many men are happy to accept the existing norms because they feel very comfortable sitting amongst men whose background they share and because they see no reason to challenge the behaviour of colleagues whom, in many cases, they have known for years. The full extent of the risks might not be uncovered until women, as outsiders, start asking more questions. As Selvik observed, the women 'slow the men down'.

This analysis opens up a wider issue. The 'business case' is put forward as an argument for more women at the top. However on examination it seems to be more accurately described as an argument for ensuring that companies are governed and managed by people from different backgrounds and with a wide range of experience. Widening the range of experience round Boardroom tables and recruiting from a wider range of people is certainly beneficial to the British economy and to individual companies. However these benefits can be achieved if more people at the top are 'outsiders' in the sense that they do not come from that rather narrow section of white male society that supplies most Board members at the moment. The 'business case' is presented as an argument for more women at the top. To some extent it is. But it also turns out to be an argument for the appointment of people with different ethnicity, from different backgrounds, with different education and with different life experiences. And some of those new appointments might reasonably be men.

Widening the talent pool to include a number of excluded groups would certainly help to correct the narrow-mindedness of some companies but that is a different issue from the need to remedy the current unfairness to women. There are actually two issues of importance – equality and diversity – and they are often confused. Indeed sometimes they can even appear in competition. At a recent seminar a head-hunter told us of his difficulties. "I have a brief from one company not only to find a woman for their Board but to find a black and ethnic member as well. They want to make their Board really diverse." We asked what the gender balance would be after these appointments. He told us that there would be two women and eight men and "one of the men will be black". Whether such a Board can be described as diverse is doubtful, but the fact that the women are outnumbered four to one by the men means that it is certainly a long way from achieving a reasonable gender balance.

Inequality and the 'Business Case'

The main problem with the 'business case' is that it is wrongly focused. It does not try to correct unfairness or promote greater equality. Indeed it scarcely recognises these faults in the present system. The 'business case' does not concern itself with the needs of women or the achievement of a fair society. It concentrates narrowly and exclusively on the needs of the company or the organisation. The 'business case' treats the appointment of women as if that issue is like any other decision that comes into the Boardroom or onto the agenda of a governing body. It encourages companies to apply the same test that would be used to evaluate any other proposal. Launch a new product, open a new office or appoint more women to the Board, and the test is the same. Never mind the wider implications, ask a single question: will it be good for business?

Judging the appointment of more women by this narrow commercial criterion is impossible to justify. The balance of power between men and women is, at its heart, a social and political issue and cannot be decided solely or mainly as if it were a conventional business decision. When Norway was debating Board membership, two social scientists – Mari Teigen and Hege Skjeie – commented on the 'business case' with a directness that is rarely heard in Britain:

> We feel quite certain that showing the will to be just and fair is good for business in the long run. But in our opinion, the slogan 'Gender equality pays off!' is hardly palatable. The idea that the end justifies the means does not work. One should not argue for gender equality by notions of money-making. Women are not here to be used, and gender equality is not about profit maximisation.[15]

The two social scientists go on to show that the 'business case', like the Emperor, has no clothes. What happens, they ask, if further research demonstrates that having more women at the top does not, in fact, lead to the business improvements that are claimed. In those circumstances, and the Norwegian academics pose the rhetorical question with a good deal of sarcasm, should we all just abandon the objective of promoting more women and allow male dominance to continue?

Countries like Norway and Britain are meant to be committed to equality of opportunity. So the over-riding reason for adopting measures that increase the number of women at the top should not be based on the argument that having more women might improve company performance or increase company profits. If we are true to the stated principles of our society, we should ensure that the female half of the population has the same opportunities as the men. That should be the principal motive for reform.

So why, in the face of these compelling arguments, have business and political leaders decided to present the case for more women at the top in terms of benefit to companies rather than in terms of fairness and equality? Perhaps part of the answer lies in the uncomfortable suspicion – fed by the revelations that followed the financial crash of 2008 – that many of the men who run large companies look at just about everything through the prism of commercial advantage. They have been taught by the imperatives of our company law and the mores of our economic system that their job is to increase the value of their company for the benefit of shareholders and nothing more. It takes a leap of imagination to look beyond the narrow confines of shareholder value and think in terms of a wider social purpose.

Attractions of the 'Business Case'

There are also more tactical considerations in play. It is a misunderstanding to imagine that the whole of the business community has been promoting the 'business case' or is interested in having more women in senior positions. In fact the case for having more women at the top has been mainly put forward by a relatively small number of business leaders from a few large companies. These 'business grandees', as we might call them, are mostly members of the 30% Club which is committed to increase the number of women on their own Boards or of Opportunity Now, an off-shoot of Business in the Community, which has been campaigning for the appointment of more women Company Directors for over 20 years. These two organisations have done a good job in publicising the case. The approach taken by the 30% Club in particular has been copied in several countries.

The trouble is that much of the business community does not share the commitment of the 'business grandees'. Instead of unity and enthusiasm we have what Harriet Harman calls "a faux consensus" with a lot of window dressing but with rather small numbers of men actively promoting the case for more women at the top. So the argument has to be framed in a manner that will make sense to the Chairmen and CEOs of companies who have, so far, done little to promote women and need some persuading to do so. We do not know what the leaders of the 30% Club and of Opportunity Now think about arguments for equality and fairness because they rarely seem to speak in these terms, but it is obvious that they think that the 'business case' – with its promise of commercial advantage – will have a better chance of winning the support of other Chairmen and CEOs. The 'business case' goes with the grain of business opinion; it challenges no prejudice and it runs little risk of generating opposition.

But the need to put together an argument that appeals to the business community does not explain why politicians in the major political Parties are similarly reluctant to talk about fairness and equality. Here a second set of tactical considerations comes into play. In the past 15 years arguments about changing the nature of society and particularly arguments about changing the way companies behave have been out of fashion. The common desire in modern politics is to be 'business friendly'. So most political leaders and many politicians are very happy to fall in behind businessmen who say they want company Boards to work better. And the rest – those politicians who can tell the difference between a reform focused on commercial advantage and the need to remedy a great injustice – might be forgiven for keeping quiet about their reservations. After all, whatever the basis of the argument, why should they complain about an initiative that will probably do some good and might lead on to better things?

Lord Davies's Target

These tactical considerations produced the Government initiative that was launched in August 2010. With some razzmatazz, the Department for Business, Innovation and Skills announced that a former Labour Government Minister, Lord Mervyn Davies, had been asked to identify 'the obstacles to women becoming Directors of listed company Boards' and to propose 'what action Government and business should take to improve the position'.

In 2011 Davies produced his Report[16] and announced that, in his opinion, Government action was not necessary and that a voluntary approach by companies would be the best way forward. Davies is a strong believer in the 'business case'. His report is full of reasons why companies will benefit from having more women in the Boardroom. He describes the intended increase in the number of women on Boards as 'a business priority'. He also believes that, with more effort, the voluntary approach can succeed. He insists that,

> *A more focused business-led approach can increase the number of women on company Boards at a much faster rate than we have seen recently.*

What about fairness and equality? Like his colleagues in the business community, Davies gives these principles little attention. His underlying assumption is that the advantages to companies of promoting women are so overwhelming that, with sweet reason and a little exhortation, more women will be appointed. He applauds the few companies that are said to be doing well; he obviously believes that, with his encouragement, the rest will quickly follow. However Davies has been shrewd enough to set a target that is very modest. He wants women to make up 25 per cent of the Board membership of FTSE 100 companies by 2015. Some commentators, who have not done the arithmetic, talk as if this would represent a major change. In fact, at the time that Davies produced his first report, all it took for his 25 per cent target to be achieved was for each of the FTSE 100 companies to appoint one additional woman to their Board at some time in the following four years.

The Government quickly endorsed the Davies approach and it has also received support from opposition Parties. Several women Labour MPs told us that the Davies initiative should be welcomed because, although its objectives are modest, it represents real progress. Most of the senior women in business whom we interviewed feel the same way. Emma Howard Boyd said she is encouraged by the Davies recommendation that CEOs should report regularly on their company's record in promoting women managers into the top jobs. She also likes the emphasis that Davies has given to creating "a bigger pipeline of women" with the necessary experience to take up senior positions. Helena Morrissey is optimistic that the Davies target of 25 per cent can be reached in the FTSE 100 companies by 2015 without undue difficulty.

It is no surprise that such a modest set of proposals should gain widespread support. In 2010, Marianne Coleman[17] reported that the 60 senior women whom she interviewed tended to 'endorse gradual rather than radical change'. A policy of slow but steady progress has an attractive ring to it. It implies moderation, caution and low risk. Very few of the women we interviewed thought that the policy would fail. But Diana Holland of the Unite trade union believes that the initiative is far too limited. "Change will come very slowly," she says, "or will be prevented by the strong cultural pressures to maintain the status quo." She believes that:

> *The necessary improvements will only be made if there is widespread commitment backed up by law, policies and rules to ensure fair and effective representation of women.*

Helena Kennedy expressed her own impatience by asking, "What are we waiting for? Do we really need more time?" Perhaps more surprisingly, Helena Morrissey, who supports the Davies initiative because she believes that the best way forward "is a voluntary approach, supported by as many business leaders as possible", nonetheless recognises that the Davies recommendations can only be the beginning of a long process:

> *More important and more difficult than increasing the number of female Non-Execs is the objective of increasing the proportion of Executive Directors who are women.*

Looking at progress so far, Helena Morrissey says that, "It has been two steps forward and one step back. The next generation may have the opportunity to be braver."

Power and Progress

This book is about power and what Helena Morrissey implies is absolutely correct. The Davies Report concentrates on increasing the number of women who sit on Boards as Non-Executive Directors. Non-Execs certainly have influence but the real power in modern-day companies is not held by the Non-Execs. It is wielded by the Executive Directors and, in particular, by CEOs and Finance Directors. Professor Annie Pye, who has led a series of three Economic and Social Research Council (ESRC)-funded studies of FTSE 100 companies across the last 25 years, makes the points that the Non-Execs must rely on Executive Directors for much of the information that they need about the company. As Annie Pye explains:

> Non-Execs are part-time directors who spend a few days a month on company business. They are meant to be challenging but if they're perceived as being too critical or probing too much, they can get a reputation for being disruptive which probably won't help Board relationships which are key to effectiveness.

When Barbara Young served as a Non-Exec on the Board of a utility company she quickly came to realise where the power lay:

> Executive Directors are there all the time and have the power; Non-Execs appear for a day every few weeks. Really they are just visiting.

Barbara Young's comment reminded us of a similar phrase used by a well-known CEO. He called the Non-Execs on his Board 'visiting dignitaries'.

Jane Fuller, who has had many opportunities as a financial journalist to study power relationships in the finance sector, thinks that the Davies programme lacks ambition. She suggests that:

> As far as redressing the balance of power between men and women in business, much of what Mervyn Davies is trying to do misses a key point.

This judgement might seem a trifle harsh. After all, Davies had to start somewhere and it is understandable that he decided to concentrate on the easiest part of the problem. A few more female Non-Execs can be appointed relatively quickly and some quick wins could be recorded. But Jane Fuller and Helena Morrissey are right to point out that, if the intention of the programme is to change the gender balance of power in business, the process will have to carry on beyond the concern for Non-Execs to more important issues. At the second stage, a thorough-going policy would have to confront the fact that the Executive Directors who hold most of the power are overwhelmingly male. A thorough-going policy would have to attempt to increase the number of women who are Chief Executives or Finance Directors of large companies, At the moment those citadels of power are almost all occupied by men. If it is to succeed, a policy of steady incremental change will have to be sustained for a very long time and through many stages.

Unfortunately each stage will prove to be more difficult than the one before. In our largest 100 companies, women hold about one in every five Non-Exec positions. By contrast women hold less than one in ten *Executive* Directorships, where the real power lies. When it comes to the two top jobs – the CEO and the Finance Director – women hold only one post in every 15. And that is just amongst the 100 biggest companies. Elin Hurvenes, who has much experience of dealing with company Chairmen and women who might serve in the future as Non-Execs thinks the real challenge starts with the next 250 companies, where the gender balance in senior management is even worse. The figures are truly daunting. Taking the FTSE 100 and the FTSE 250 companies together we could find only 31 women who hold the post of either CEO or Finance Director. The other 669 CEOs and Finance Directors, making 95 per cent of the total are all men. So women at that level are outnumbered by more than 20 to one. After the relatively simple task of sorting out the Non-Execs there are no easy wins; it is all uphill and the going quickly gets very tough indeed.

The advocates of an incremental approach must hope that, as it rolls forward, the campaign will gather support like the proverbial snowball. But a long campaign also provides ample opportunity for the build-up of resistance, for arguments to be contested and for programmes to unravel. The systemic weakness of the Davies approach is that it relies on the willingness of the men in power to believe that the benefits of the 'business case' are worth having and – more to the point – on their willingness to make the necessary changes. Early indications have not been encouraging. After the Davies Report was published in 2011, there was a small increase in the number of female Non-Execs in FTSE 100 companies but by 2012 the process had stalled. After further exhortation from Davies and the politicians there was another small increase. Then the process stalled again. More exhortation was followed by another small increase. And then the cycle was repeated. There is no sign whatsoever of the surge of enthusiastic support amongst businessmen that Davies and the business grandees clearly hoped for. Mervyn Davies must feel that he is a modern-day Sisyphus: pushing a large boulder uphill with his nose.

Reluctance of the Business Community

What seems to be happening is that many big companies are happy enough to make some gesture in support of Davies but have not been convinced that thorough-going action is either necessary or desirable. A woman who was close to the Davies process told us that Davies had been shocked by the reaction of some businessmen. One man apparently asked Davies why he was 'faffing around with this stuff'. Rumours keep circulating that companies who have appointed another woman Non-Exec to their Board say that they have, 'done diversity' (sic) and have little intention of displacing long-standing male Board members to meet a target that seems to produce no particular benefits to their business.

This is the heart of the matter. The key question is: does the mainly male business community see much practical value in the 'business case'? Our depressing conclusion is that most businessmen do not share Davies's faith in the 'business case' and they cannot see much reason to change. This conclusion was reinforced when we spoke to Andrew Mackenzie, now CEO of the huge mining group BHP Billiton. He said, "We need to be ruthless in applying positive discrimination. Companies need to look again at how they evaluate women and how women evaluate themselves."

What some advocates of the 'business case' do not seem to appreciate is that there is a real divergence of view between what some senior men in FTSE 100 companies and some senior politicians claim is good for companies and how it looks to most of the men who actually run the companies and sit on the Boards. The evidence that we have seen suggests that the likely effect of having more women in senior positions is that companies will become more conservative in their decision making and more risk averse. This might be in the long-term interests of many companies and a good outcome for the British economy but it is by no means certain that many senior businessmen would welcome a more cautious approach. Under current bonus arrangements many men in top positions have been able to benefit enormously from high-risk policies and rarely pay much of a financial penalty for failure. Even a temporary surge in profits or in the share price can put millions of pounds in the pockets of Britain's top Executives.

The same divergence of interest bedevils the argument that having more women in the Boardroom improves the effectiveness of the Board. Looked at from the outside the benefits appear to be substantial. However, the view from inside the Boardroom is quite different. In practice, greater effectiveness means longer Board meetings, more detailed discussion of each decision and a more diligent consideration of every change in the Governance Codes. This will not be to everyone's taste. Professor Annie Pye, who led the 2009–2011 ESRC-funded study of FTSE 100 corporate directing,[18] reports that one Senior Executive explained how his company had recently appointed a woman to their Board but that in his view, 'All she has done so far is ask lots of pointless questions.'

Even that no-brainer of the 'business case', the promise of a wider talent pool for company recruitment, sounds more convincing in a speech from a politician or a business grandee than it seems in a male-dominated Boardroom. The truth is that in most big companies the salary levels for Executive Directors are stupendous and there is no shortage of enthusiastic candidates pressing for promotion or, as they prefer to put it, 'looking for a new challenge'. The talent pool argument might have more resonance in a debate about the recruitment of graduate trainees but here the considerations are very different. Many large companies already recruit a high proportion of women graduates and the problem is not recruitment but the rapid attrition of talented women. As we explained in Chapter 4, 'After five years, so many of the women have left that the men typically outnumber the women by two to one.' How to stop the women who might eventually be candidates for Executive positions from leaving the company is, in real life, a much bigger problem than putting one or two extra women onto the Board as Non-Execs.

Surprisingly, the biggest problem of all is scarcely ever mentioned. Indeed the enthusiasm with which politicians and business grandees ignore the elephant standing in the corner of the room is breath-taking. The simple and obvious truth is that the more women who are promoted into the Boardroom or into senior Executive management, the fewer jobs will be available to the men. It might be possible to fudge the figures a little by creating more Non-Executive positions on a Board but when it comes to the powerful Executive positions the rules of arithmetic apply. The Business Secretary might make a speech detailing the public and business reasons for appointing more women to the top but the balance of advantage looks very different to a man who believes that he is in line for promotion and sees that promotion being taken by a woman. Widening the talent pool means increasing the competition for the top jobs. It would be more honest if those people who talk so enthusiastically about the benefits of having more women at the top also mentioned the disappointment that will be suffered by many men.

These simple and obvious facts explain why the Davies programme offers no solution to the imbalance of power in the business sector. While the Davies programme confines itself to Non-Executive appointments and to small numbers it will be tolerated and might even achieve a measure of support but, if it were ever to tackle the more important issues of Executive Director and Chief Officer appointments, the opposition will muster and progress will be frustrated. For many men the stakes are very high. As Jane Fuller put it to us:

> *There are about 2,000 jobs in the private sector that are very desirable. They are powerful and extraordinarily well paid. Men will fight hard to keep them.*

The Outcome

It might be premature to speculate about the precise tactics that will be used to frustrate the programme of incremental change. Many defensive moves are available. The most effective is probably the expression of heartfelt regret voiced by many men in top-most jobs that they 'cannot find suitable women' to promote. Elin Hurvenes, who has helped many companies in Norway, the UK, The Netherland and Switzerland to find female Board members, has heard that phrase on many occasions. She often found that the level of qualifications and experience required of potential women Board members was significantly higher than the requirements set for men. Often Chairmen are very limited in their search. As Sue Vinnicombe confirms, most Chairmen want women who are finance specialists. Many more women work in HR but, since Davies started his work, only four Board members had been recruited from that important function compared with over a dozen finance specialists. Solving these problems is relatively easy if the will is there to do so, but the problems can also be magnified and used as blocking tactics if men want an excuse for delay.

Whatever the results of the Davies programme, there is unlikely to be any dramatic confrontation between business leaders and the Government. No one in the business community will want to provoke the Government into more resolute action and the Government shows no indication that it wants to fight the business community on the issue. The outcome is a likely to be a considerable focus on Davies's modest target of 25 per cent women Board members by 2015. When the 25 per cent figure is reached we can expect enormous mutual congratulation and many solemn assertions that the voluntary approach has worked. At that stage the Government will no doubt launch a substantial consultation about next steps. The consultation will probably be followed by a lengthy period of reflection. Several years might easily slip by.

Reaching the Davies target means that the number of female Non-Execs will be outnumbered by three to one. Whether this is rated as a significant success or an irrelevance will depend on a person's views on gender equality and the development of British society. Most people will probably think that the initiative has been worthwhile and will very likely believe that a platform has been built for further progress in the future. Unfortunately this apparently common sense judgment might turn out to be wrongheaded. Putting a few more women in senior positions without strong follow-up action might prove to be damaging to the cause of gender equality instead of being helpful.

Heavily Outnumbered

In 1977, Rosabeth Moss Kanter[19] wrote a ground-breaking study of life in a large American company called *Men and Women of the Corporation*. In one famous chapter Kanter described what happened to women who worked in occupations where they were surrounded and outnumbered by men. Kanter found that the pressure on these women was considerable. The women felt very visible and were aware that they being closely watched. Everything they did was liable to be the subject of gossip. They carried a heavy burden of responsibility because they knew that any failure would be used to demonstrate that women were not suitable for that particular job. They were also apprehensive that they would be treated badly if they attempted to outshine the men. Many women played down their abilities to avoid jealousy and recrimination.

The men were of little help. They tended to be doubtful about whether they could trust the lone woman: when she was present, the men were more circumspect in their criticisms of the company. In private the men would give the woman some stereotypical label – 'emotional', 'hard', 'sexy' or 'motherly'. The men made little attempt to involve any woman in activities that took place outside the workplace and it was quite common for the men to go off together leaving the woman on her own. So it is not surprising that most of the women in this position felt isolated, pressurised and uncomfortable. Many just left: women were twice as likely to resign from the company compared with men in similar jobs.

Much has changed since the 1970s but subsequent research has confirmed that, more than a generation later, a woman working alone or with another woman amongst a large group of men still faces many of the problems that Kanter described. Research by Alison Konrad and colleagues[20] in 2008 gave many examples of the pressures felt by a lone woman on a company Board. She was often made to feel like an outsider:

> It felt like I was always playing catch-up … it was an old boy network (making decisions).

> It is hard … to get your voice heard.

> (The male Board members) asked each other about their wives but were very uncomfortable asking about husbands.

And a familiar story:

> When new auditors were introduced, they shook hands with the men, 'skipped me and shook hands with the next guy'. One man admitted that he had noticed but he did nothing.

Konrad and her colleagues found that having two women on a Board was better but they noted that the two women were still not treated as individuals. It was not until three or more women were appointed that the women felt that they could behave naturally. 'Three is a kind of charm,' said one Board member, 'When the third woman came, it was easier.' Others talked about a 'critical mass' and the 'tipping point'.

The importance of a 'critical mass' was emphasised by several of the women we interviewed. Some like Sally Barnes warned that a woman on her own quickly feels alone and isolated. "There has to be a 'critical mass' and the women should have proper support to match the support that men have built up over many years." In their research into the role of women on Boards, Huse and Solberg[21] confirmed that a woman serving on her own amongst a large number of men often feels very lonely. Sarah Anderson agreed that the feeling of isolation can be very damaging but added that there are also strong practical reasons for appointing a group of women rather than just one. "Three women can cover more ground, divide up the work and press a point more effectively than a woman on her own."

Deirdre Hutton gave us a fascinating insight into the importance of this 'critical mass'. She sat on the Board of the Financial Services Agency with two other women and says that, while there were three women, they could all behave perfectly naturally, agreeing or disagreeing as necessary. However, when one of the women left, Deirdre Hutton and the other woman Board member noticed a change in the atmosphere. Any disagreement between the two remaining women, however reasonably expressed, now seemed to be regarded by the men not as a disagreement between members of the Board but as a 'cat fight' between two women. In the end Deirdre Hutton and her colleague met in private and decided that public disagreements had to be kept to an absolute minimum.

Future Policy

The work of Kanter, Konrad and others, taken together with the personal experiences that we heard in our interviews, has important implications for future policy. It seems that the best way to ensure that women operate effectively and feel a reasonable measure of comfort when surrounded by a large number of men is not to appoint the women in ones and twos but to appoint them as a group so that they form this important 'critical mass'. This conclusion undermines the validity of any programme of slow incremental change, including the Davies initiative.

Appointing a single woman member to a Board made up of men will result in that woman feeling isolated and having to bear the unreasonable responsibility for representing the view of her gender as a whole – the 'woman's view' – to the majority of men. Increasing the number of women from one to two will not be much better and, according to the research, those women will still be under pressure to behave in a manner that is forced and unnatural. Of course this might not be much of a problem if the intention were to move on quickly to the appointment of a third and fourth member of each Board. But this is not being contemplated. Davies has struggling to persuade some companies to appoint even one woman to the Boardroom and the arithmetic of his target, whenever that is achieved, will mean that few large companies will have a 'critical mass' of three women or more on their Board.

Some unsympathetic individuals might argue that the women concerned, having gained the Board position they wanted, should put up with whatever problems arise. And of course most of them will do exactly that. As we noted in Chapter 9, successful women do not spend much time complaining. However the Davies programme, and the 'business case' that supports it, is based on the expectation that having more women at the top brings benefits to companies. It would be curiously counter-productive if a programme with that particular objective ended up by appointing women in a manner that reduced their effectiveness. Moreover, women put in this constrained and uncomfortable position might well decide that there is little point in continuing in the role of a token woman and might decide to leave the Board and seek more fulfilling work elsewhere. The reaction of the men is also likely to be unhelpful. Some men will take due note of the limited impact made by a lone woman and conclude, rather conveniently, that there is no point in repeating the experiment.

A policy that seems to be based on sweet reason sometimes turns out to be nothing of the kind. A programme of modest incremental change appeals to the cautious element in most of us. The programme initiated by the Government might not be very exciting but most people seem to believe that having a few more women on company Boards will make the next stage easier to achieve. In fact the current programme might well serve to impede future progress rather than prepare the way ahead. A few more isolated women Non-Execs sitting rather uncomfortably on a few more Boards is unlikely to bring any discernible business benefit and the enthusiasm of those politicians and the business grandees who promoted the 'business case' is likely to decline rather rapidly. Instead of moving on to the much more difficult and more important task of achieving a better gender balance in the appointment of Executive Directors, the protagonists for the 'business case' are likely to decide that enough is enough. Another opportunity to remedy a great injustice will have been missed.

The 'business case' was designed to win some easy support by holding out the possibility of commercial advantage. Incremental change is a comfortable policy for those men with power but is likely to provide little justice for those women on the outside. As benefits fail to emerge and the going gets more difficult, the policy of incremental change will probably end up satisfying only those who want to preserve a convenient status quo. It may be expedient for political and business leaders to shy away from any mention of fairness and equality and to clothe their policy in the language of business requirements but gender issues are more important than that. Women deserve better than this puny initiative.

For nearly a decade, more enlightened countries across the world have been improving the rights and opportunities of women and women in Britain have been left behind.[22] To halt this miserable slide and to create a more civilised country, Britain needs a stronger programme, more solidly based on better principles.

Chapter 11

The Glass Ceiling and Beyond

The Glass Ceiling

The phrase 'the glass ceiling' was first used 30 years ago by Gay Bryant[1] in her book, The Working Woman Report, which examined the status of women in employment in the US. Bryant said:

> *Women have reached a certain point – I call it the glass ceiling. They're in the top of middle management and they're stopping and getting stuck.*

Bryant's idea was that women were stopped from progressing by an invisible barrier. They were not sure exactly what was stopping them but they could get no further.

In 1986 the phrase was picked up and used by Carol Hymowitz and Timothy D. Schellhardt in an article in the *Wall Street Journal*.[2] After that it spread rapidly. The same phrase was used repeatedly in the media and in 1991 it achieved official recognition when the US Department of Labour set up the Federal Glass Ceiling Commission. The Commission extended the concept beyond women to other groups: it examined disadvantage, 'on the basis of gender, race or ethnicity'.

'Glass Ceiling' is a vivid and captivating metaphor. Its popularity helped to publicise the difficulties that women face in business and elsewhere. Unfortunately it also gives a misleading impression of the nature of those difficulties. As we have shown in this book, talented and determined women can not only see the jobs at the top of organisations, but they can also get to them. However, as we described in Chapter 9, the journey that women have to travel to reach the top is rarely as direct or as straightforward as it is for talented and determined men. The description we quoted from Helena Kennedy is apt and graphic. "It's not in the front door and up the stairs as it is for many men. For women, it is more likely to be in the door, out of the window and up the draïnpipe." The route is convoluted with many hazards to navigate and wrong turnings to avoid. So the image of a labyrinth, as suggested by the American academics Alice Eagly and Linda Carli,[3] is more accurate and revealing than the picture of a 'glass ceiling'. Thoughtful and determined progress through a labyrinth is a better representation of how women actually achieve success than the dramatic violence needed to smash a panel of glass.

The authors of the *Wall Street Journal* article used the image of the 'glass ceiling' to suggest that the problem faced by women is a barrier that blocks their path. Indeed, the title of their article is:

> *The Glass Ceiling: Why Women Can't Seem to Break The Invisible Barrier That Blocks Them From the Top Jobs.*

In reality the difficulties faced by women are much more complicated than that. The external barriers are real enough but so are the pressures on women to conform to a stereotype that puts them in second place supporting the men who occupy senior positions rather than working alongside them. In our culture women are expected to conform to norms of appearance and behaviour that are scarcely compatible with what society expects of its leaders. And because career pathways are organised to suit men, the birth of children acts as a maternal wall that slows progress, halts careers and restricts opportunities. Men have made the rules and women have to fit in. It is not just a matter of removing the ceiling. As one woman put it to us, if women are to achieve equality the whole edifice of contemporary society needs to be rebuilt, "from the skirting boards up to the roof".

The Wrong Direction

In 1995, when the glass ceiling was rapidly becoming the normal explanation for the small number of women at the top of organisations, the American academic Patrice Buzzanell[4] argued that the concept of the glass ceiling was taking policy initiatives in the wrong direction. She suggested that the task of achieving equality had come to be defined solely in terms of increasing the numbers of women who have broken through the glass ceiling into senior positions. Attention was being focused on how more women could be helped to succeed under the present system rather than on how to change the system itself. In Buzzanell's view this is why women are advised to take extra training, to find a mentor to guide them, to promote themselves constantly and to network enthusiastically. As she explains, all this might help individual women to achieve success in a man's world but it does little to deal with the deeper cultural problems that cause inequality. Indeed Buzzanell characterises the conventional package of advice that is offered to women as, in effect, asking women to do more to compensate for not being men.

Not everyone would be quite so dismissive of the advice that is given to ambitious women, but Buzzanell highlights the central question that has to be addressed in any debate about what should be done to achieve equality. Either we attempt to help individual women to succeed in the current system or we reform the system to make it fair to women. In short, we either fix the women or we fix the system. Buzzanell argues that it is the system that needs changing and we agree with her.

During our research we have uncovered a complex of organisational, cultural and attitudinal constraints faced by women in British society. The present system suits most men but in many respects is profoundly unfriendly to women. Giving women advice on how to make the best of the difficulties that a man-made society has created for them will confine women to a secondary position for all time. Such an approach is inadequate, patronising and deeply unfair. The barriers certainly need to be removed but we also need policies that change many of the customs, processes and attitudes in our society which restrict and penalise women. A great deal needs to be done and much of it will involve changing long-standing conventions and habits of mind.

Uncertain Commitment

Does any British Government that is likely to be elected in the foreseeable future have the necessary appetite for such a programme of radical reform? In the present state of British politics it appears unlikely. Several of the women we have interviewed have given us an insight into how successive British Governments have dealt with gender issues in the past 25 years. The commitment to gender equality has been patchy and uncertain.

In 1992, when it seemed that Labour might win the Election and create a Ministry for Women, the Civil Service started preparatory work. From what we have been told by insiders it seems that the Ministry for Women was conceived by the Civil Service as rather small with a Deputy Secretary rather than a more senior official in charge. The civil servant who was developing these plans was quoted as saying, 'We (the Civil Service) haven't anything to worry about but I expect we will need to bring others up to our level.' The unmistakable impression was that senior civil servants regarded the policy as of secondary importance.

In the event the Conservatives won the General Election and Prime Minister John Major had no plans for a Ministry for Women or any similar initiative. Women were outnumbered by 20 to two in Major's Cabinet and equality hardly figured on the Government's agenda. Apparently there was a Cabinet Committee with an oversight of equality issues but we can find no evidence that it developed policies of benefit to women.

A Ministry for Women was finally created by Tony Blair in 1997. It followed one of those sad little episodes that is so revealing. The first list of ministerial appointments made no mention of a Minister for Women and the post was only created after Harriet Harman reminded the Prime Minister that a Manifesto commitment had been given and needed to be honoured. By that time the Government had already appointed the maximum number of paid ministerial posts allowed by law. So Joan Ruddock, the new Minister for Women, received no ministerial salary. This move, which was highlighted by the Prime Minister's office, was widely regarded as an indication that the Minister for Women had a lower status than other ministers.

The record of the Blair Governments on gender issues is mixed. Women benefited considerably from policies like the National Minimum Wage, tax credits and Sure Start but there is a persistent impression that the central issue of inequality was not being faced and that these helpful policies were implemented for other reasons. The long argument that companies should be required to undertake equal pay audits was not successful and symbolic issues like page 3 of *The Sun* were side-stepped. Moreover, in spite of the Ministry for Women and the Equalities Unit in the Cabinet Office, Downing Street seemed quite content when parts of the media referred to Labour women MPs as, 'Blair's babes'.

The Coalition Government added a new element of incoherence to this story of uncertain commitment. The Coalition has made some attempt to increase the number of women on Boards but, at the same time, and in spite of the Prime Minister's well-publicised 'determination' to appoint more women Ministers, the number of women in the Cabinet has remained depressingly low. Mixed messages abound. The Coalition Government aims to increase tax relief for childcare but the poorest women will get little benefit and those are the women who have been hardest hit by the Government's austerity programme.

Changing the Culture

Can this rather uninspiring period be brought to an end and is it possible for a new Government to develop a coherent policy to achieve equality in Britain? Much depends on whether politicians are prepared to take a more positive view of the capacity of Government to make changes in our society.

Achieving equality involves transforming our current culture. Although modern politicians seem to believe cultural changes are too difficult to contemplate, there is in fact plenty of evidence that substantial changes can be accomplished. Sixty years ago, racism was an accepted part of British life. Black people were called 'darkies' and were regularly excluded from jobs and accommodation. Homosexuals were called 'queers', homosexual activities were against the law and prison sentences were often severe. Abortion was illegal and people carrying out abortions were regularly jailed. Persons stopped for drunken driving usually gained a good deal of public sympathy for being 'picked on' by the police. The majority of the adult population smoked and the atmosphere in most workplaces was as polluted as the air above our major cities.

The common feature of all these significant cultural changes is that they were achieved, in part or in full, by a change in the law. Either legislation led public opinion or it consolidated a change in the public mood. In each case the Government of the day was warned by traditionalists that the reform would cost votes. But that never seemed to happen. The change was accepted by most people and the traditionalists soon found that voters had other things on their minds when they went into the polling booth.

These examples offer an important corrective to the prevailing view of what is possible in politics. They also demonstrate the importance of legislation in achieving cultural change. Of course changes in the law are rarely sufficient on their own: legal changes need to take public opinion along with them. And governments will not succeed if the electorate as a whole feels that a new law is fundamentally unfair; the Conservative Government of the 1980s learnt that lesson as it tried to implement the Poll Tax. But leadership by Government can often be successful if it is determined, skilful and seen to be correcting an injustice.

However, for a new law to command support, the public must understand the nature of the injustice that is being addressed. This requires explanation and publicity. As we have shown, the customs, processes and attitudes that hold women back have a long history. They are deep-rooted and familiar. In many cases they are not thought of as unfair because they are not thought about at all. Therefore, an important element in any programme of reform must be a determined attempt to expose the flaws in many of the cosy platitudes that we have been taught to accept. For instance, we are always told that appointments of company Board members are made on merit. In fact, as we revealed in Chapter 3, nearly half of all the Non-Executive Directors on company Boards have been recruited through personal friendships and contacts. Even more startling is the revelation that only one out of every 25 Non-Executive Directors has been appointed after a formal interview and only a miniscule one in a 100 has been appointed after answering an advertisement. So are these appointments really being made on merit? Of course not. Most of the jobs go to insiders: to the friends, colleagues and acquaintances of men who are already Board members. A host of well-qualified people, men as well as women, will not even know that a vacancy exists until after it has been filled. The idea that merit is the main criterion for appointment is revealed as one of those comforting myths that are used to justify the status quo. The truth needs to be publicised. The public is entitled to know what really goes on in our important organisations and the Government has a responsibility to tell them.

Timetable for Reform

Space needs to be made for public explanation and debate. However strong the arguments for reform, a challenge to long-held patterns of thought and behaviour is certain to provoke antagonism and resistance. Rushing ahead with reforms before the case is fully made is likely to mean that the programme stalls before it is complete. On the other hand, giving women a message that they should not worry because everything will be sorted out at some distant date is arrogant, insulting and foolish. Stella Creasy MP[5] asks, 'Why is progress so agonisingly slow? I look at my two and a half year old niece and I think, she'll be drawing her pension before we have equality – and we can't wait that long.'

Deciding on an appropriate timescale is a matter of careful political judgment. Our preference is for a programme that aims for equality not in two or three generations – the timescales implied by current policies and lamented by Stella Creasey – but in one. A single generation should be long enough for the explanation, justification and implementation of far-reaching reforms but short enough to give the programme credibility and maintain momentum. Even that timescale, which is much shorter than anything contemplated by most politicians, means that girls now in Primary school will be nearly 40 years of age before the programme of equality measures is fully complete. Men who think we need longer should try to justify that cautious view to their daughters and granddaughters.

It would also be a mistake to start with minor changes that are the least contentious. The here and now is very important in politics. A programme will not be taken seriously if it relies on what is planned to happen in 2040 or 2050. Most important is the issue of fairness. The sooner that Britain gets rid of some of the most objectionable examples of inequality, the better it will be for the women of Britain. Women are entitled to expect real benefit in the first few years of any serious programme of reform.

Equality in the Workplace

Many of the worst examples of inequality occur in employment and that is a good place to start a new programme of reform. In Chapter 2 we applauded the passing of the Equal Pay Act and the Sex Discrimination Act.[6] However, we regret that those two reforming Acts of the 1970s have never delivered the improvements they promised. The failure is easily explained. Under the present system, the enforcement of equal rights requires individual women to take their cases to Tribunal, a costly process in itself. Once in a Tribunal they will be cross-examined – often mercilessly – and their case will attract personal publicity that can blight their career. It is not surprising that most victims of discrimination decide that the emotional and financial costs of going to Tribunal are just too high.

Two changes are necessary. The first concerns transparency. Employers should be required to declare in their Annual Reports the numbers of men and women at the various levels in their organisation. They should also be required to declare the number of women and men at each salary level. This information would be very easy to compile – in most cases it will already be on a spreadsheet in the HR department or in Accounts – and will give a clear indication of the relative career opportunities and salaries of men and women in each organisation. If employers consider that the impression given by these raw statistics is unfair, no doubt they will add footnotes of explanation to demonstrate how much better they are than they appear to be.

The publication of these figures is our first proposed reform. It should prompt a public debate about how far equal opportunities have been achieved in the British workforce and this will be valuable. We suspect that very many organisations will show the classic signs of job segregation, with women in large numbers in junior jobs and men occupying almost all of the most powerful positions. But the primary aim should be to give a specialist public agency the opportunity to examine the figures, to identify organisations with the worst record and to take action if there is evidence of discrimination. The public agency should have the right to take class actions to Tribunal, meaning action not just on behalf of an individual but on behalf of a section of the workforce. Trade unions should also have the right to take class actions on behalf of groups of their members. Setting up the specialist agency and allowing it to take class actions to Tribunal is our second reform.

The right of individuals to take equal pay or discrimination cases to Tribunal could remain but the whole emphasis of the legislation would change from a focus on discrimination against individuals to discrimination against groups. The public agency should have the task of encouraging improvement rather than engaging in litigation. If it does its job well, it is unlikely that many cases will have to go to Tribunal. However the change of approach would have a bracing effect on gender policies in the workplace. Employers would be encouraged to examine their practices and interrogate their HR specialists about recruitment, promotion and salary fixing procedures. A new urgency might be given to the development of adequate equality policies and action plans. Those companies that boast about their progressive policies but are reluctant to produce figures will have their claims tested in public.

Opening Career Opportunities

Effective enforcement of the Sex Discrimination Act will ensure that employers give more attention to the experience and abilities of women when considering candidates for promotion. This should open up more career opportunities for women, particularly in middle management. However some commentators and a few of the women we interviewed regretted that women seem to lack the ambition to go for the topmost positions. In the rather repugnant jargon of the business world, a lot of women seem happy to get stuck in the 'marzipan layer' and never really try to get through to 'the icing'.

We see things differently and so do most of the women from the corporate world whom we interviewed. One factor above all others seems to have a significant influence on whether women in middle management think that they can get to the top: whether or not women hold senior positions in their own organisation. "Seeing a woman in a top job is the only way to convince people that it is possible," is Dianne Thompson's conclusion. Many others agreed. One interviewee made a related point. Girls and young women are not shown enough of what women can achieve. The tabloids tend to focus on celebrities who seem to have done little of real consequence yet girls are encouraged to look on these celebrities as the main examples of female success. And, as we showed in Chapter 6, even those women who achieve career success tend to be presented as oddities, with the focus often on how they look rather than on what they have achieved.

The only way to overcome this cluster of problems is to make rapid progress so that it becomes just as common to see a woman in a senior position as it is to see a man. The slow and steady process favoured by the major political Parties will not do that, or at least not for an inordinately long time. Appointing women in ones and twos has the added disadvantage of leaving many senior women more or less isolated and surrounded by men. The best solution is to appoint a number of senior women quite quickly so that there is a critical mass of highly visible women at the top of every organisation. If the stereotype is to be shattered, seeing women in senior positions must become normalised as an everyday fact of life.

Quotas

In 2002 Norway faced a similar problem: the number of women sitting on the Boards of their large companies was small and needed to be increased. At first, as in Britain, the Norwegians encouraged companies to take voluntary action. That produced little change. Eventually Ansgar Gabrielson, the Minister of Trade and Industry, became so frustrated at the lack of progress that he persuaded (some say bounced) the Norwegian Government into introducing a system of quotas, enforced by law, guaranteeing that at least 40 per cent of the Board members of companies listed on the Oslo Stock Exchange would be women.[7] The new law took effect in 2008 and has aroused great interest throughout the world. One academic[8] has said that the quota policy has been like 'a snowball that has continued to grow'. In 2013 the EU Commission asked Member States whether they would support the introduction of a similar system of quotas throughout the EU. The British Coalition Government was adamant that it would not accept quotas enforced by law and reiterated the Government's policy of following a voluntary approach through the efforts of Lord Davies.

Most of the women we interviewed were against quotas for women on company Boards and in respect of public appointments. They said that giving women special treatment would mean that women in senior positions would be regarded as inferior to men. They also feared that quotas would undermine the principle that appointments should be made on merit. One woman said that the whole idea of promoting a large number of women by introducing quotas made her "feel a bit queasy".

We do not agree with these objections. During research for this book we looked in depth at what had happened in Norway. In 2013 we organised a Conference[9] at the House of Commons where five Norwegian experts explained and reflected on the Norwegian initiative. What they told the conference was illuminating and reassuring. The Norwegian experts were able to dispel many of the myths that seem, for whatever reason, to have been circulating in UK Government circles and amongst the British business establishment.

In the first place, the introduction of quotas did not damage Norwegian business. Considerable efforts have been made to demonstrate that harm has been done but no convincing evidence has been found. A particular canard, often repeated by the British press, is that quotas meant that a small number of women scooped up most of the Directorships and became what they called 'golden skirts'. In fact, as the figures presented to the Conference by Professor Morten Huse clearly show, the number of women who hold multiple Directorships in Norway is very similar to the figures for men. Most remarkable has been the way in which opposition to quotas, initially strong in the Norwegian business community, has faded away. Nowadays the consensus view in Norway is that Boards work better than they did before the change. Having women from a variety of backgrounds in the Boardroom has improved the nature of debate and the quality of decisions.

What about the fear that women who get into the Boardroom as a result of the quota law would be regarded as second class Directors, lacking the authority of their male colleagues? Professor Agnes Bolsø told the Conference that in Norway the fear has proved to be groundless. Businesswoman Mai-Lill Ibsen added that in her experience the reputation of women Directors depends entirely on their performance and not on the route they travelled to reach the Boardroom.

Unfortunately – and perhaps this is the intention – the discussion of the alleged problems with quotas has tended to obscure the considerable advantages of the Norwegian policy. Quotas were introduced in Norway to increase the number of women who sit on company Boards. It achieved that objective after other initiatives had failed. The proportion of women who sit on the Boards of the major companies in Norway is double the proportion of women on the Boards of big companies in Britain.

The case for quotas needs to be debated in the light of the evidence. People who dislike quotas should stop searching for deficiencies in a system that is working well in Norway and should be challenged to suggest an alternative which is as effective as quotas in improving the gender balance. Chi Omwurah MP quoted a former French Minister for Business to us. He said, 'Quotas are terrible but we're going to have them.' Terrible or not, until someone finds an alternative that works as well, the choice facing Britain will be between quotas and decades of continuing inequality. That is why the introduction of quotas for Stock Exchange-listed companies is our third reform.

Quotas are valuable but policy makers must keep their eyes on the main objective: how to change the balance of power in business. As we argue in Chapter 10, increasing the number of women serving as Non-Executive Directors on the Boards of our largest companies will not, in itself, make a huge difference to who wields power in corporate Britain. The redistribution of power will only begin in earnest when company Boards start appointing significant numbers of women to be Chief Executives and Senior Executive Directors.

Some commentators have suggested that Boards containing a critical mass of women are more likely to appoint women to be Senior Executives than Boards dominated by men. The good news is that this common sense conclusion is now supported by evidence. Research presented by Atul Gupta, and Kartik Raman[10] in 2013 showed that a Board containing three women is 20 times more likely to appoint a woman CEO than a Board with only one woman.[11] Admittedly, even with three women on the Board, a male CEO is still more likely than a woman to be appointed. Nevertheless the research by Gupta and Raman supports the view that a good way to get more women CEOs is to make sure that company Boards comprise not just one or two women but that vital critical mass of three or more.

To complete the transformation, a new openness should be introduced into the appointment of Company Directors, both Non-Executive and Executive. This is our fourth reform. Job requirements should be defined, posts should be advertised and formal selection procedures should be used. The whole process should be publicised on the company website so that everyone can see that the normal obligation to behave in an unbiased and equal manner is being fulfilled. To observe the quota requirements, some of the appointments will have to specify gender, but the rigour of the new system should reassure the doubters that the most able women are being appointed instead of some insider who happens to be a friend, colleague or acquaintance of an existing Board member.

Public Appointments

In Britain, Government policy has focused heavily on company Boards and much less media attention has been given to appointments to public bodies, where Governments have the power to change the gender balance very quickly. At first sight there have been some encouraging signs. The Prime Minister has spoken of the need to increase the number of women who are appointed and in 2013 the Cabinet Office stated that it was 'supporting efforts' to raise the proportion of women on public Boards to 50 per cent by 2015.

However, when we looked at the statistics, we found a familiar gap between rhetoric and delivery. The figures for 2012/13[12] show that 354 women were appointed or reappointed as members of public Boards out of a total of 964 appointments. In other words nearly two men were appointed or re-appointed for every woman. As the number of men already outnumber women on public Boards by nearly two to one[13] the current rate of appointment will merely consolidate the existing imbalance and do nothing to improve it.

The full story is even more depressing. In most public bodies a good deal of power rests with the Chair and the figures show that appointments and reappointments of Chairs of public bodies were even more heavily weighted towards men. In the year 2012/2013, 112 appointments or re-appointments of Chairs were made and only 29 of them were women. This means that three men were appointed as Chairs for every woman. Yet again, Government practice is acting to consolidate the dominance of men in positions of power instead of changing it.

Most observers will wonder why the Cabinet Office, which is responsible for gender policy, is trumpeting its attempts to close the gender gap while, with very few exceptions, the other 21 Departments of State which sponsor public bodies are doing too little. An obvious conclusion is that Ministers and senior civil servants do not feel any great commitment to meet the target set by the Cabinet Office. But, whatever the reason, this is a failure of government process. The Prime Minister should declare a target date for the achievement of a gender balance on public bodies and put his personal weight behind the policy. Because of ministerial and departmental apathy, the Cabinet Office's target of gender parity by 2015 is unachievable but there is no reason why the target could not be reached soon afterwards. After all, appointments to public bodies are usually made for only three years and that gives the Government a good deal of discretion. Crucially, the Government's commitment should not just be about the members of public bodies. To ensure a redistribution of power, a second target date should be set. Across the range of public bodies, we should seek to achieve parity in the number of men and women appointed to Chair public bodies. These two targets constitute our fifth reform.

Political Parties

Establishing a new policy for public appointments and carrying it through successfully requires the exercise of moral authority. This is where the Leaders of all the big political parties face a challenge. Introducing quotas for the membership of company Boards and delivering what is meant to be a determined policy on public appointments leaves the Party Leaders open to the question of exactly what they are doing to reduce inequality in their own backyard. Over three-quarters of Members of Parliament are male and only Labour has any firm constitutional arrangement to increase the number of women candidates; the Conservatives and the Liberal Democrats apparently intend to rely on exhortation and persuasion, a soft policy that stands little chance of success and is taken by many to signify a lack of commitment.

Attempts to persuade business and the institutions to reduce inequality are unlikely to carry much weight if politicians are comfortable with male dominance in Parliament and in other elective assemblies. But changing the gender balance in the House of Commons and in local Councils is much more important than that. It is idle to talk about a redistribution of power in Britain unless it takes place in the heart of national and local government. Moreover the best way to combat the half-expressed prejudice that women are not suited to leadership is for the public to see women wielding political power as often as men. Unless the political parties take more decisive action, realistic calculations suggest that women will not achieve even 40 per cent of the seats in Parliament until after 2030, and it could be very much later. Parity is an even more distant prospect.

It is tempting to recommend a preferred method to change the gender balance in Parliament and in local government. The system of women-only shortlists that the Labour Party has used for the selection of parliamentary candidates has proved effective in changing the gender balance. As a result of women-only shortlists, the Labour Party in Parliament has a much better gender balance than the other Parties. Thirty-four per cent of Labour MPs are women compared with fewer than 15 per cent of Conservative MPs and fewer than 13 per cent of LibDem MPs.

Like most positive action to correct discrimination, women-only shortlists proved controversial. Plenty of men and some women suggested that women who had been selected from a women-only shortlist would not be taken seriously by voters and, if they were elected to Parliament, they would have a second class status in the House of Commons. Rachel Reeves, who sits on the Labour Front Bench, says that, in the event, she and other colleagues who have been selected from women-only shortlists faced neither of these problems. The statistics support her view. An analysis of voting trends gives no indication that voters are any less likely to support a women-only shortlist candidate than a candidate selected using the traditional procedure. Once in the House of Commons, MPs who come from constituencies operating women-only shortlists seem to be treated no worse than other women MPs.

It would be a big step forward if the Conservatives and the Lib Dems introduced the device of the women-only shortlist and if Labour used it more intensively. However each Party has its own view of democracy and other methods might work as well and be more acceptable to Party members. We suggest a more flexible approach. Successive governments have been strongly attracted to the idea of setting targets. A target has been set by Lord Davies for the gender balance in company Boardrooms, albeit at an undemanding level, and a rather more encouraging target has been set for public appointments by the Cabinet Office, albeit without much political weight behind it. Our sixth reform is that, as a stage on the journey to equality, a 40 per cent target should be set as the minimum proportion of women (and men) in each Party in the House of Commons and in local Councils. The target should be achieved by the 2020 General Election or, in the case of local councils, by the first local elections after that date. This reform will mean that Britain will start the next decade with the most representative House of Commons and, soon after, with the most representative local councils that we have had at any time in our history.

Parliament has two Chambers and there is no reason why the House of Lords could not achieve parity rather more quickly than the House of Commons. This is the intention behind our seventh reform. The Lords demonstrated flexibility in reducing the number of hereditary peers who can attend and a similar process could be adopted to achieve gender balance: the male peers would vote to elect the required number. An adjustment could be made to this process to take account of Party allegiance if that were considered appropriate.

As the composition of the Houses of Parliament moves towards gender parity, we also presume that the Government of the day will ensure that ministerial and Cabinet appointments move in the same direction. The scandal of allowing women in Cabinet to be outnumbered by five or six to one must never be repeated.

In this policy area, as in others, the particular change is important not only in itself but to create the circumstance where other helpful changes are made as a matter of course. A Parliament that includes a high proportion of women will be more likely to concern itself with issues that women as a whole consider important and a Cabinet that includes a high proportion of women is more likely to act on those issues. As many more women become MPs, Councillors, Cabinet members and Council Leaders, the priorities of Government should come a good deal closer to reflecting the realities of women's lives.

Contrary Demands

We found in our research that one over-riding priority requires to be tackled. As most women know, it is when babies are born that the full extent of gender inequality is revealed. Because of long-standing traditions and a good deal of prejudice, the world of work has never taken proper account of the need for women to have babies and to look after their children. Earlier in this book we labelled that deficiency as arguably the biggest failure in western society.

Almost all women want to work and many want to build a career. But when they become mothers, women *have* to take time off work to have children but they also *want* to take time off when the children are young and, perhaps just as important, when the children are going through the pressurised teenage years. Most women do not want to stop work entirely during these periods but they often want to reduce their hours of work so that they can spend more time with their children.

It is when women try to implement these necessary changes that the inadequacy of our current system of work is displayed in all its miserable clarity. Employers often act as if work breaks and changes in hours pose significant problems that are difficult to accommodate. Suggestions are rejected or are granted grudgingly. Women feel that they are asking for favours and are inordinately grateful if the organisation – or more often a particular individual – is sympathetic and cooperative. Yet viewed in terms of the public good, these are not requests or requirements for which women should be expected to apologise. Indeed, ensuring that women have the time and space to look after their children is a good way to build a cohesive, civilised and happy society.

The second part of this miserable story is that even if women manage to get the time off and the shorter hours that they often need, they find themselves penalised in terms of pay and promotional opportunities. Any move away from a full-time contract usually means a career setback or, at best, what one woman called a "stalling period". Compromises are worked out, some not very happily, and leave most mothers with the feeling that they do not have proper control of their lives. The contrary demands from work and home are never entirely predictable and stress is a constant companion.

Flexible Working Practices

These problems can be reduced if employers adopt more flexible practices. As one politician argued, making part-time work and job-shares readily available and attractive for men – particularly those in middle management and above – would help to change the male impression that 'short hours are only worked by wimps'. With a little imagination and proper guidance, part time and job-shares can be used much more extensively. Many jobs in the service sector involve seven-day, around the clock, activity and that means that the responsibility already has to be split between different managers. In many cases it is not much more difficult and might even be more efficient to divide the responsibility between a mix of full-timers and part-timers rather than just employing full-timers.

The pattern of hours throughout the day might be varied so that mothers and fathers are able to cope more easily with that stressful time in the afternoon when children come out of school. We spoke to one civil servant who had negotiated a break in the afternoon so that she could pick up her child from school, deliver him home and then return to the office. More work might be task-based rather than involving the commitment to be present in a particular workplace. Few people want to lose social contact with colleagues but a greater flexibility about where work can be done would help many parents and carers.

Good will and imagination can produce many helpful ideas but, as so often in employment matters, best practice takes a long time to spread. Legislation can help to drive the necessary changes. The notion that people need a statutory right before they can ask for flexible working has always seemed somewhat strange: any good employer should surely be open to suggestions on any work-related issue. However the legal obligation on every employer to consider each proposal for flexibility in a serious and systematic way is helpful, as is the rule that a suggestion may only be rejected if the grounds for rejection are clearly stated. These requirements nudge employers in the right direction.

The trouble is that the letter applying for more flexible hours has to be written by an individual and this often takes a lot of courage. Making an application is more straightforward if the employing organisation has an equal rights policy and is accustomed to receiving such requests. But many organisations have no published policy and little experience of handling applications. The first request is likely to be unwelcome and the first applicant will have to explain and justify every sentence in her letter. In this respect, as in many others that we have noted, it is difficult being a pioneer.

The culture has to be changed so that equal rights and flexible working form an essential part of every employers HR practices. It is easy to see how this might be done because a useful precedent is available. Forty years ago when the number of deaths and accidents at work was considerably higher than it is now, the pressing need was to persuade employers to take safety issues much more seriously. The solution was to require every employing organisation to have a published safety policy with a senior manager directly accountable for safety matters. To make sure that the workforce as a whole was involved and that the organisation listened to the staff, safety representatives were elected. Some employers protested but a great deal of independent research has demonstrated that the system works well. Most important, Britain's accident rate fell quickly after the new system was introduced.

A similar system would certainly improve Britain's equal rights performance. Every employing organisation should be required to have an equal rights policy and a senior manager responsible for equality issues. An equality representative should be elected by the staff and equality issues should be considered as a matter of routine through the organisation's consultative arrangements. The new system should be backed by a law giving the equality representative the right to be involved in all discrimination complaints and to be consulted on all applications for flexible working. The information about the distribution and pay of women and men throughout the organisation, which we have proposed as our first reform, would provide the basis of a continuing discussion about the organisation's equality performance. These measures would ensure that every employer gives proper consideration to gender and equality issues and that all women employees have a reasonable expectation that applications for flexible working and complaints of discrimination will be treated seriously. The creation of this workplace-based system of equal rights accountability and consultation is our eighth reform.

All this would give a new momentum to equal rights improvements and, if there is a trade union to ensure that the spirit as well as the letter of the law is observed, so much the better. Working hours and working practices should become more flexible and this would be very worthwhile. But no one should believe that the introduction of more flexible working practices will, in itself, eliminate inequality. Flexible working helps to mitigate the problems faced by women but will not solve them. Even in sympathetic and progressive workplaces, women with children will still face difficulties that do not affect men. Broken career paths and the fact that women take the prime responsibility for childcare will ensure that some inequality remains.

Limited Solutions

In our research we considered a number of policies which, it is claimed, would usher in complete equality. The most popular on the political left is the creation of a more extensive set of legal rights for working women, with heavy penalties for any employer who is found in breach. There is no doubt that legal rights, properly enforced, can bring substantial benefits and we have advocated a number of changes in this and earlier chapters. But the limitations of this approach need to be taken seriously. When Lord Alan Sugar said that he knows of many employers who are determined not to recruit women of child-bearing age because they want to avoid the costs and inconvenience of maternity leave, he was understandably shouted down. Many said that he should be leading calls for equality not acting as an apologist for discriminatory employers. But it was also noticeable that after Sugar's outburst a significant number of small employers joined the debate and stated that indeed they were wary of appointing women of child-bearing age to key positions.

We believe that companies should be required to publish figures showing how many women are employed and at each level in the organisation. An examination of these figures would reveal which companies were operating discriminatory policies. But this type of pressure works best with bigger organisations. A very large number of job opportunities exist in small firms which operate below everybody's radar. A more active use of equality legislation would certainly bring benefits to many women but the attitudes that Sugar and his supporters have expressed will continue to deprive many other women of the chance of worthwhile jobs in smaller companies. Spreading equality of opportunity to the less visible parts of the economy is extremely difficult.

An alternative approach gets more publicity and has become the preferred solution in the minds of many commentators. If taking primary responsibility for childcare is what puts women at a disadvantage, then surely the best solution is for men and women to share childcare, balancing the burden and equalising the disadvantage. It is an attractive idea, elegant in its simplicity. Unfortunately some people who have tried to put it into effect have told us that it works much less well in practice than the optimists expect.

The main problem is that neither partner really wants to share the responsibility equally. The father will offer help but this offer is usually limited by remarks about what he cannot or should not do – like getting the school clothes ready each day or remembering when the PE kit is needed or making up the lunch box or leaving work early on a regular basis to pick up the children from school. It soon becomes clear that lodged in almost every man's brain is the belief that, although it is reasonable for him to help, it is only right that the bulk of the routine work should stay with the mother.

As we described in Chapter 8, the mother's position is more complicated. The mothers we interviewed wanted to retain their role as the principal carers. They want the final say on what the children eat and what they wear and they want to know immediately if their child is ill or badly upset. Some women confessed to us that, when the father took over, they had to fight the compulsion to keep giving advice and instructions. Sometimes this desire to retain control is exhibited through lists and post-it notes to 'remind' the father what needs to be done, when it needs to be done and how it should be done. We quoted Suzanne Warner's conclusion in Chapter 8. She had "never met a mother who was not the default carer". Our research strongly suggests that this is what both partners want and any attempt to build a policy initiative on a different assumption will cause unhappiness to women, discontent amongst men and would almost certainly fail.

If this analysis is correct, no clever fixes are available and we must simply find a way to ensure that women can take the necessary breaks without damaging their job and promotional prospects. This means that a career containing the pauses, the deviations and the changes from full time to part time and back again that women need, is valued as highly as the linear uninterrupted career conventionally worked by men. We can imagine how work can be reorganised to achieve this outcome but the necessary changes are so dramatic and so far-reaching that it would be foolish to pretend that they add up to a realistic programme for the near future.

Fortunately, an opportunity might come from an entirely different direction. Substantial changes will be taking place in the working lives of men and women in the next few decades. These changes might force a rethink of our attitude to work and a re-examination of what is still thought of as 'a normal career'.

The Explosion in Longevity

Girls born this year are likely to live to 100. The life expectancy of boys will not be far behind. This explosion in longevity will force massive changes in our social and economic life. This book is not the place to speculate in detail about all the consequences but it is obvious that we do not have the institutions, the customs or the psychological know-how to cope with such a large and rapid increase in the average lifespan. There will be a need to make substantial changes in the way society is run and this creates a major opportunity for reform and improvement. If a wise approach is adopted, we may be able to use the necessary changes to increase the life chances of the British people, to foster greater wellbeing and, in the terms of this book, to produce a society where women are treated equally with men.

However the outcome could be very different. The obvious consequence of the longevity explosion is that, by the end of this century, the people of Britain will be expected to work for 20 years longer than they do now. Only time will tell whether people will accept a working life of 60 years instead of 40 but a steady increase in the working life of the average person seems to be what is intended by Government. At the moment the only political response to the explosion in longevity has been the downbeat and small-minded conclusion that existing pension arrangements will be unaffordable and that the retirement age be raised and then raised again.

During the next few decades technological change, which already seems so rapid, is likely to accelerate further. This puts an enormous strain on our education and training systems. Throughout a much longer working life, people will experience a regular need to bring their academic and vocational skills up to date. The world of work will require a flexible system that makes education and re-education, training and retraining readily available for the majority of men and women who will need it. Britain does not have such a system. Education is typically delivered between the ages of 5 and 22. There are very few second chances. Colleges and universities take some 'mature students' (the name explains everything) but there are too few places and not many adults have the resources to fund themselves through further or higher education.

Employers could meet the demand for continuing education and training but at present most typically do not. The modern notion is that education and training is the responsibility of the individual. The message is that if you think you need it, you should access it and pay for it yourself. This is manageable if the person concerned is relatively affluent and the training is of short duration but anything that is substantial and costly means a struggle for almost everyone and is usually impossible for people without significant resources.

How does all this affect women? The short answer is that, in this arduous new world, women might face even greater difficulties than men. More women are going to university and that is encouraging but, as we showed in Chapter 4, women make much less progress once they get into work and in some occupations the attrition rate is very high. Many families continue to give a higher priority to the man's employment than to the woman's so many women will not have the resources to fund their own training and retraining. Women who take career breaks to have children and want to return to work will increasingly find that they need education or training courses to catch up with latest developments in the sector. At present few such courses are available and those that exist are costly.

Frances O'Grady told us that the creation of second and third chances for people who missed out on education in their teens would be of enormous value in increasing the life chances of women. So it would – and it would also be of considerable value to many men and to the sustainability of the British economy. This single policy change would begin to correct the inadequacies of our education and training systems and begin to prepare Britain for the greater challenges that will be faced by the next generation. So our ninth reform is the creation of a scheme of funded work breaks that will improve the educational attainment of the British population and, in time, deliver other social and economic benefits.

Work Breaks

A work break scheme need not be particularly complicated. Adults should be given the opportunity to apply for a paid sabbatical from work for up to three years to study for an academic or vocational qualification. A salary would be paid related to previous earnings subject to a minimum and maximum. It would be unreasonable to put this financial obligation on the current employer so the scheme would have to be funded by the Government. The obligation of the employer would be to offer a job comparable to the one that had been left when the employee returns with their new qualification. This should be no hardship. An employee, reinvigorated by a break with time to think, learn new skills and develop their talents should be of benefit to any forward-looking employer in any field. Conditions could be imposed to meet the inevitable objections and a system could even be introduced to recover part of the cost if the Government of the time happened to be too blinkered to see the enormous economic and social benefits of such a scheme.

Not everyone will wish to take advantage of the work break scheme, particularly in the early days. Many people identify heavily with their career. They see themselves as drivers, doctors, builders, teachers, lawyers, IT specialists, cooks, politicians, gardeners, managers or the rest. This fixed identity gives them stability and a recognised place in society. They know where they are on the rungs of a promotional ladder. At a deeper level many people are emotionally and intellectually committed to their job and have a clear vision of how to further their career and how to increase the value of their work. For these people it could be unsettling to abandon their plans and focus on something new. They might feel that their ambition is being frustrated or that they are being pressurised to do something that does not accord with their view of themselves.

However there is another way of thinking about a long lifetime of work and we believe that, as the years of employment lengthen, this alternative view will become increasingly important and attractive. Some people trap themselves into a job which is not suitable and need to change direction. Some people find that they become stale in a job that has lost its satisfaction and want to try something else. People rightly need a period of reflection or to test themselves out against a new challenge or to rekindle their ambition. The work break scheme will be an invitation to try new ventures, develop neglected talents or simply have time to delve more deeply into familiar work.

Most of us change as we grow older, and it is perverse to expect a person of 60 or 70 to have the same work priorities as she or he had at age 20 or 30. Work breaks will provide second and third chances as well as the opportunity to adjust our working lives to match the changes in the way we view ourselves and the world about us. Offering women and men the chance to deepen knowledge, to develop talents, to reflect on their opportunities and to change direction will make Britain happier and more productive. We should not condemn our children and grandchildren to work for such a very long time within the cramped and inflexible system that we have created. If we are prepared to be bold, we can ensure that the working lives of the next generation will be more fulfilling and more equal.

The work break scheme could be extended beyond education and training. Individuals with plans to set up a new business could be granted a paid break. Conditions would be imposed to ensure that the project is genuine and viable, with suitable milestones to monitor progress. More ambitiously the work break concept might be opened to people who wanted to volunteer their services to charities at home and abroad. Perhaps places could also be found for people who want to set up arts and drama projects. No doubt other ideas will be put forward. The scheme should start with education and training because knowledge, understanding and skills top the list of our most desperate needs but it could be extended substantially as the scheme grows in popularity and if the Government has the necessary imagination. The test should be whether the projects enhance the economic, cultural and social wellbeing of the people of Britain.

Of course, once paid work breaks are judged by such a test, people will ask whether maternity and paternity breaks should be fitted into the scheme. In a better world, with many more women in positions of power, we trust that the question will be taken seriously. Would maternity and paternity breaks pass the test of enhancing the wellbeing of Britain? Of course they would. Having time off to bear children and to look after them is of overwhelming importance in a society that wants its young people to grow up as secure and communal citizens.

In fact the benefits of properly funding maternity and paternity go much deeper. For almost every woman the birth of a child is a matter of joy and wonder, a defining moment of life, never to be forgotten. Our society should celebrate childbirth and give it complete legitimacy, not surround it with doubts and difficulties. It is neither sensible nor reasonable for society to make pregnancy and childbirth into periods of economic stringency as household income falls and money worries increase. An equal society would stop applying financial penalties to childbirth. An equal society would force the world of work to change its culture so that there is a reconciliation between employment practices and the self-evident fact of life that women have babies. An equal society would stop making the birth of each child into a 'career crisis'. And an equal society would also offer proper periods of paid time off to partners so that they can offer help and support for months rather than for a miserable few days. For all these reasons, extending the work break scheme to include maternity and paternity leave is our tenth reform.

Extra Advantage

Everyone should benefit from a work break scheme but women will gain some extra advantage. With better maternity pay women will be able to decide when to have children without so much financial pressure. They might decide to use part of their maternity leave to gain new learning and new qualifications; the scheme should be sufficiently flexible to encourage that combination. Greater equality will also come from changes in the nature of men's careers. In time many men will see the benefit of taking work breaks to improve their skills or to change direction. As the working life grows longer, men as well as women might have several careers and will reach particular points at different ages. So women who have taken a work break to have children might not always find themselves six or so years behind the men they started out with. It would be too much to claim that a work break scheme will destroy the notion that normal careers are continuous and unbroken but the scheme should at least encourage more people to see breaks from work as a good thing for themselves and for society rather than as an inconvenient 'woman thing' that interrupts the smooth operation of business.

We think that, once the implications of the longevity explosion are understood and as people face the prospect of an ever-increasing working life, the work break scheme will be decidedly popular. But opposition is easy to anticipate. We will be told that Britain cannot afford the cost. We suspect that the idea of paying mothers a significant proportion of their former earnings for up to three years will be the subject of particular criticism. No doubt we will be assured that this is not a matter of prejudice, but just a matter of finance. And no doubt the opposition will forget to remind us that Britain is the sixth richest country on the planet. Some critics will suggest that large numbers of women will 'exploit the scheme' by having lots of babies. And no doubt these critics will forget to mention that this does not happen in Scandinavian countries where maternity benefits are already much better than in Britain.

We hope that people will see through the objections and appreciate the benefits. A scheme of work breaks will ensure that we are better prepared to achieve success in an even more demanding world. Women will have better career opportunities and so will men. The chance to learn more, train more and reflect more will take some of the drudgery and unfairness out of working life in Britain. Perhaps it will even help to make us a better, happier and more successful country.

Positive action

The recommendations we make in this chapter for a programme of reform – for the better enforcement of equality legislation, for a greater transparency in appointments and pay, for the introduction of quotas, targets and in-house equality programmes to achieve a better balance of power in companies, public sector organisations and in Parliament, and for the introduction of a scheme offering work breaks – will all contribute to the correction of a long-standing injustice.

For hundreds of years women in Britain have suffered discrimination, both directly and indirectly. To achieve equality of opportunity, not only should the barriers that impede women be removed but we must also change the customs, processes and attitudes that frustrate achievement and success. We understand the desire to move cautiously but a programme of incremental change is too uncertain and too slow. Even the programme of more radical and positive action that we propose in this chapter may take a generation before the full benefits are felt. To make women wait longer for equality is unreasonable insulting and unfair.

In this chapter we have recommended ten far-reaching reforms. However the question that hovers ominously in the background is whether a British Government can be persuaded to implement such a radical programme of positive action. We accept that the prospects are not good. Earlier in this chapter we noted that recent British Governments have been inclined to show what we called, 'an uncertain commitment' to gender equality. That is why we should look for guidance at the two periods in the last 100 years when significant gains have been made. We find that in each case sustained pressure was exerted on the Government: by the suffragettes in the early part of the twentieth century and by the Women's Liberation Movement in the 1960s and 1970s. The lesson of history seems to be that sustained pressure produces significant benefits but that without sustained pressure, progress is slow, improvements tend to be small and, on occasion, the position of women may even get worse.

So, in our next and last chapter, we consider the state of feminism in Britain today and whether it is possible to build a substantial and cohesive campaign that will be powerful enough and persistent enough to persuade the political parties to take gender equality seriously and to implement the far-reaching changes that are necessary to transform the lives of women in Britain.

Chapter 12

Reports of the Demise of Feminism Have Been Greatly Exaggerated

I myself have never been able to find out precisely what feminism is. I only know that people call me a feminist whenever I express sentiments that differentiate me from a doormat.

Rebecca West

So how difficult is it to decide that you are a feminist?

One Woman's Feminist Awakening

Writing as a member of what is now called 'the second wave' of feminists who were active in the 1960s and 1970s, my experience of becoming a feminist was complicated, disturbing, uplifting and certainly neither straightforward nor easy to describe.

Over 40 years ago, in 1971, a close friend gave me a copy of *The Female Eunuch* saying, 'You have got to read this.' After some hesitation, worried that I may be disturbed by Germaine Greer[1] but not realising how substantially she would challenge my view of the world, I did.

My immediate reaction was, 'I can't cope with this. My relationship with my husband will have to change. I'm not sure I want that.'

At the time I was at home, having left teaching when my first child was born, looking after my two daughters aged three and four. My husband was a successful Head Teacher and the much admired secretary of the largest NUT branch in the country. To be honest I enjoyed basking in his reflected glory. I was no shy retiring flower and had always been politically active and had a large circle of friends. The last thing I needed was to be dragged out of my comfortable life as a fairly contented mother and housewife.

But there was no escape. I kept going back to Germaine Greer's words: 'The fear of freedom is strong in us.' It was this fear that I was initially gripped by. Independence should have been an attractive proposition but if I were to be truly independent would I still recognise myself? It all seemed far too risky.

Then I found Betty Friedan's[2] *The Feminist Mystique*. Published in 1963, seven years before *The Female Eunuch*, this book spoke to me in a way I could not ignore. Writing in a less confrontational style than Germaine Greer, Betty Friedan explores the lives of suburban American housewives in the 1950s and early 1960s. They suffer from 'the problem that has no name' which each woman struggles with alone. Fitting in with the American dream they complement their successful husbands who are out at work all day. 'The problem,' she writes, 'was with the mystique of waxed floors and perfectly applied lipstick. They are afraid to ask, even of themselves, the silent question, "Is this all?"' Simone de Beauvoir's[3] revolutionary *The Second Sex* had been published in France in 1949 and began to be read on this side of the Channel in the 1950s. It is difficult to imagine the emotions evoked in readers of Simone de Beauvoir in the kind of climate where in 1955 the readers of *Woman's Own* voted for their favourite radio voice. The winner was a family favourite. 'Jean Metcalfe's voice depicts all the qualities every woman ought to have. Sincerity, humour, understanding, reliability and tact.' According to *Family Britain 1951–75* by David Kynaston,[4] women were 'dutiful companions, wives, uncomplaining homemakers'.

The world of Betty Friedan's housewives was still very much alive and well in Britain in the 1960s and I understood and sympathised with the situation of the women she wrote about: isolated, bored and unfulfilled in their gleaming, pristine homes, feeling unable to speak out about their frustration. I also understood that I could no longer justify sitting on the side-lines, bleating and doing nothing.

I joined the nascent Women's Liberation Movement, taking part in demonstrations and marches calling for 24-hour nurseries, equal pay and making women from every class visible. In my mind's eye I remember that some of us were wearing pretty, flowing Laura Ashley styles and others were looking more severe in dungarees. But whatever our outward appearance we were all united in our central aim: equality.

I attended women's consciousness-raising groups which often made me feel uncomfortable. Sometimes that discomfort could be attributed to the number of women I met who seemed to have disappointing relationships with the men they lived with. I did not share their disaffection and anger with their husbands and partners. However there was a deeper disquiet. As a teenager in the 1950s I had been brought up to regard most girls and women as competitors for the approval and affection of men. Gradually I found that the strong philosophical and emotional bonds that brought us together intensified. I began to see women as real friends, sisters on whom I could rely. The confidence and feelings of solidarity which came from working together in a just cause helped me to overcome my initial hesitation. A trust developed which overwhelmed me at first and then sustained me in my new-found beliefs and changing identity.

It is indeed probable that my own and other women's belated but heady recognition of solidarity came from our as yet unspoken understanding that we lived in a male-dominated society.

I began – tentatively at first and then defiantly and proudly – to call myself a feminist. Having to defend both what I saw as my new identity and the concept of feminism itself against patronisingly dismissive reactions was daunting. Then, as women working together appeared to gain strength and perhaps become threatening, I faced more scornful comments but this only confirmed me in my commitment. I have never turned back.

So Are You a Feminist?

That is my story but how do other women feel?

To gauge the reaction to the concept of feminism among the women we interviewed, we asked each of them whether they would regard themselves as feminists.

A majority of the women we interviewed said that they did regard themselves as feminists. But their responses varied from those for whom feminism has become an intrinsic part of their philosophical and moral outlook to those for whom there are still strong misgivings about its meaning and a few who adamantly refuse any such label.

> *Yes, of course I'm a feminist. Other people opened doors for me and I want to do the same. And give women a platform. (Maggie Baxter)*

Of course I am a feminist. We all want to do something to make people's lives better, I suppose. (Dr Wendy Savage)

I suppose so. I think everyone else regards me as a feminist. (Baroness Jenny Tonge)

And for women like Frances O'Grady, the first female General Secretary of the TUC, being a feminist is taken for granted. The question simply does not arise. She and her deputy Kay Carberry consider it to be part of their job. Both of them mentor young women. Part-time workers (usually women) are accorded proper respect by the TUC and after having a career break for children women are usually welcomed back at the same level they left.

However, others expressed doubts about feminism:

I do regard myself as a feminist but I don't like the kind of feminism described by the slogan 'A woman needs a man like a fish needs a bicycle' – though perhaps we need some strident pioneers when attempting to change society. Feminism has to mean equality as a matter of course, not sound bites. (Maura McGowan QC)

I don't know. It's so often perceived negatively to do with aggression and burning bras. If it's about showing respect and love for one another, then I am a feminist. (Revd Rose Hudson Wilkin)

I suppose I am, in that I want to encourage women to aim high and to help other women achieve their potential, but I am uncomfortable with the sort of bra burning strident feminism of the past where men are always seen as oppressors. (Sue Street)

I suppose I am but I am not in favour of that Germaine Greer, let it all hang out, sort of stuff. (Corinne Swain)

I Do Not Call Myself a Feminist

Barbara Young, Chief Executive of Diabetes UK is pleased that a number of senior people in the organisation she leads are women. "Of course I want other women to have the opportunities I had," but she firmly denies being a feminist. Similarly Sally Martin, a Vice President of Shell Global tells us, "I do not consider myself to be a feminist. I do work hard to help women navigate their careers ... for me this is about encouragement and support rather than rights."

Other women replied in much the same vein.

Does it matter that Barbara Young and Sally Martin, two women wielding considerable power, are reluctant to describe themselves as feminists although they gladly use their influence to promote other women? Possibly not, but as former banker, now consultant, Mary Chadwick points out "Of course I'm a feminist: unless you have a theory of life, you see everything as personal." The solidarity that comes from being part of a group of like-minded people gives confidence and helps to sustain one through set-backs. It is also likely that adopting the feminist label encourages us to be more proactive in changing the status quo instead of tinkering around the edges. Feminism as a guiding 'theory of life' may help us to be braver in challenging structures in a society that appear immutable.

Feminist Myths

Even from this small sample of successful women mainly aged over 50, it is clear that people are still unsure and uneasy with the concept of feminism. The word still provokes feelings of discomfort and these are fed by a number of notable myths. In order to understand why there are still so few women in positions of power in Britain we need to be clear what feminism means, unravel those myths and misinterpretations and reclaim its potential as a force for good.

BRA BURNING

Let us start with the ubiquitous myth of 'bra burning'. The myth that feminists of the 1960s and 1970s burned their bras, wore dungarees and had hairy armpits still persists. In fact there is no evidence that any woman actually burnt her bra. The truth is more mundane. Feminists protesting about the 1968 Miss America contest in Atlantic City on the grounds that it degraded all women, were pictured throwing not just bras but girdles, curlers, tweezers and high heels into a 'freedom trashcan'. These articles were seen as inhibiting their freedom to appear natural and un-constricted – unlike the women taking part in the beauty contest. As it happens these annual displays of human flesh did eventually cease, so the protesters could legitimately claim success. So why is it that what has been stored in the collective memory is some image of wild women 'burning' their bras? A possible explanation might be that the deliberately misleading propaganda based on these myths allowed some women to avoid engagement with a more accurate reading of feminism.

Crudely, it is easier to understand the reaction of some men for whom fantasies about women in bras may be appealing: difficult to imagine curlers or tweezers producing the same effect! For some men and indeed some women to dismiss feminism and feminists with disparaging references to 'bra burners' is, to a certain extent, understandable, though it is as infuriating as it is simplistic.

MAN HATING

Some women were concerned that being a feminist implies disliking men: Sue Street thought that impression was extremely unhelpful and feminists needed to correct it. Other women voiced similar objections. Asked about being a feminist, Clarissa Williams said, "No, I've never given myself that label. I've never felt that men and women should see each other as enemies." Lesley Wilkin was worried that, "A lot of feminist rhetoric seems to be women blaming men for too many of their problems."

While it is true that in the 1970s a very small minority of feminists felt that all men were oppressors, the majority certainly did not. In order to make sure that women's voices were heard, women's sections were established in some political parties, trade unions and other institutions. Women were given a platform where they learned to be confident in airing their views without interruption or intimidation – a novel experience for many. Gaining from this experiment with female support, speaking assertively in mixed sex groups gradually became less daunting for them and enabled them to take a more active role on an equal footing with their male colleagues. They were not hostile to men but they did want to appear more visible in mixed company.

As Bea Campbell puts it, "We believe in the best of ourselves. We believe in the best of men."

Brenda Hale took us back to the heart of the matter. "I have no problem at all about calling myself a feminist. A feminist is someone who believes women are equal to men in terms of potential and entitlement. I dislike the idea that women do not want to be called feminists – it has nothing to do with hating men ..."

This succinct interpretation of feminism means that women and men should have equal chances in life and that we can all work together to achieve this aim. At its simplest level, this is what feminism should be about.

For those of us who were active in the second wave, the Women's Liberation Movement facilitated the urge to unite behind different concerns.

Women's Liberation

The Women's Liberation Movement of the late 1960s and 1970s served as an umbrella for those of us who were seeking some kind of solidarity with others who were having new, and what Glenys Kinnock called, "allowable thoughts". Many of us who had read and been moved, disturbed and excited by Simone de Beauvoir's[5] *The Second Sex*, had also fallen gratefully upon Doris Lessing's[6] *The Golden Notebook*, which presented a different way of interpreting a woman's life story. The press described the more active among us as 'women's libbers': a casual rather than insulting way to include any woman who was fighting for equality on various fronts; the title seemed more affectionate than offensive.

But gradually, as some rights were gained and a general consensus about the need for greater equality and fairness was accepted, in principle at least, the Women's Liberation Movement seemed to fade away. Lesley Stern,[7] writing about how women are portrayed on the screen in *Feminism and Cinema Exchanges* as early as 1980, asks: 'To think of oneself as a feminist has been to assume links with The Women's Liberation Movement but ... where is it now?'

The security of an overarching cover was disappearing as we introduced our new found certainties into our family and social life, the workplace and political parties. However, during the massive social and economic upheaval led by Margaret Thatcher in the 1980s, the power of the second wave of feminism began to dissipate. Some of us thought that the momentum started in the 1970s would continue to introduce improvements in the lives of women. But Britain's first woman Prime Minister promoted few women and seemed very happy to be surrounded by men. She was contemptuous of feminism and feminists. Her own son described her with approval as 'the toughest man in the Government'. Many feminists were involved in forming support groups for miners in the 1984 strike and many protested outside

Greenham Common against the siting of cruise missiles. They took an active part in politics against what we saw as major and deliberate infringements of rights in society as a whole. It is not surprising that feminism without a political context went out of fashion. It certainly seemed to lose its power to attract younger women.

The Essence of Feminism

One of the most recent publications to reflect on feminism is *Fifty Shades of Feminism* edited by Lisa Appignanesi, Rachel Holmes and Susie Orbach.[8] Compiled in response to the unnervingly vast sales of *Fifty Shades of Grey* to a mainly female readership, the three Editors asked 50 well-known women from different walks of life to contribute short pieces on feminism. 'Fifty years after the publication of Betty Friedan's *The Feminine Mystique* have we as women really exchanged supposed purity and maternity to become vacuous desiring machines inspired only by variations of sex, shopping and masochism?', they ask in their introduction.

The answer is a resounding 'no' but just as with the comments from the women we interviewed, quoted above, there are many variations in perceptions of feminism in their book. For some the question is redundant. The premise is that feminism is a given in their lives and the main problem is using that belief to improve their own lives and those of others.

For Linda Grant, "Feminism has been the defining political principle of my life." Martha Spurrier says, "I find feminism to be a source of strength, empathy and principle."

"Feminism gave me a light to shine into dark corners of the law," writes Helena Kennedy.

It gives Gillian Slovo "a determination to change the world". Susie Orbach is clear that, "Feminism saved my life and it gave me life," but she admits that, "inner conflicts thwarted us." And Josie Rourke makes a plea for the right to be uncertain. For her, "The private sphere is where I most need feminism's ideas."

It is worth making a guess at what the 'uncertainty' and 'inner conflicts' mean.

The Obstacles

If we take feminism to mean equality between men and women, their potential and aspirations recognised and fulfilled as far as possible: clearly beneficial and worthwhile, what is getting in the way?

To return to the women we spoke to – remember they are all successful in their fields – about two-thirds seemed initially disconcerted when asked whether they would regard themselves as feminists. Many of them asked us, 'What do you mean by feminist?' In discussion, all settled for equality between the sexes as being an acceptable aim. No quarrel with that. However, as we have seen, several referred to the militant behaviour of the small (but vital) minority who, for them, appear to represent feminism in the 1970s. For some, the idea that to be a feminist involved campaigning is the main deterrent. Many others had a lingering feeling that being a feminist implies action of some sort. This worried many of them. Rosa Luxembourg's uncompromising statement: "Those who do not move, do not notice their chains" would seem irrelevant to them. They are aware of, and disapprove of, some injustices they see but taking action is a stage too far. They know that things are gradually improving: certain assumptions about fairness have become embedded in our society; we watch our language more carefully – at least in public; job advertisements are not allowed to imply that they are more suitable for male or female candidates; aggressive or crude sexism is frowned upon by women and men.

In a recent radio interview, journalist Safraz Manzur described himself as a 'lazy feminist'. He had always agreed in principle with equality between men and women but it did not touch him deeply enough for him to act upon his beliefs until the recent birth of his baby daughter. (We met or heard of several men for whom becoming fathers of girls acted as a wake-up call about gender issues.)

Probably many of us could admit to 'laziness' in taking our beliefs to the stage of actively promoting them – particularly if we suspect that we may meet resistance.

Standing Up for Your Beliefs

Sharon Haywood, a freelance Canadian feminist writer, says, "I fervently defended my beliefs in equality by tagging on the disclaimer, 'Yes, but I'm not a feminist,' lest I be ostracised from mainstream society." Living in Argentina

– with a female President who insists that she is 'feminine' not a 'feminist', where women occupy almost 40 per cent of the seats in the Senate but where the gender disparity in wages is one of the highest in the world – forced Haywood to reconsider. "Since I've owned feminism, my life has changed for the better … It has improved the quality of my personal relationships with others and myself."

Becoming part of a group taking collective action was less daunting than she feared. She now feels that, as a result of standing up for her beliefs, she can not only help to enhance the life chances of others but also claim a new positive image for herself.

There is a slow burning excitement about taking the plunge and committing oneself to new ways of thinking which helps to sustain one through moments of self-doubt. No one is expected to change fundamentally by relinquishing a well-rehearsed and cherished view of themselves. Femininity need not clash with feminism. As Helena Kennedy writes, "My departure from feminist orthodoxy was that I maintained a visceral pleasure in dressing up. I loved lipstick and mascara, high heels and push up bras, nail polish and scent."

Her credentials as a celebrated feminist Human Rights Lawyer, speaking out against injustice, are too well known and established for anyone to criticise her style of dress. Indeed it might be claimed that her very femininity adds strength to her cause.

An incident from my own experience from the time when I was working as a gender adviser for teachers in the 1980s and 1990s tells us something about what a feminist might be expected to look like. Always conscious of deflecting prejudice, however petty, I never wore trousers when working in schools.

I was running an in-service day on gender issues in Lyme Regis's comprehensive school. It was being held in the school library and I was not helped by the enthusiastic young deputy head who introduced me to the staff by telling them that what I had to say 'will be good for you'. Two male teachers sat, without removing their coats, behind a large book stack from where I could not be seen. 'They don't want to be contaminated,' laughed one of their colleagues.

Remaining invisible but making audible derogatory noises most of the morning, whilst refusing to join in any conversations, they went to see the Head Teacher in some distress at lunchtime to complain about me: 'That woman may not look like one, but she's a feminist you know!'

There is no doubt that Helena Kennedy and other feminists are driven by what Lorine Pruette calls the spirit of "flaming audacity". Strongly-held convictions add a necessary impetus which helps them to unite with others who share their beliefs. Together they can brush aside ignorant taunts and jibes from those who are discomfited by their confident assertions.

As we have demonstrated throughout this book, without concentrated effort by women, little of significance is likely to change. There is no point in waiting for someone to offer improvements. Equality should not be seen as a 'gift' but as a right or entitlement.

In *Why Feminism?*, Lynne Segal[9] warns, '… It is unlikely that we can ever repackage feminism in a neat or orderly fashion.' Perhaps this implied untidiness, hinting at chaos, is alienating. Most of us like to feel in control of events that impinge on our lives and feminism takes us out of a safe and ordered existence. It takes courage to be genuinely receptive to new ideas. It takes even more courage to allow those new ideas to become so firmly and deeply fixed in our minds that our self-concept begins to alter. A new identity emerges with which we are not familiar and the temptation is to squash it. When we finally understand that this new self is not easily suppressed and we even start to feel happy with all it may entail in terms of changes in demeanour and behaviour, the change gradually seems inevitable and complete.

I remember during the time that I had begun to define myself as a feminist, an old and respected friend aggressively attacked the whole idea of feminists and feminism as, 'Yet another 'ism' we'll have to endure. What's wrong with these women?' My heart sank. I realised that I had to defend my new principles with conviction and in a way that would help my friend to understand how important the concept of feminism was to me. I cannot recall my exact words but I can still remember her confused expression and, more importantly, the strength that I gained from stating my principles. Hearing my own voice defend my beliefs deepened my commitment to feminism. It is a necessary, if daunting, part of the process experienced by anyone taking on a new idea which changes one's identity.

Publicly owning feminist beliefs becomes a source of pride. Being ready and willing to challenge the forces holding us back should mean that we are now ready to make the next step and take on power.

Power

Like feminism, the notion of power makes some women feel nervous. Dictionary definitions include vigour, strength, control, influence and authority: strong words – not for the fainthearted. As we have said in this book, many men feel that they are entitled to power. Women, if they aspire to power, feel that it is something they have to work hard to achieve. They feel that they have to prove to themselves and to others that they are worthy of it. However, the connotations of influence over others, the ability to make decisions possibly affecting large numbers of people, can feel overwhelming. So it is not so much that women think they are incapable of wielding power but they are anxious about what that power might say about them. We are used to hearing about the abuse of power and women are often the victims of that abuse. They do not want to find themselves being accused of the callous treatment they resent and attempt to combat.

There is also the danger as Gloria Steinem points out that, "Women might end up simply with an equal share of the action in the competitive, dehumanizing, exploitative system that men have created."

My contention is that this is where taking on the mantle of feminism comes into its own. Previous generations of women, some who might nowadays be called feminists and some who have simply striven to correct a particular injustice, have fought to voice their concerns and to be heard. They have pulled aside an unseen veil that hitherto had rendered them invisible. Blatant inequality has been identified and had entered the public consciousness in a way that can no longer be denied.

As campaigning broadcaster Joan Bakewell writes in *Fifty Shades of Feminism*, 'I have battled male entitlement, resentment, laziness and indifference.' She, and others like her, has used her power to pave the way for younger feminists.

Young Women and Feminism

Jay Morton, a 28-year-old architect says, "I regard myself as a feminist. I don't see why people have problems with that word. I expect to be treated in the same way as a man. I don't want to be looked at as a female architect. I'm just a person. I really don't see this is an issue." Acknowledging that her views are not universally accepted, she adds that most of her friends, male and female, are feminists. "So I exist most of the time in an equality bubble."

Many of the women we interviewed, however, told us that although they themselves are feminists, their daughters seem to reject the feminist label.

One Senior Executive says with some regret, "I've always thought of myself as a feminist, though I'm not sure I interpret the word as some do: for example, my daughter tells me her generation regards it as a term of abuse."

Deborah Hargreaves, Director of The High Pay Centre, echoes her concern. "I certainly would consider myself to be a feminist. I am amazed that all women do not feel that way! I find it very odd that we make up half of the population and yet are so under-represented in public life," she says. "Unfortunately, I'm not sure my daughters agree with me."

Sharon Shoesmith, former Director of Children's Services in Haringey, told us that she is a feminist but her daughters are not and quoted her eldest daughter, "If women really want power they could go out and get it. Women debilitate themselves."

Of course we are quoting from a small sample of women, but it should be a matter of concern that daughters are disengaging so vehemently from the idea of feminism with which their own mothers identify and which in all probability contributed to their success.

Other women told us that that many young women feel the same way:

"Yes I'm obviously a feminist," says Joan Ruddock MP, "but for a while younger women refused to use the label feeling that the battles had been won. However there is a new group of younger women MPs who blog furiously as feminists."

"Yes of course I am a feminist, but for many young women it's a dead battle," said Patricia Hollis. "That is until they have children. And then the traditional female roles kick in. Where both in a couple work, I don't see many men taking responsibility for organising family childcare. Maybe, when younger women again learn the meaning of the Personal is Political ... we would all be gainers."

"I get depressed when I hear young women say they have nothing further to say," adds Ivana Bartoletti. And referring to my experience, she says, "I envy your generation of women. You had the privilege of making your own beliefs." She is concerned that very many younger women really believe that the battles are behind them and that their opportunities are limitless. What causes this anxiety attached to the word 'feminist' that is felt by many younger women in particular? Many assume that the battle for equality has been won by a previous generation of women and that the need for action is now over. And anyway it is a bit embarrassing to be associated with the 'bra burning' militants of the past. The danger is that if young women really believe that equal rights are theirs for the asking, when they do not succeed they will tend to blame their failure on themselves. Tackling the problems of inequality as individuals leaves them unsupported. In the opinion of the daughter of one prominent woman we spoke to, all women have to do is to try harder: "Surely if women really want to get ahead they just have to go for it." One might argue that her optimism is to be applauded and encouraged but, sadly, such lonely courage does not always end in positive results. Indeed the evidence from our research is that it rarely succeeds.

The New Feminists

This discontent with the arguments and methods of the feminism of the second wave seems to persist but in the past few years a new women's movement has been growing. Very much based on action and not always connected to an underlying theory, younger women are successfully campaigning against page 3, against the display of 'lads' mags, against violence towards women, and in making sure that we will have a woman other than the queen appearing on our currency.

Fortunately there is also a vociferous minority among younger women who are not afraid to use what they call the 'f' word to promote a variety of causes. They conduct their campaigns with enviable imagination. Kat Banyard[10] is a co-founder of UK Feminista. Interviewed by journalist Kira Cochrane she says that, 'A generation of girls like me had grown up thinking that discomfort about sexism was their problem.' The main theme of her book,[11] *The Equality Illusion: The Truth about Women Today*, is the objectification of women's bodies, how this hampers us and takes up inordinate time. 'The rituals women go through are necessary because their sense of self hinges on the gaze of others'. She goes on to consider the labyrinthine paths women have to travel in order to reach any kind of parity with men in the workplace. Rejecting the notion of the glass ceiling as only being applicable to a fortunate few who get close to the top, she describes what she calls 'the sticky floor' of women's work as the five Cs: cleaning, caring, clerical work, cashiering and catering.

Recent books by younger feminists tackle many of the problems previously exposed and publicised by writers like Germaine Greer, Gloria Steinem and Lynne Segal but their approach is different and they tend to focus on single issues.

The main thrust, for instance, of Kat Banyard's book and subsequently of her campaigning organisation, UK Feminista, is to raise greater awareness of violence against women. Interestingly, she advocates the importance of including men in 'the feminist struggle', saying that, 'Gender equality forces them into a mould of dominance, aggression and control.' Even though many men may deny feeling 'forced' into such a mould, Laura Bates[12] in her book based on her blog, *Everyday Sexism*, reminds us 'not to underestimate the degree to which our young men are affected by the cumulative force of normalized misogyny'. So Kat Banyard is right to try to involve them in campaigning rather than seeing them implacably as the enemy.

Eighteen months after the article by Kira Cochran, Kat Banyard[13] herself wrote in *The Observer* to introduce Anna van Heeswijk, CEO of 'Object', the feminist organisation spearheading the fight against what she calls the 'pornification' of society. Working with The Fawcett Society, they successfully lobbied for a bill to strengthen the laws that control the licensing of lap dancing clubs.

Kat Banyard and Anna van Heeswijk are serious women conducting serious campaigns which will be beneficial to us all – women and men. However Object's position on pornography was dismissed as 'nuts' by Caitlin Moran,[14] whose best-selling book *How to be a Woman* has the aim, she says, of giving feminism a more acceptably human face. Moran's book is easy to read and sometimes very funny but regrettably it never really addresses the issues that more thoughtful feminists strive to publicise and rectify.

Be Awesome: Modern Life for Modern Ladies by Hadley Freeman[15] is a witty and provocative book written for and about younger women. She tackles matters that are of genuine concern to younger women and her advice is more serious than the chapter titles would lead us to believe: viz 'You don't need Winona Ryder to tell you how to live your life,' 'You're never too old for Topshop,' 'Ten signs you are having a none-awesome date'.

Hadley Freeman's chapter on eating disorders, 'Talking about eating disorders without using a single photo of Kate Moss,' is powerfully written and she bravely refers to her own experience of anorexia to illustrate her argument and emphasise her points. Freeman is honest about her illness but, as she says, 'Having worked so hard to recover, I'd rather not spend the rest of my life being seen through the prism of my past, permanently labelled "ex-anorexic".' She can be caustic, as she occasionally is in her book, but she appeals to women (and, I suspect, to some men too) as an engaging writer, showing attentive consideration when answering their questions in her weekly column in *The Guardian*. She uses humour very effectively in her book, but her intention is not to amuse at a superficial level: she is suggesting ways in which young women may conduct themselves safely in a society which is full of traps for the unwary.

In *What Should We Tell Our Daughters? The Pleasures and Pains of Growing Up Female*, Melissa Benn[16] – describing herself as a 'middle-aged feminist' – considers the pitfalls facing her own two daughters (and all our daughters) in a potentially hostile twenty-first century. She warns of the 'myth of perfection' and of 'love in a cold climate'. Melissa Benn speaks with the benefit of years of campaigning against discrimination and a sensitive understanding of young women's needs. She is reassuring about their chances of success as long as they possess 'backbone, resilience, optimism and endurance'. Life experience teaches one how to gain and retain these qualities and also the best times to put them into practice. Again, this is serious (but not solemn) stuff, written in a style that is accessible, inviting the reader to ponder and react.

When Laura Bates[17] started her blog *Everyday Sexism*, describing some of her own experiences, she expected that perhaps about 50 people would reply. In fact she was deluged with thousands of responses from women who had suffered in similar fashion and in many cases much worse. The significance of this is important: women realised that what they had regarded as their own individual experiences were replicated by many, many others. Reading about personal insults and violations suffered by other women reassured them that they were no longer alone. The book she has published based on these responses makes difficult reading. In the section entitled 'Politics' she cites a girl saying, 'I was told, "If you want to be in politics, you could be an MP's secretary".' Another says, 'Went on a trip to the Houses of Parliament as part of our Government and Political Studies A-Level … The guide said, "There is a bookshop over there, there are recipe books for the girls".' These examples are irritating but the responses she quotes under the headings 'Women in public spaces' and later 'Women under threat' are frankly alarming in their openly derogatory sexual comments made by men to girls as young as nine.

Here are three examples sent to Laura Bates's blog:

When I was nine a man asked 'the girl with the dick sucking lips' to come here.

And, 'I was raped by my father as a child. When I first told this to someone I felt comfortable with, my current boyfriend, he made a rape joke and said, "Well, you shouldn't have led him on ... "'

'Sexting and sexual pressure is common,' writes one school girl. 'In my school when my friend was thirteen pictures of her were circulated ... she was called a slut very often by boys in our class. If they were having an argument or banter, they'd just bring up the name of the guy she lost her virginity to. You could just see the colour drain from her face when they mentioned his name ... A boyfriend is something to shame you after, but for him it's like a victory.'

Later in her book, Laura Bates writes: 'I'd like them (people who attempt to laugh off these and other similar incidents) to know about a girl of just fourteen ... who killed herself because of worries about the size and shape of her beautiful teenage body.'

It is interesting that since the abuses committed by Jimmy Savile have come to light, newspapers are full of stories about men in their sixties and seventies being brought to trial for historical sexual offences against girls and women. It seems to me that it is no coincidence that campaigns led by Laura Bates, Kat Banyard and Anna van Heeswijk are gaining ground at the same time as attempts are being made to bring perpetrators of sexual misconduct to justice. The men being tried have used their power to abuse and intimidate trusting, vulnerable women and girls. Max Clifford's open arrogance throughout his trial exemplifies the opinion of these men that they are omnipotent and invulnerable. His conviction and imprisonment should act as a warning to other predators that the world is beginning to change.

Using Humour

The new younger feminists write in vigorous and lively fashion, often using humour to great effect. Perhaps this is intended to be a response to another canard: that as feminists we take ourselves too seriously and lack a sense of humour. There is undoubtedly a stereotype of women not being funny.

The cause of women's equality is, of course, a serious matter and no apology should be made for our endeavours in seeking it. Our loud protests may make us appear grim at times, but to counteract the accusation that feminists never laugh at ourselves, I vividly remember attending a conference on a bitterly cold and snowy day in London in 1983. A large gathering of women had fought their way through atrocious conditions to arrive at London University. All of us were wearing several layers of protective clothing – none of us looked at all conventionally 'feminine'.

We had come to hear Cora Kaplan, a well-known American feminist with strong views which she was never afraid to state. There was a feeling of optimistic idealism and even of militancy in the air. Cora Kaplan arrived clad in snow boots and wrapped in a huge overcoat.

We all waited, expecting to be instantly galvanised by her reputed rhetorical skills.

She looked slowly round the room and then said, 'Put your hands up if you watched Thornbirds last night?' After an explosion of sheepish laughter a forest of hands went up: then, 'Now keep your hands up if you enjoyed it!' Most hands stayed in the air. She looked at us and smiled and then began to dissect the extremely popular Australian soap that was appearing weekly on our television screens, and the reasons for its appeal.

Her point was that our emotions can be pulled in various conflicting directions. Romantic fiction has a powerful emotional sway: to slightly misquote Noel Coward, 'Strange how potent cheap *fiction* is.' Kaplan's unexpected opening question released the tension in the air, made us relax and brought us together. We were still engaging with serious issues but in a comfortable environment where 'weaknesses' were both admitted and permitted.

Nearly a century ago the Italian political theorist, Antonio Gramsci,[18] called such conflicting emotions – 'contradictory consciousness'. In general he meant that, however much we may subscribe intellectually to a social theory, we are still unable to resist the seduction of other potent, though contradictory, forces. Women's exposure to stories, films and plays from a young age, portraying ultimately compliant women seeking 'happy endings', made a television series like Thornbirds hard to resist. The appeal of the current popular series Downton Abbey relies on viewers denying uncomfortable facts about the class system in the first part of the twentieth century in order to soak up the romantic story lines.

The social conventions implicit in this and other similar books, films and plays should be recognised, even while we allow ourselves the illicit pleasure of enjoying them. We can have the best of both worlds if we manage to detach ourselves from their subliminal message and persevere in our endeavours on the road to equality. Easier said than done, as Kaplan[19] illustrates in *Sea Changes: Culture and Feminism*:

> ... *I discovered in puberty ... (that) ... narrative pleasure lost its innocence; adult fictions with their gripping scenarios of seduction and betrayal held me captive. I read with heart pounding and hands straying, reducing the respectable and the popular to a basic set of scenarios. Peyton Place, Jane Eyre, Bleak House, Nana: in my teens they were all the same to me, part of my sexual and emotional initiation, constructing my femininity ...*

The answer of course is to enjoy romantic fiction in all its forms with as little guilt as possible, try to analyse what produces conflicting emotions, smile indulgently at ourselves and move on.

Humour is a useful tool but should be used to supplement argument not to replace it. Rhiannon Lucy Coslett and Holly Baxter, whom Melissa Benn describes as 'the witty and irreverent' founders of *Vagenda* (magazine), tell us that, "Feminism has a PR problem that needs sorting ... young women are telling us that 'feminism is a dirty word ... too complex and alienating ... '."

Frankly, this sounds too much like a plea not to be disturbed. Wit and irreverence are both necessary and we cannot afford – nor do we wish – to be po-faced. But wit and irreverence are pernicious if they are used to disparage any kind of earnest debate. A recent newspaper article by Rhiannon Lucy Coslett[20] entitled *Feminism has to make space for the half arsed* and written in a faux, world weary manner trivialises the meaning of feminism, which she says needs 'rebranding'. She pleads for the necessity in her life of twerking and dieting.

No wonder Melissa Benn[21] says, 'Something about contemporary feminism nags at me. I like ... light-heartedness but fear perhaps that some of the new politics is too accommodating of those who find feminism "angry" or "difficult".'

Melissa Benn goes on to quote Ellie Mae O'Hagan: 'If being sexy and funny are the two cornerstones of a new feminist movement, we may as well all pack up and go home now. At its core, feminism should be angry. It should be angry because women are still being taken for a ride.'

Certainly there is still plenty to be angry about, as we have demonstrated in this book.

Reinvigorating Feminism

How can feminists and feminism reignite and reinvigorate what Airlie Hoschild[22] memorably termed, 'the stalled revolution'?

Whether greater equality can come about through rapid action or more slowly through incremental change was examined in our last two chapters. We note that many people think that it is politically wise to move slowly and carefully. Some women agree but others would retort that they have waited long enough to seize what they are entitled to. There can be no intellectually valid argument for yet more protracted delay. However we also have to accept that effective transformations in social attitudes do not come about by accident and they inevitably invite resistance. Winning hearts and minds is necessary for lasting success. Deborah Mattinson, the highly regarded political and social commentator, has stressed on many occasions that 'if you want to carry people along with you, you must start from their position not from yours'.

Sensible advice. Let us explore the implications of her words for feminism by returning to more of the women that we interviewed.

We have already seen that some women who spoke to us do not want to be associated with the unflattering image, which unfortunately still persists, of humourless, aggressive, man-hating feminists. Michaela Bergman, Director at the European Bank for Reconstruction, regrets what she called, "A wrong turning for feminism in the 1970s when in some parts of the world feminism and femininity seemed to part company."

Many women still seem to think that 'the battle' has been won, although exactly which battle is not often specified. Elisabeth Kelan of Cranfield University, feels that women are a bit tired of discussing gender discrimination again and again. She calls this phenomenon "gender fatigue".[23] The reaction seems to be, 'Oh no, not more about the problems we all know about.'

A New Direction for Feminism

The past few years have seen a scattering of newspaper and magazine articles commenting on a renewed interest in feminism. The tone is generally optimistic. It is surprising how often Simone de Beauvoir's[24] *The Second Sex*, published over 60 years ago, is still a reference point for commentators: Joanna Biggs[25] in her article *Feminism is on a high – but it needs a strong intellectual voice* is no exception. She applauds 'feminism's newfound ebullience' which has resulted in legislation to enable couples to share parental leave, renewed calls for equal pay and the courage of the members of Pussy Riot, unrepentant and outspoken in their campaign against undemocratic processes in Russia. However, she nevertheless reminds us of the intellectual theories underlying Beauvoir's seminal text which seem to be missing in today's rhetoric. In Joanna Biggs's view, this has led to many campaigns which she says are 'legion but uncoordinated, related but not connected'. She asks whether aiming at what she describes as 'scattershot goals' are more likely to dissipate energy rather than to focus it and goes on to suggest that 'maybe it is time for another national women's liberation movement conference to coordinate efforts and define aims'.

Part of the problem for current campaigners is the existence of modern technology which facilitates easy and quick responses. An excellent way to bring issues to the attention of a potentially vast audience, eliciting immediate support for numerous valid causes, 'clicking' agreement requires little thought and no discussion. Tweeting has its uses as long as it enhances rather than replaces discussion. Real solidarity entails face to face contact, engaging verbally with others, being able to argue, reassess and perhaps to redefine one's position.

So is the pessimistic prediction of feminism's imminent demise 'greatly exaggerated' or is there a continuation, even a renaissance, of the ideals that impelled our forebears to act? How does the concept of feminism impinge on women gaining power: the main subject and purpose of this book?

According to Bob Connell[26] in *Gender and Power*, feminists in the 1960s and 1970s posed theoretical questions under headings such as 'sexual politics,' 'oppression' and 'patriarchy'. These were useful concepts in helping to frame the arguments but seem rather stale today. We probably need to express ourselves in language that speaks to younger women and men, although as he says, 'Sexist stereotypes are still with us, showing impressive toughness and resilience.' There has been genuine progress on many fronts but Connell's words still ring true nearly 30 years after they were written. He is also right when he says, 'Equality is an absolute concept. It allows of no qualifications however well intentioned.' So 'getting there' is not enough. Whatever the difficulties, we should surely now be at the stage where no prevarication is tolerated.

What About the Men?

It might be fruitful at this stage to return to Kat Banyard's invitation to men to join the feminist struggle.

A generation ago Janet Radcliffe Richards[27] caused some upset in her hard hitting *The Sceptical Feminist* challenging men to, 'Do what is good for women in spite of themselves ... Feminists will believe men's good intentions when they make *offers* not *rules*.' Her book was an open call to men to change their ways but men and women at the time reacted against what was seen as its aggressive tone. Now her comments, though strongly expressed, probably seem blindingly obvious.

In *Men and Masculinity*, Joseph Pleck[28] and Jack Sawyer reminded us that the 'traditional male pursuit of power, prestige and profit will not fulfil their (men's) lives'. Ruth Hartley in the same book writes that, 'Manliness seems to carry with it a chronic burden of stress ... What is expected of boys and men is adventure, production, noise, dirt, decision making, courage, strength and a "good business head"'. In a later chapter Gloria Steinem takes this a stage further, saying, 'An obsession with winning turned into an even greater obsession with not losing' – an even more depressing description of the pressures men find themselves under at work and elsewhere.

One woman we interviewed made a similar point when she alerted us to an aspect of feminism that has caused her great concern. She regards herself as a feminist but "dislikes the way that earlier feminists regarded work as all important and everything else as secondary". The message to feminists is that, in striving for equality with men, they must not trap women in the same obsessions that damage men. The aim must be a better society for both women and men. The message to men is that they need liberation too.

Ultimately there has to be a shift in the relationships between men and women from dominance and subservience to interdependence. However obvious and desirable this would seem, there remain underlying tensions and contradictions which makes the problems difficult to resolve.

Sheila Rowbotham,[29] an active campaigner for women's rights, whose writing in the 1970s and 1980s was extremely influential in persuading women of the relevance of feminism, says in *The Trouble with Patriarchy*, 'Some aspects of male–female relationships are evidently not oppressive, but include varying degrees of mutual aid.' A salutary reminder that intelligent cooperation benefits women and men.

This is not the place to be agonising about the travails of men but we cannot afford to ignore or dismiss how men feel and behave because it has a major impact on the lives of women.

The Political Challenge

In planning a future course for feminism, some kind of synthesis of the approaches – confrontational in the case of Radcliffe Richards and more emolliently expressed by Pleck and Sawyer – needs to be achieved. And as MP Chi Onwura argued, one of the great weaknesses of the campaign for gender equality is that it has never managed to achieve the high level of importance that it deserves in current political debate. Speaking as a black feminist politician she says, "I've found out that civil rights gets more sympathetic treatment in the media than gender."

If feminism is to become the force for effective reform that we contemplate in Chapter 11, it needs to win greater support. Several themes have emerged during the course of this chapter which explain the reticence in pursuing equality and some of the reasons why women hesitate to embrace feminism.

How should feminists respond?

First of all, it is time for us to consign pejorative comments about feminism to the bin. They have always been used by people of both sexes hostile to progress in order to obstruct and confuse. Let us expose them for the lies that they are and move on. We should not allow infantile jibes to colour our perceptions of the case for greater justice.

Many battles have been won and we can celebrate the gains we have made, but we need to concentrate on the obstacles yet to be faced and overcome. It is much easier to achieve this focus by working together. Not only is this more effective but it is more enjoyable too. Those who are opposed to feminist ideals are far more likely to bend under the pressure of visible concerted effort by a determined and unified force. Collective effort is more likely to succeed than individual heroism.

Gramsci's idea of 'contradictory consciousness' may hold us back, but being aware of and understanding our own reactions to people, ideas and events can help us control our responses. We owe it to one another and to future generations of men and women to be constantly vigilant and to be unafraid of raising necessary questions when we see or hear about discrimination, however subtle. There is no need for aggressive tactics: indeed one of the positive outcomes of women getting together to challenge sexism socially and at work has been acknowledging and practising an assertive rather than aggressive approach. Instead of provoking a defensive response, this strategy almost always results in some form of engagement with the problems and their perpetrators.

Ultimately we have to recognise the structures in our society which are barriers to progress. For some of us this is a question of politics. To quote Bob Connell[30] again, 'in the liberal capitalist countries … there is enough tolerance and enough intermittent support. It will sustain a feminist … presence at the level of pressure group politics.' In other words we can make gains which, however small, are gratifying and should be encouraged but the bigger picture is complex and daunting and we cannot avoid confronting the fact that powerful vested interests will continue to control the debate unless they are recognised and challenged on a political level.

For me, feminism has always formed part of a wider political commitment. There is a connection in my mind between the fight for equality in terms of working conditions and pay and the fight for equal recognition of men and women. It would seem to me that they are naturally entwined.

In Chapter 11 we propose a programme of positive reforms which require a shift in emotional, intellectual and political attitudes.

In a society where to be a feminist and to believe deeply in equality is the normal stance for women to take, rather than seen as an eccentric position adopted by a few fanatics, the ten reforms we set out in Chapter 11 would seem modest, reasonable and irresistible.

Perhaps a quiet revolution is required in our thinking which embraces the concept of feminism as part of a radical change in our political direction. The logic seems clear. All we need is the courage to act on our beliefs. As Bea Campbell puts it: 'That's the work of women's liberation: *reasonable and revolutionary.*'

I was 18 when I first read Virginia Woolf's[31] *A Room of One's Own*, first published in 1928 long before even *The Second Sex*. In that year Woolf was asked to give a lecture on fiction to women at Girton College, Cambridge University. She arrived early and was walking in the grounds of one of the men's colleges. This is her famous description of that 'transgression':

> *It was thus that I found myself walking with extreme rapidity across a grass plot. Instantly a man's figure rose to intercept me. Nor did I at first understand that the gesticulations of a curious looking object in a cut-away coat and evening shirt were aimed at me. His face expressed horror and indignation. Instinct rather than reason came to my help; he was a Beadle; I was a woman. This was the turf; there was the path. Only the Fellows and Scholars are allowed here; the gravel is the place for me.*

My reaction to that first reading was one of amusement rather than outrage. Feminism and feminists have taught me not only to be less tolerant of such ludicrous discrimination but to campaign against it.

This is not a revolution that will happen naturally or by accident. It will have to be fought for. Many men may offer support but the campaign will have to be led and sustained by women. As Harriet Harman said to us, "Women must still control the fight for equality. Women have to be the engine of their own liberation." Laurine Pruette suggests that we become 'flaming audacious' and so we must. We should spread the message and win the intellectual argument. But in matters of gender that is never enough. If we are to do justice to ourselves and to future generations we need to muster the power to match the strength of our cause.

Notes

Preface

1   To emphasise prominence, information provided by our interviewees is displayed throughout the book in double quotation marks. Any other quote is shown in single quotation marks.

Chapter 1

1   On 20 September 2013, UKIP withdrew the party whip after Godfrey Bloom referred to his female audience as "sluts" and struck a journalist in the street.

2   Global Gender Gap Report 2014, published by the World Economic Forum.

3   Cable, Vince, Secretary of State for Business, Innovation and Science, 28 March 2012.

4   Friedan, Betty: *The Feminine Mystique*, HarperCollins, 1963.

5   Barnett, Rosalind and Gareis, Karen C.: Work–family conflict and enhancement, Chapter 10. In Pitt-Catsouphes, M., Kossek, E.E. and Sweet, S. (Eds), *The Work and Family Handbook: Multi-disciplinary Perspectives and Approaches*, Lawrence Erlbaum Associates, 2006.

Chapter 2

1   Article by Nick Hopkins in *The Guardian* of 29 November 2011.

2   In 2014 Zara Lamont became a Vice President of ICE and she can be expected to become President in due course. However that will not be until 2018 at the earliest as men have been named as proposed Presidents until that date.

3   Interview for 'The Life Scientific', Radio 4, 25 October 2011.

4   Nick Hopkins – op. cit.

[5] Most of these figures are for 2012 but the figures for Government, political parties and private companies are for 2014.

[6] There are 28 Davids and 20 Michaels adding up to 48, the number of women MPs in the Conservative Party.

[7] 'Sex and Power 2013' examines the position of women across much of British society. 'Sex and Power 2014' focuses on government and politics. Both reports were researched and written by the Centre for Women and Democracy on behalf of the Counting Women in Coalition (CfWD, the Electoral Reform Society, the Fawcett Society, the Hansard Society and Unlock Democracy). They were funded by the Joseph Rowntree Charitable Trust.

[8] 'Debbie Jevans tops *Guardian* list of most influential women in UK sport', *The Guardian* of 7 March 2014.

Chapter 3

[1] Rapoport, Rhona, Bailyn, Lotte, Fletcher, Joyce and Pruitt, Bettye: *Beyond Work Family Balance: Advancing Gender Equality and Workplace Performance*, Jossey Bass, 2002.

[2] Larry Elliott in *The Guardian* of 24 April 2014.

[3] The Kelly Review, Sir Christopher Kelly, May 2014.

[4] Schein, Virginia: *A global look at psychological barriers to women's progress in management*, Journal of Social Issues, Vol 57, No. 4, 2001.

[5] Kelan, Elisabeth: *The discursive construction of gender in contemporary management literature*, Journal of Business Ethics, Vol 81, 2008.

[6] Reskin, Barbara F.: Bringing the men back in – sex differentiation and the devaluation of women's work. In Kimmel, M. and Aronson, A. (Eds) *The Gendered Society Reader*, Oxford University Press, 2008, p309, 2004.

[7] The Higgs Review, *Role and Effectiveness of Non-Executive Directors*, Derek Higgs, 2003.

[8] Article by Nick Hopkins in *The Guardian* of 29 November 2011.

[9] Interview for 'The Life Scientific', Radio 4, 25 October 2011.

[10]   Rosin, Hanna: *The End of Men – and The Rise of Women*, Viking, 2012.

[11]   Vinnicombe, Susan and Bank, John: *Women with Attitude*, Routledge, 2003.

[12]   Kelan, Elisabeth: Informal research project.

[13]   Leadbetter, Charles: *A Piece of Action. Employee Ownership, Equity Pay and the Rise of the Knowledge Economy*, Demos papers, 1997.

[14]   Gill, Rosalind: *Cool, creative and egalitarian? Exploring gender in project based new media work in Europe*, Information Communication and Society, Vol 5, No. 1, 2002.

Chapter 4

[1]   Article by Nick Hopkins in *The Guardian* of 29 November 2011.

[2]   Barsh, Joanna and Yee, Lareina: *Unlocking the Full Potential of Women in the US Economy*, Special report for McKinsey, April 2011.

[3]   Sturges, Jane: *What it means to succeed: Personal conceptions of career success held by male and female managers at different ages*, British Journal of Management, Vol. 10, 1999.

[4]   Cornelius, Nelarine and Skinner, Denise: *The careers of senior men and women – a capability theory perspective*, British Journal of Management, Vol, 19, 2008.

[5]   Private conversation with Lynne Segal, 2012.

[6]   Frankel, Lois P.: *Nice Girls Don't Get the Corner Office*, Warner, 2008.

[7]   Sandberg, Sheryl: *Lean In – Women Work and the Will to Lead*, WH Allen, 2013.

[8]   Quoted in Vinnicombe, Susan and Bank, John: *Women with Attitude*, Routledge, 2003.

[9]   Singh, Val, Vinnicombe, Susan and James, Kim: *Constructing a professional identity: how young female managers use role models*, Women in Management Review, Vol. 21, No. 1, 2006.

[10]   Lockwood, Penelope: *'Someone like me can be successful': Do college students need same-gender role models?* Psychology of Women Quarterly, Vol. 30, pp. 3036–40, 2006.

[11]   Singh et al. – op. cit.

[12]   See for instance Chapter 8 of Kanter, Rosabeth Moss: *Men and Women of the Corporation*, Basic Books, 1977. The research is nearly 40 years old but most of us have seen something similar happening in a wine bar or pub.

[13]   Coleman, Marianne: *Women at the Top – Challenges, Choices and Change*, Palgrave Macmillan, 2011.

[14]   Reported in Thomson, Peninah and Lloyd, Tom: *Women and the New Business Leadership*, Palgrave Macmillan, 2011.

[15]   Cormier, Denise: *Retaining top women business leaders. Strategies for ending the exodus*, Business Strategy series 2007: Focus on leadership, Vol. 8, No. 4, 2007.

Chapter 5

[1]   The gap in bonus payments is larger at senior levels. Female Directors' bonuses are on average £27,430 less than the bonuses paid to men.

[2]   Babcock, Linda, Laschever, Sara, Gelfand, Michele and Small, Deborah: *Nice girls don't ask*, Harvard Business Review, October 2003.

[3]   Bowles, Hannah, Babcock, Linda and Lai, Lei: *Social Incentives for gender differences in the propensity to initiate negotiations: Sometimes it does hurt to ask*, Organisational Behavior and Human Decision Processes, Vol. 103, No. 1, 2007.

[4]   Sealy, Ruth: *Changing perceptions of meritocracy in senior women's careers*, Gender Management, Vol. 25, No. 3, 2010.

[5]   Quoted in *Made in Norway*, the report of the Conference held in the House of Commons in January 2013. PDF is available from websites of Fabian Society (Fabian Women's Network) and of the Labour Finance and Industry Group (LFIG).

[6]   Fitzgerald, Louise, Gelford, Michelle and Drasgow, Fitz: *Measuring sexual harassment: Theoretical and psychometric advances*, Basic and Applied Social Psychology, Vol. 17, 1995.

[7]   Rhodes, James in *The Guardian Blog*, 4 April 2014.

[8]   Rudman, Laurie and Glick, Peter: *The Social Psychology of Gender*, Guilford, 2008.

[9]   Rowbotham, Sheila: *Woman's Consciousness, Man's World*, Pelican, 1973.

[10] After Mervyn King retired the new Governor, Mark Carney, quickly announced that the Bank planned to feature a portrait of Jane Austen on the £10 note, probably in 2017.

Chapter 6

[1] Berger, John: *Ways of Seeing*, BBC and Penguin Books, 1972.

[2] Bates, Laura: *Everyday Sexism*, Simon and Schuster, 2014.

[3] Dyhouse, Carole: *Glamour: Women, History, Feminism*, Zed Books Ltd, 2010.

[4] Harper, Brit and Triggerman, Marika: *The Effect of Thin Ideal Media Images on Women's Self-Objectification, Mood, and Body Image*, Sex Roles, 2008.

[5] Orbach, Susie: *Fat is a Feminist Issue*, Paddington Press, 1978.

[6] Szekely, Eva: *Never Too Thin*, The Women's Press, 1988.

[7] Dawson, Jill: *How Do I Look?*, Virago Press Ltd, 1990.

[8] Bates, Laura – op. cit.

[9] Murray, Jenni on *Woman's Hour*, BBC Radio 4, 13 January 2014.

[10] Hall, Valerie: *Dancing on the Ceiling: A Study of Women Managers in Education*, Paul Chapman Publishing Ltd, 1996.

[11] Hakim, Catherine: *Erotic capital*, European Sociological Review, Vol. 26, No. 5, 2010.

[12] Rowling, J.K. on *Woman's Hour*, BBC Radio 4, 28 April 2014.

[13] Bell Burn, Jocelyn on 'The Life Scientific', BBC Radio 4, 25 October 2011.

[14] Bates, Laura – op. cit.

[15] Trott, Laura: This much I know, *The Observer*, 4 August 2013.

[16] Trott, Laura: What I see in the mirror, *The Guardian*, March 2014.

[17] Fredrickson, Barbara et al.: *That swimsuit becomes you: Sex differences in self-objectification, restrained eating and maths performance*, Journal of Personality and Social Psychology, Vol. 75, 1998.

[18] Banyard, Kat: *The Equality Illusion*, Faber and Faber, 2011.

[19] Rosin, Hanna: *The End of Men and the Rise of Women*, Viking, 2012.

[20] Miller, Jane: *Crazy Age, Thoughts on Being Old*, Virago, 2010.

[21] Segal, Lynne: *Out of Time*, Verso, 2013.

[22] Hall, Valerie – op.cit.

[23] *The Guardian*, 10 June 2013.

[24] *The Observer*, 17 November 2013.

Chapter 7

[1] Eagly, Alice H. and Carli, Linda L.: *Through the Labyrinth. The Truth about How Women Become Leaders*, Harvard Business School, 2007.

[2] Belotti, Elena: *Little Girls*, Writers and Readers Publishing Cooperative Ltd, 1975.

[3] Cormier, Denise: *Retaining top women business leaders. Strategies for ending the exodus*, Business Strategy series 2007: Focus on Leadership, Vol. 8, No. 4, 2007.

[4] Rowbotham, Sheila: *Woman's Consciousness, Man's World*, Penguin, 1973.

[5] Fine, Cordelia: *Delusions of Gender*, ICON, 2010.

[6] Bell Burnell, Jocelyn on 'The Life Scientific', Radio 4, 5 October 2011.

[7] Dorothy Wedderburn in David, Miriam and Woodward, Diana (Eds): *Negotiating the Glass Ceiling: Careers of Senior Women in the Academic World*, Routledge, 1998.

[8] Ninette de Valois in Genne, Beth: Ninette de Valois's theories of dance. In Cave, R. and Worth, L. (Eds): *Ninette de Valois: Adventurous Traditionalist*, Dance Books, 2012.

[9] Baxter, Judith: *The Language of Female Leadership*, Palgrave Macmillan, 2010.

[10] Tannen, Deborah: *You Just Don't Understand: Men and Women in Conversation*, Virago Press Ltd, 1991.

[11] Davies-Netzzly, Sally Ann: *Women above the glass ceiling: Perceptions on corporate mobility and strategies for success*, Gender and Society, Vol. 12, No. 3, 1998.

[12] Bescoll, Victoria L. and Uhlmann, Eric Luis: *Can angry women get ahead? Status conferral, gender and expression of emotion in the workplace*, Psychological Sciences, Vol. 19, No. 3, 2008.

[13] Heilman, Madeline: *Description and prescription: How gender stereotypes prevent women's ascent up the organisational ladder*, Journal of Social Issues, Vol. 57, No. 4, 2001.

[14] Haigh, Jo: *Tales from the Glass Ceiling: A Survival Guide for Women in Business*, Piatkus, 2008.

[15] Baron Cohen, Simon: *The Essential Difference*, Basic Books, 2003.

[16] Fine, Cordelia – op. cit.

[17] Rudman, Laurie and Fairchild, Kimberley: *Reactions to counterstereotypic behavior: The role of Backlash in cultural stereotype maintenance*, Journal of Personality and Stereotype – Social Psychology, Vol. 87, No. 2, 2004.

[18] Tannen, Deborah – op.cit.

[19] Heilman, Madeline – op.cit.

[20] Tannen, Deborah: Put down that paper and talk to me, Chapter 21. In Monaghan, L. and Goodman, J.E. (Eds) *A Cultural Approach to Inter-Personal Communication*, Blackwell, 2007.

[21] Eagly, Alice and Carli, Linda – op. cit.

[22] Quoted in Eagly, Alice and Carli, Linda – op. cit.

[23] Hall, Valerie – op. cit.

[24] Rosin, Hanna: *The End of Men and the Rise of Women*, Viking, 2012.

[25] Tichenor, Veronica Jarvis: *Earning More and Getting Less: Why Successful Wives Can't Buy Equality*, Rutgers University Press, 2005.

[26] Bell Burnell, Jocelyn – op. cit.

[27] de Valois, Ninette in Genne, Beth – op. cit.

[28] de Valois, Ninette: *Step by Step*, WH Allen, 1977.

[29] Ryan, Michelle, Haslam, Alex, Wilson-Kovacs, M. Dana, Hersby, Mette and Kulich, Clara: *Managing Diversity and the Glass Cliff*, School of Psychology, Exeter University, CIPD publication, 2007.

[30] Ellen, Barbara, We're doomed if most women want male bosses, *The Observer*, 15 August 2010.

[31] Quoted by Branson, Douglas M: *No Seat at the Table – How Corporate Governance and Law Keep Women Out of the Boardroom*, New York University Press, 2007.

[32] *The Guardian*, May 2011.

[33] Madeleine Allbright – Quoted in a Cable TV Report of her Keynote Address to the Women's National Basketball Association Luncheon in July 2006.

[34] Hoschild, Dr Airlie: *The Second Shift*, Piatkus, 1989.

[35] Tichenor, Veronica Jarvis – op. cit.

[36] Hoschild, Airlie – op. cit.

Chapter 8

[1] Crittenden, Ann: quoted in Branson, Douglas: *No Seat at the Table*, NY University Press, 2007.

[2] Catalyst and Opportunity Now: *Breaking the Barriers*, 2000.

[3] Biernat, Monica, Crosby, Faye and Williams, Joan: *The maternal wall*, Journal of Social Issues, Vol. 60, No. 4, 2004.

[4] Vinnicombe, Sue and Colwill, Nina L.: *The Essence of Women in Management*, Prentice Hall, 1995.

[5] As reported in Mail Online, June 2014.

[6] Cornelius, Nelarine and Skinner, Denise: *The careers of senior men and women – a capability theory perspective*, British Journal of Management, Vol. 19, 2008.

[7]   Gaw, Matt, *The Guardian*, 17 August 2011.

[8]   Rosin, Hanna: *The End of Men and the Rise of Women*, Viking 2012.

[9]   One–Poll, March 2013.

[10] Miller, Fiona: *The Secret World of the Working Mother*, Vermillion, 2009.

[11] Benn, Melissa: *Madonna and Child: Towards a New Politics of Motherhood*, Vintage, 1999.

[12] Sandberg, Sheryl: *Lean In – Women Work and the Will to Lead*, WH Allen, 2013.

[13] Rosin, Hanna – op. cit.

[14] Tichenor, Veronica Jarvis: *Earning More and Getting Less: Why Successful Wives Can't Buy Equality*, Rutgers University Press, 2005.

[15] Steinem, Gloria in Fine, Cordelia: *Delusions of Gender*, ICON, 2010.

[16] Catalyst and Opportunity Now – op. cit.

[17] Hinsliffe, Gaby, Do it by halves, *The Guardian*, 17 December 2011.

[18] Anderson, Deirdre. Vinnicombe, Susan and Singh, Val: *Women partners leaving the firm: Choice, what choice?* Gender in Management, Vol. 25, No. 3, 2010.

[19] Eagly, Alice H. and Carli, Linda L.: *Through the Labyrinth: The Truth about How Women become Leaders*, Harvard Business School, 2007.

[20] Burrows, Gideon: *Men Can Do It*, NGO Media Ltd, 2013.

[21] Barnett, Rosalind and Gareis, Karen C.: Work – Family Conflict and Enhancement, Chapter 10. In Pitt-Catsouphes, M., Kossek, E.E. and Sweet, S. (Eds), *The Work and Family Handbook: Multi-disciplinary Perspectives and Approaches*, Lawrence Erlbaum Associates, 2006.

[22] Anderson, Deirdre et al. – op. cit.

[23] Miller, Fiona – op. cit.

[24] Crittenden, Ann: *The Price of Motherhood: Why the Most Important Job in the World is Still the Least Valued*, Picador, 2001.

[25] Sandberg, Sheryl – op. cit.

[26] Gangl, Markus and Ziefle, Andrea: *Motherhood, labor force behaviour, and women's careers: An empirical assessment of the wage penalty for motherhood in Britain, Germany and the USA,* Demography, Vol. 46, No. 2, 2009.

[27] Branson, Douglas – op. cit.

[28] Interview for 'The Life Scientific', Radio 4, 25 October 2011.

[29] Booth, Cherie: All women should have the chance to have a family and a career, *The Observer,* 20 October 2013.

[30] Gill, Rosalind: *Cool, creative and egalitarian? Exploring gender in project based new media work in Europe,* Information Communication and Society, Vol. 5, No. 1, 2002.

[31] Steinem, Gloria: quoted in Rosin, Hanna – op. cit.

Chapter 9

[1] Ryan, Michelle, Haslam, Alex, Wilson-Kovacs, M. Dana, Hersby, Mette and Kulich, Clara: *Managing Diversity and the Glass Cliff,* School of Psychology, Exeter University, CIPD publication, 2007.

[2] Presented by Michelle Ryan as part of 'Gender and the Boardroom' symposium at Department of Economics, Sheffield University, 9 June 2014.

[3] Stead, Valerie and Elliott, Carole: *Women's Leadership: Sociological Construction,* Palgrave Macmillan, 2009.

[4] Eagly, Alice H. and Carli, Linda L.: *Through the Labyrinth: The Truth about How Women become Leaders.* Harvard Business School, 2007.

Chapter 10

[1] Vinnicombe, Susan and Bank, John: *Women with Attitude,* Introduction by Harriet Harman, Routledge, 2003.

[2] Hakim, Catherine: *Feminist Myths and Magic Medicine,* Centre for Policy Studies, 2011.

3   Private conversation with an insider who examined the operation of the RBS Board.

4   Childs, Sarah, Lovenduski, Joni and Campbell, Rosie: *Women at the Top: Changing Numbers, Changing Politics?*, for the Hansard Society, 2005

5   Terjesen, Siri, Sealy, Ruth and Singh, Val: *Women directors on corporate boards: A review and research agenda*, Corporate Governance: An International Review, Vol. 17, No. 3, 2009.

6   Konrad, Alison, Kramer, Vicki and Erkut, Sumru: *The impact of three or more women on corporate boards*, Organisational Dynamics, Vol. 37, No. 2, 2008.

7   Quoted in Tutchell, Eva and Edmonds, John (Eds): *Made in Norway*, the report of the Conference held in the House of Commons in January 2013. PDF is available from websites of Fabian Society (Fabian Women's Network) and of the Labour Finance and Industry Group (LFIG).

8   Catalyst: *The Bottom Line: Connecting Corporate Performance and Gender Diversity*, 2004.

9   Deloitte: *Only Skin Deep: Re-examining the Business Case for Diversity*, 2011.

10 Huse, Morten and Solberg, Anne Grethe: Gender related boardroom dynamics: How Scandinavian women make contributions on corporate boards. In Huse, Morten (Ed.) *The Value Creating Board's Corporate Governance and Organizational Behaviour*, Routledge, 2009.

11 Terjensen et al. – op. cit.

12 Credit Suisse: *Gender Diversity and Corporate Performance*, Research Institute, 2012.

13 *Made in Norway* – op. cit.

14 Coates, John: *The Hour between Dog and Wolf: Risk Taking, Gut Feelings and the Biology of Boom and Bust*, Random House, 2012.

15 Quoted in *Made in Norway* – op. cit.

16 Davies, Mervyn – Baron Davies of Abersoch: *Report on Women on Boards*, 2011.

17 Coleman, Marianne: *Women at the Top*, Palgrave Macmillan, 2011.

18 The latest report in the series is: Pye, Annie, Kaczmarek, Szymon and Kimino, Satomi: *Leading FTSE Companies: The Continuing Study of Corporate Directing*. Centre for Leadership Studies, University of Exeter Business School, 2011.

[19] Kanter, Rosabeth Moss: *Men and Women of the Corporation*, Basic Books, 1977.

[20] Konrad et al. – op. cit.

[21] Huse and Solberg – op. cit.

[22] Global Gender Gap Report 2014, published by the World Economic Forum.

Chapter 11

[1] Bryant, Gay: *The Working Woman Report*, Simon and Schuster, 1984.

[2] Hymowitz, Carol and Schelhardt, Timothy D: The glass ceiling: Why women can't seem to break the invisible barrier that blocks them from the top jobs, *Wall Street Journal*, March 1986.

[3] Eagly, Alice H. and Carli, Linda L.: *Through the Labyrinth: The Truth about How Women become Leaders*. Harvard Business School, 2007.

[4] Buzanell, Patrice: *Reframing the Glass Ceiling as a socially constructed process; Implications for understanding and change*, Communications Monographs, Vol. 62, No. 4, 1995.

[5] *The Observer*, 13 April 2014.

[6] Equal Pay Act, 1970 and Sex Discrimination Act, 1975.

[7] It is rarely explained that the Norwegian legislation also guarantees the position of men. Boards have to include 40 per cent men as well as 40 per cent women.

[8] Morten Huse, who spoke at the Conference described below.

[9] *Made in Norway*, the report of the Conference held in the House of Commons in January 2013. PDF is available from websites of Fabian Society (Fabian Women's Network) and of the Labour Finance and Industry Group (LFIG).

[10] Gupta, Atu and Raman, Kartik: *Female CEOs*, Bentley University Ma, USA, delivered as a paper at the European Financial Management Association in Reading, UK, in June 2013.

[11] Op. cit. The chances of a Board containing one woman appointing a woman CEO were only one in 80. The chances of a Board containing three women appointing a woman CEO were one in four.

[12] Annual Survey of Ministerial Appointments and Reappointments to the Boards of Public Bodies regulated by the Commission for Public Appointments – Statistics and Analysis, 2012–13.

[13] *Public Bodies 2012*, published by the Cabinet Office.

Chapter 12

[1] Greer, Germaine: *The Female Eunuch*, HarperCollins, 1970.

[2] Friedan, Betty: *The Feminine Mystique*, HarperCollins, 1963.

[3] Beauvoir, Simone de: *The Second Sex*, first published in 1949 as *Le deuxième sexe*, Editions Gallimard, Paris.

[4] Kynaston, David: *Family Britain 1951–75*, Bloomsbury, 2010.

[5] Simone de Beauvoir – op. cit.

[6] Lessing, Doris: *The Golden Notebook*, Michael Joseph, 1962.

[7] Stern, Lesley: *Feminism and cinema exchanges*, Screen Winter 1979/80, Vol. 20 No. 3/4.

[8] Appignanesi, Holmes Rachel and Orbach, Susie (Eds): *Fifty Shades of Feminism*, Virago, 2013.

[9] Segal, Lynne: *Why Feminism?* Polity Press, 1999.

[10] Banyard, Kat: *The Guardian*, 10 September 2010.

[11] Banyard, Kat: *The Equality Illusion: The Truth about Women and Men Today*, Virago, 2013.

[12] Bates, Laura: *Everyday Sexism*, Simon and Schuster, 2014.

[13] Banyard, Kat: *The Observer*, 15 September 2012.

[14] Moran, Caitlin: *How to be a Woman*, Ebury Press, 2011.

[15] Freeman, Hadley: *Be Awesome- Modern Life for Modern Ladies*, Fourth Estate, 2014.

[16] Benn, Melissa: *What Should We Tell Our Daughters? The Pleasures and Pains of Growing Up Female*, John Murray, 2013.

17 Bates, Laura – op. cit.

18 Gramsci, Antonio: quoted in Femia, Joseph V: *Hegemony and political consciousness in the thought of Antonio Gramsci*, Political Studies, Vol. 23, No. 1, 1975.

19 Kaplan, Cora: *Sea Changes: Culture and Feminism*, Verso, 1986.

20 Goslett, Rhiannon Lucy: *The Guardian*, 25 November 2013.

21 Benn, Melissa – op. cit.

22 Hoschild, Airlie – op. cit.

23 Kelan, Elisabeth: 'Gender Fatigue – The Ideological Dilemma of Gender Neutrality and Discrimination in Organisations', *Canadian Journal of Administrative Sciences*, 26:3, 197–210, 2009.

24 De Beauvoir, Simone – op. cit.

25 Biggs, Joanna: *The Observer*, 30 December 2013.

26 Connell, Bob: *Gender and Power: Society, the Person and Sexual Politics*, Stanford University Press, 1987.

27 Radcliffe Richards, Janet: *The Sceptical Feminist: A Philosophical Enquiry*, Routledge and Kegan Paul, 1980.

28 Pleck, Joseph and Sawyer, Jack: *Men and Masculinity*, Prentice Hall, 1974.

29 Rowbotham, Sheila: *The Trouble with Patriarchy*, New Statesman, 1979.

30 Connell, Bob – op. cit.

31 Woolf, Virginia: *A Room of One's Own*, Hogarth Press, 1928.

Select Bibliography

Acker, Joan: *Hierarchies, jobs, bodies: A theory of gendered organisations.* In Kimmel, M. and Aronson, A. (Eds) *The Gendered Society Reader*, Oxford University Press, 2008.

Anderson, Deirdre, Vinnicombe, Susan and Singh, Val: *Women partners leaving the firm; Choice, what choice?* Gender in Management, Vol. 25 No. 3, 2010.

Appignanesi, Holmes Rachel and Orbach, Susie (Eds): *Fifty Shades of Feminism,* Virago, 2013.

Babcock, Linda, Laschever, Sara, Gelfand, Michele and Small, Deborah: *Nice girls don't ask,* Harvard Business Review, October 2003.

Banyard, Kat: *The Equality Illusion: The Truth about Women and Men Today*, Faber, 2010.

Barnett, Rosalind and Gareis, Karen C.: *Work – Family conflict and enhancement,* Chapter 10. In Pitt-Catsouphes, M., Kossek, E.E. and Sweet, S. (Eds), *The Work and Family Handbook: Multi-disciplinary Perspectives and Approaches,* Lawrence Erlbaum Associates, 2006.

Baron Cohen, Simon: *The Essential Difference*, Basic Books, 2003.

Barsh, Joanna and Yee, Lareina: *Unlocking the Full Potential of Women in the US Economy*, Special report for McKinsey, April 2011.

Bates, Laura: *Everyday Sexism*, Simon and Schuster, 2014.

Baxter, Judith: *The Language of Female Leadership*, Palgrave Macmillan, 2010.

Beauvoir, Simone de: *The Second Sex*, first published in 1949 as *Le deuxième sexe*, Editions Gallimard, Paris.

Belotti, Elena: *Little Girls*, Writers and Readers Publishing Cooperative Ltd, 1975.

Benn, Melissa: *Madonna and Child: Towards a New Politics of Motherhood*, Vintage, 1999.

Benn, Melissa: *What Should We Tell Our Daughters? The Pleasures and Pains of Growing Up Female*, John Murray, 2013.

Berger, John: *Ways of Seeing*, BBC and Penguin Books, 1972.

Bernardi, Richard, Bosco, Susan and Colomb, Veronica: *Does female representation on boards of directors associate with the most ethical companies?* Corporate Reputation Review, Vol. 12, No. 3, 2009.

Bescoll, Victoria L. and Uhlmann, Eric Luis: *Can an angry woman get ahead? Status conferral, gender and expression of emotion in the workplace*, Psychological Sciences, Vol. 19, No. 3, 2008.

Biernat, Monica, Crosby, Faye and Williams, Joan: *The maternal wall*, Journal of Social Issues, Vol. 60, 2004.

Biernat, Monica and Fuegen Kathleen: *Shifting standards and the evaluation of competence: Complexity in gender-based judgment and decision making*, Journal of Social Issues, Vol. 57, 2001.

Bohren, Oyvind and Staubo, Siv: *Changing Organisational Form to Avoid Regulatory Constraints: The Effect of Mandatory Balance in the Boardroom*, October 2012.

Bohren, Oyvind and Staubo, Siv: *Female Directors and Board Independence: Evidence from Boards with Mandatory Gender Balance*, October 2012.

Boulden, Richard, Hawkins, Beverley, Gosling, Jonathan and Taylor, Scott: *Exploring Leadership*, Oxford University Press, 2011.

Bowles, Hannah, Babcock and Lai, Lei: *Social incentives for gender differences in the propensity to initiate negotiations: Sometimes it does hurt to ask*, Organizational Behavior and Human Decision Processes, Vol. 103, No. 1, 2007.

Branson, Douglas: *No Seat at the Table*, NY University Press, 2007.

Bryant, Gay: *The Working Woman Report*, Simon and Schuster, 1984.

Burrows, Gideon: *Men Can Do It*, NGO Media Ltd, 2013.

Buzzanell, Patrice: *Reframing the glass ceiling as a socially constructed process; Implications for understanding and change*, Communications Monographs, Vol. 62, No. 4, 1995.

Cameron, Deborah: *The Myth of Mars and Venus*, Oxford, 2007.

Catalyst and Opportunity Now: *Breaking the Barriers*, 2000.

Childs, Sarah, Lovenduski, Joni and Campbell, Rosie: *Women at the Top: Changing Numbers, Changing Politics?* for the Hansard Society, 2005.

Coates, John: *The Hour between Dog and Wolf: Risk Taking, Gut Feelings and the Biology of Boom and Bust*, Penguin, 2012.

Coleman, Marianne: *Women at the Top. Challenges, Choices and Change*, Palgrave Macmillan, 2011.

Connell, Bob: *Gender and Power: Society, the Person and Sexual Politics*, Stanford University Press, 1987.

Cormier, Denise: *Retaining top women business leaders. Strategies for ending the exodus*, Business Strategy Series 2007: Focus on Leadership, Vol. 8, No. 4, 2007.

Cornelius, Nelarine and Skinner, Denise: *The careers of senior men and women – a capability theory perspective*, British Journal of Management, Vol. 19, 2008.

Cranfield University: *The Female FTSE Board Report*, 2010.

Crittenden, Ann: *The Price of Motherhood: Why the Most Important Job in the World is Still the Least Valued*, Picador, 2001.

Crosby, Faye, Williams, Joan and Biernat, Monica: *The maternal wall*, Journal of Social Issues, Vol. 60, 2004.

Cuddy, Amy, Fiske, Susan and Glick, Peter: *When professionals become mothers, warmth doesn't cut the ice*, Journal of Social Issues, Vol. 60, 2004.

David, Miriam and Woodward, Diana (Eds): *Negotiating the Glass Ceiling: Careers of Senior Women in the Academic World*, Journal of Social Policy, Vol. 27, No. 4, 1998.

Davies-Netzzly, Sally Ann: *Women above the glass ceiling: perceptions on corporate mobility and strategies for success.* Gender and Society, Vol. 12, 1998.

Dawson, Jill: *How Do I Look?* Virago Press Ltd, 1990.

Deaux, Kay and Emswiller, Tim: *Explanation of successful performance in sex-linked tasks; What is skill for the male is luck for the female.* Journal of Social Psychology, Vol. 29, p. 80, 1974.

Dulewiez, Victor and Herbert, Peter: *Current practice of FTSE 350 Boards concerning the appointment, evaluation and development of Directors, Boards and Committees post the Combined Code,* International Journal of Business Governance and Ethics, Vol. 4, No. 1, 2008.

Dyhouse, Carole: *Glamour: Women, History, Feminism,* Zed Books Ltd, 2010.

Eagly, Alice H. and Carli, Linda L.: *Through the Labyrinth: The Truth about How Women become Leaders,* Harvard Business School, 2007.

Faludi, Susan: *Backlash – The Undeclared War against Women,* Chatto and Windus, 1991.

Fausto-Sterling, Anne: *Myths of Gender,* Basic Books, 1987.

Femia, Joseph V.: *Hegemony and political consciousness in the thought of Antonio Gramsci,* Political Studies, Vol. 23, No. 1, 1975.

Figes, Eva: *Patriarchal Attitudes – Women in Society,* Faber, 1970.

Fine, Cordelia: *Delusions of Gender,* ICON, 2010.

Fitzgerald, Louise, Gelford, Michelle and Drasgow, Fitz: *Measuring sexual harassment: Theoretical and psychometric advances,* Basic and Applied Social Psychology, Vol. 17, 1995.

Ford, Jackie: *Discourses of leadership: Gender, identity and contradictions in a UK public sector organisation,* Leadership, Vol. 2, No. 1, 2006.

Frankel, Lois P.: *Nice Girls Don't Get the Corner Office,* Warner, 2008.

Fredrickson, Barbara L., Roberts, T.A., Noll S.M., Quinn, D.M. and Twenge, J.M.: *That swimsuit becomes you: Sex differences in self-objectification, restrained eating and math performance*, Journal of Personality and Social Psychology, Vol. 75, pp. 1269–84, 1998.

Freeman, Hadley: *Be Awesome – Modern Life for Modern Ladies*, Fourth Estate, 2014.

Friedan, Betty: *The Feminine Mystique*, HarperCollins, 1963.

Gangl, Markus and Ziefle, Andrea: *Motherhood, labor force behaviour, and women's careers: An empirical assessment of the wage penalty for motherhood in Britain, Germany and the USA*, Demography, Vol. 46, No. 2, 2009.

Genne, Beth: Ninette de Valois's theories of dance. In Cave, R. and Worth, L. (Eds) *Ninette de Valois: Adventurous Traditionalist*, Dance Books, 2012.

Gill, Rosalind: *Cool, creative and egalitarian? Exploring gender in project based new media work in Europe*, Information Communication and Society, Vol. 5, No. 1, 2002.

Glick, Peter, Larsen, Sadie, Johnson, Cathryn and Branstiter, Heather: *Evaluations of sexy women in high and low status jobs*, Psychology and Women Quarterly, Vol. 29, 2005.

Golden, Claudia and Rouse, Cecilia: *Orchestrating impartiality: The impact of 'blind' auditions on Female Musicians*, American Economic Review, Vol. 90, No. 4, 2000.

Goodwin, Stephanie, Fiske, Susan, Rosen and Rosenthal, AM: *The eye of the beholder: Romantic goals and impression biases*, Journal of Experimental Psychology, Vol. 38, 2002.

Gorman, Elizabeth H. and Kmec, Julia A.: *We (have to) try harder: Gender and required work effort in Britain and the United States*, Gender and Society, Vol. 21, No. 6, 2007.

Greenhaus, Jeffrey H. and Powell Gary N.: *When work and family collide: Deciding between competing role demands*, Organisational Behaviour and Human Decision Processes, Vol. 90, Number 2, 2003.

Greenhaus, Jeffrey H. and Powell, Gary N.: *When work and family are allies: A theory of work-family enrichment*, The Academy of Management Review, Vol. 31, Number 1, 2006.

Greer, Germaine: *The Female Eunuch*, HarperCollins, 1970.

Groesz, Lisa, Levine, M.P. and Murnen, Sarah: *The effect of experimental presentation of thin media images on body satisfaction – a meta-analytic review*, International Journal of Eating Disorders, Vol. 3 p.1, 2002.

Gupta, Atu and Raman, Kartik: *Female CEOs*, Bentley University Ma, USA, delivered as a paper at the European Financial Management Association in Reading, UK, in June 2013.

Haigh, Jo: *Tales from the Glass Ceiling: A Survival Guide for Women in Business*, Piatkus, 2008.

Hakim, Catherine: *Honey Money: The Power of Erotic Capital*, Penguin, 2011.

Hakim, Catherine: *Myths and Magic Medicine*, Centre for Policy Studies, 2011.

Hall, Valerie: *Dancing on the Ceiling: A Study of Women Managers in Education*, Paul Chapman Publishing, 1997.

Harper, Brit and Tiggermann, Marika: *The effect of thin ideal media image on women's self-objectification, mood and body image*, Sex Roles, Vol. 58, 2008.

Heilman, Madeline: *Description and prescription: How gender stereotypes prevent women's ascent up the organisational ladder*, Journal of Social Issues, Vol. 57, p.657, 2001.

Heilman, Madeline E.: *Gender bias in evaluation*, Journal of Social Issues, Vol. 57, No. 4, 2001

Heron, Liz (Ed): *Truth, Dare or Promise – Girls Growing up in the Fifties*, Virago, 1985.

Hoschild, Dr Airlie: *The Second Shift*, Piatkus, 1989.

Huse, Morten and Solberg Anne: *Gender related boardroom dynamics: How Scandinavian women make and continue to make contributions on corporate boards*, Women in Management Review, Vol 21, No. 2, 2002.

Huse, Morten and Solberg, Anne: Gender related boardroom dynamics: How Scandinavian women make contributions on corporate boards, in Huse, Morten (Ed.) *The Value Creating Board's Corporate Governance and Organizational Behaviour*, Routledge, 2009.

James, E.L.: *Fifty Shades of Grey*, The Writers' Coffee Shop, 2011.

Kanter, Rosabeth Moss: *Men and Women of the Corporation*, Basic Books, 1977.

Kaplan, Cora: *Sea Changes: Culture and Feminism*, Verso, 1986.

Kaplan, Gisela and Rogers, Lesley J.: *Gene Worship – Moving beyond the Nature/ Nurture Debate over Genes, Brain and Gender*, The Other Press New York, 2003.

Kelan, Elisabeth: *Emotions in a rational profession: The gendering of skills in ICT world*, Gender, Work and Organisation, Vol. 15, No. 1, 2008.

Kelan, Elisabeth: *The discursive construction of gender in contemporary management literature*, Journal of Business Ethics, Vol. 81, 2008.

Kelan, Elisabeth: *Gender Fatigue – The Ideological Dilemma of Gender Neutrality and Discrimination in Organisations*, Canadian Journal of Administrative Sciences, 26:3, 197–210, 2009.

Kerr, Ron and Robinson, Sarah: *Leadership as an Elite Field: Scottish Banking and the Crisis of 2007–2009*, Sage Publications, 2011.

Klenke, Karin: *Women in Leadership: Contextual Dynamics and Boundaries*, Emerald (Review by Valerie Stead).

Konrad, Alison, Kramer, Vicki and Erkut, Sumru: *Impact of three or more women on corporate boards*, Organisational Dynamics, Vol. 37, No. 2, 2008.

Kynaston, David: *Family Britain 1951–75*, Bloomsbury, 2010.

Lamsa, Anna and Hillos, Minna: *Career counselling for women managers at mid-career: Developing an auto-biographical approach*, Gender in Management, Vol. 23, No. 6, 2008.

Leadbetter, Charles: *A Piece of Action. Employee Ownership, Equity Pay and the Rise of the Knowledge Economy*, Demos papers, 1997.

Lessing, Doris: *The Golden Notebook*, Michael Joseph, 1962.

Lockwood, Penelope: *Do college students need same gender role models?* Psychology of Women Quarterly, pp.3036–40, 2006.

Lyton, Hugh and Romney, David M.: *Parent's differential socialisation of boys and girls: a meta-analysis*, Psychological Bulletin, 1991.

Mallon, Mary and Cohen, Laurie: *Time for a change? Women's accounts of the move from organizational careers to self-employment*, British Journal of Management, Vol. 12, 2001.

Maltz, Daniel N. and Borker, Ruth A.: Chapter 20. In Monaghan, L. and Goodman, J.E. (Eds) *A Cultural Approach to Inter-Personal Communication*, Blackwell, 2007.

MccGwire, Scarlett: *Best Companies for Women*, Pandora, 1992.

Metcalf, Andy and Humphries, Martin (Eds): *The Sexuality of Men*, Pluto Press Ltd, 1985.

Mill, John Stuart: *The Subjection of Women*, 1869. Several scholars have suggested that the tract may have been written jointly with his wife, Harriet Taylor Mill, although it was published several years after her death.

Millar, Fiona: *The Secret World of Working Mothers*, Vermilion, 2009.

Miller, Jane: *Women Writing About Men*, Pantheon, 1986.

Miller, Jane: *Crazy Age, Thoughts on Being Old*, Virago, 2010.

Millett Kate: *Sexual Politics*, Granada Publishing, 1968.

Moran, Caitlin: *How to be a Woman*, Ebury Press, 2011.

O'Connor, Victoria J: *Women and Men in Senior Management*, online document.

Opportunity Now: *Breaking the Barriers – Women in Senior Management*, Opportunity Now.

Orbach, Susie: *Fat is a Feminist Issue*, Paddington Press, 1978.

Palmer, Barbara and Simon, Dennis: *Breaking the Political Glass Ceiling*, Routledge, 2006.

Pitt-Catsouphes, Marcie, Kossek, Ellen E. and Sweet, Stephen: Charting new territory: advancing multi-disciplinary perspectives, methods and approaches in the study of work and family. In Pitt-Catsouphes, M., Kossek, E.E. and Sweet, S. (Eds) *The Work and Family Handbook: Multi-disciplinary Perspectives and Approaches*, Lawrence Erlbaum Associates, 2006.

Pleck, Joseph and Sawyer, Jack: *Men and Masculinity*, Prentice Hall, 1974.

Pye, Annie: *Leadership and Organising: Sensemaking in Action*, Leadership, 2005.

Pye, Annie, Kaczmarek, Szymon and Kimino, Satomi: *Leading FTSE Companies: The Continuing Study of Corporate Directing*, Centre for Leadership Studies, University of Exeter Business School, 2011.

Radcliffe Richards, Janet: *The Sceptical Feminist: A Philosophical Enquiry*, Routledge and Kegan Paul, 1980.

Rapoport, Rhona, Bailyn, Lotte, Fletcher, Joyce and Pruitt, Bettye: *Beyond Work Family Balance: Advancing Gender Equality and Workplace Performance*, Jossey Bass, 2002.

Reskin, Barbara F.: Bringing the men back in – sex differentiation and the devaluation of women's work. In Kimmel, M. and Aronson, A. (Eds) *The Gendered Society Reader*, Oxford University Press, 2008, p.309.

Rosin, Hanna: *The End of Men and the Rise of Women*, Viking, 2012.

Rowbotham, Sheila: *Woman's Consciousness, Man's World*, Pelican, 1973.

Rowbotham, Sheila: *The Trouble with Patriarchy*, New Statesman, 1979.

Rowbotham, Sheila: *A Century of Women – A History of Women in Britain and the United States*, Viking, 1997.

Rudman, Laurie and Fairchild, Kimberley: *Reactions to counterstereotypic behavior: The role of Backlash in cultural stereotype maintenance*, Journal of Personality and Stereotype – Social Psychology, Vol. 87, No. 2, 2004.

Rudman, Laurie A. and Fairchild, Kimberley: *The F word: is feminism compatible with beauty and romance?* Psychology of Women Quarterly, Vol. 31, 2007.

Rudman, Laurie and Glick, Peter: *The Social Psychology of Gender*, Guilford, 2008.

Ryan, Michelle and Haslam, S. Alexander: *The Glass Cliff: Evidence that women are over-represented in precarious leadership positions*, British Journal of Management, Vol. 16, No. 2, 2005.

Ryan, Michelle, Haslam, Alex, Wilson-Kovacs, M. Dana, Hersby, Mette and Kulich, Clara: *Managing Diversity and the Glass Cliff*, School of Psychology, Exeter University, CIPD publication, 2007.

Sandberg, Sheryl: *Lean In – Women Work and the Will to Lead*, WH Allen, 2013.

Schein, Virginia: *A global look at psychological barriers to women's progress in management*, Journal of Social Issues, Vol. 57 No. 4, 2001.

Sealy, Ruth: *Changing perceptions of meritocracy in senior women's careers*, Gender Management, Vol. 25, No. 3, 2010.

Segal, Lynne: *Why Feminism?* Polity, 1999.

Segal, Lynne: *Out of Time*, Verso, 2013.

Sharan-Jeet, Shan: *In My Own Name*, The Women's Press Ltd, 1985.

Singh, Val, Vinnicombe, Susan and James, Kim: *Constructing a professional identity: How young female managers use role models*, Women in Management Review, Vol. 21, No. 1, 2006.

Spender, Dale: *Invisible Women – The Schooling Scandal*, Writers and Readers Cooperative, 1982.

Stead, Valerie and Elliott, Carole: *Women's Leadership: Sociological Construction*, Palgrave Macmillan, 2009.

Steinem, Gloria: *Outrageous Acts and Everyday Rebellions,* Holt, Henry,1983.

Stern, Lesley: *Feminism and cinema exchanges,* Screen Winter 1979/80, Vol. 20, No. 3/4.

Sturges, Jane: *What it means to succeed: Personal conceptions of career success held by male and female managers at different ages*, British Journal of Management, Vol. 10, 1999.

Sturges, Jane, Conway, Neil and Liefooghe, Andreas: *Organizational support, individual attributes, and the practice of career self-management behavior*, Group and Organization Management, Vol. 35, No. 1, 2010.

Szekely, Eva: *Never Too Thin*, The Women's Press, 1988, published in 2007 by Wiley-Blackwell.

Tannen, Deborah: *You Just Don't Understand, Women and Men in Conversation*, Virago, 1991.

Tannen, Deborah: *Gender and Discourse*, Oxford University Press, 1994.

Tannen, Deborah, *Put down that paper and talk to me*, Chapter 21. In Monaghan, L. and Goodman, J.E. (Eds) *A Cultural Approach to Inter-Personal Communication*, Blackwell, 2007.

Terjesen, Siri, Sealy, Ruth and Singh, Val: *Women directors on corporate boards: A review and research agenda*, Corporate Governance: An International Review, Vol. 17, No. 3, 2009.

Thomson, Peninah with Lloyd, Tom: *Women and the New Business Leadership*, Palgrave Macmillan, 2011.

Tichenor, Veronica Jarvis: *Earning More and Getting Less: Why Successful Wives Can't Buy Equality*, Rutgers University Press, 2005.

Tonge, Jane: *Barriers to networking for women in a UK professional service*, Gender in Management, Vol. 23, No. 7, 2008.

Tutchell, Eva and Edmonds, John (Eds): *Made in Norway*, the report of the Conference held in the House of Commons in January 2013. PDF is available from websites of Fabian Society (Fabian Women's Network) and of the Labour Finance and Industry Group (LFIG).

Valois, Ninette de: *Step by Step*, WH Allen, 1977.

Vinnicombe, Susan and Bank, John: *Women with Attitude*, Routledge, 2003.

Vinnicombe, Sue and Colwill, Nina L.: *The Essence of Women in Management*, Prentice Hall, 1995.

Walker, Sir David, *A Review of Corporate Governance in the UK Banks and other Financial Industry Entities*, HM Treasury, 2009.

Weisberg D.S., Keil, Frank C., Goodstein, Joshua, Rawson, Elizabeth and Gray, Jeremy R.: *The seductive allure of neuroscience explanations*, Journal of Cognitive Neuroscience, Vol. 20, No. 3, 2008.

Wharton, Amy: *Work – Family Conflict*, Chapter 2. In Pitt-Catsouphes, M., Kossek, E.E. and Sweet, S. (Eds) *The Work and Family Handbook: Multidisciplinary Perspectives and Approaches*, Lawrence Erlbaum Associates, 2006.

Williams, Christine L.: *The glass escalator: Hidden advantages for men in the female professions*. In Kimmel, M. and Aronson, A. (Eds) *The Gendered Society Reader*, Oxford University Press, 2008.

Woolf, Virginia: *A Room of One's Own*, Hogarth Press, 1928.

Index

An asterisk against the name of a person indicates that s/he was interviewed by the authors and appears in the list of interviewees on pages vii–xiv.